T0285311

PRAISE FOR
SUPER **PSYCHED**

"Connection is at the heart of everything we want. This book is our key."

—**Lori Gottlieb,** *New York Times* bestselling author of *Maybe You Should Talk to Someone*

"In a world brought down by disconnection and distraction, Adam Dorsay offers an uplifting guide to reclaiming genuine connection. *Super Psyched* is packed with practical wisdom and creative exercises to help you rediscover joy and meaning."

—**Daniel H. Pink,** #1 *New York Times* bestselling author of *The Power of Regret, Drive,* and *When*

"It's time for you to truly enjoy life again! Dr. Adam Dorsay combines incredible insight with thousands of hours of therapeutic experience to bring you this highly actionable blueprint for deeper, more meaningful connections."

—**Mel Robbins,** *New York Times* bestselling author and host of *The Mel Robbins Podcast*

"Drawing from his unique experience, research, and insights, Dr. Adam Dorsay guides readers to identify their unique 'connection formula' in this empowering invitation to embrace the remarkable work of living fully."

—**Guy Kawasaki,** *New York Times* bestselling author of *The Art of the Start* and *Think Remarkable*

"The greatest predictor of both long-term happiness and success is the same: social connection. In a world awash with disconnection, *Super Psyched* provides a comprehensive and practical approach to creating more and better connections in every domain of life."

—**Shawn Achor,** *New York Times* bestselling author of *The Happiness Advantage* and *Big Potential*

"From the perspective of the author of *Super Psyched*, connection is ontological, meaning it is 'reality,' not just an emotional-cognitive bond. Not only does this make sense to me—I agree with it absolutely. Connecting is being. That means we cannot actually disconnect, but we can and do 'experience' disconnection, for the variety of reasons listed by Dr. Dorsay. This experience of disconnection is the source of all forms of human discontent and suffering, about which the author offers an encyclopedic discussion of the sources that restore connection. Not often does a book come along that is so fundamentally important. We recommend it to everyone."

—**Harville Hendrix, PhD,** and **Helen LaKelly Hunt, PhD,** *New York Times* bestselling coauthors of *Getting the Love You Want* and cocreators of Imago Relationship Therapy

"If T. S. Eliot was correct in his claim that 'hell is the place where nothing connects,' could it be, then, that heaven is a place where everything connects? In *Super Psyched*, Adam Dorsay makes a strong case for connection being the fundamental building block of happiness. Brick by brick, this book can help you construct a happier, healthier, and more successful life."

—**Tal Ben-Shahar,** *New York Times* bestselling author of *Happier*

"We crave connection more than anything in life, and I first found it in my deeply rewarding career as the founding drummer of Maroon 5. But I ultimately had to grapple with the loss of that connection when I was forced to walk away from the band due to a physical and psychological breakdown. Grieving that loss of identity, I learned to reconnect with myself, allowing me to find new purpose as a therapist, author, and advocate for mental health. My experience of reconnecting to the world has made all the difference in feeling contented and fulfilled by my life. Dr. Adam has written a book that deeply resonates with my personal experience. I'm super psyched he's written it and that so many people will benefit!"

—**Ryan Dusick, MA, AMFT,** and founding drummer of Maroon 5

"*Super Psyched* connected with my soul. It feels like a conversation with a therapist who sees things you don't know about yourself and a loyal friend who loves you no matter how messed up you are. If we could all have therapists like Dr. Adam Dorsay, there would be no mental health crisis."

—**Dr. Zoë Chance,** author of *Influence Is Your Superpower*; senior lecturer, Yale School of Management

"*Super Psyched* is full of good advice for living a happier and more meaningful life. At the heart of the book is the importance of connection—to oneself, to others, to one's work, etc. This may seem obvious, but every connection we make is also a constraint on our freedom to do exactly what we want. And Americans so worship freedom that we pass up opportunities for connection. So to me, the big message of the book is to embrace constraint—in the form of connection."

—**Barry Schwartz,** author of *The Paradox of Choice* and *Why We Work*; professor, UC Berkeley Haas School of Business

"Connection is what we all crave, and science shows us that connection is a fundamental need if we want to live happy and fulfilled lives. Adam is a master at connection—as anyone who knows him can tell you—and there is no one better to show us the way. With warmth, wisdom, science, and practicality, Adam takes our hand and shows us how to connect both to ourselves and others with riveting stories that will transform the way you relate to the world."

—**Emma Seppälä, PhD,** science director, Stanford Center for Compassion and Altruism Research and Education, and bestselling author of *The Happiness Track*

"Connection is much talked about yet little understood as a key part of living a happy and healthy life. In *Super Psyched*, Adam Dorsay reveals an innovative new framework for thinking about what might just be the silver bullet for many of our societal woes. Written with deep empathy and stories drawn from his real-life experience as a longtime therapist to Silicon Valley's elite, this book is an urgent and necessary antidote to our culture of disconnection and despair."

—**Dorie Clark,** *Wall Street Journal* bestselling author of *The Long Game* and executive education faculty, Columbia Business School

"Connection is a complex phenomenon that intrigues us all; yet, despite our desire for it, we often fail to explore its true significance. Dr. Adam Dorsay brilliantly delves into the intricacies of connection, guiding readers on a journey to discover their personal interpretations of this vital aspect of human experience. With clarity and insight, Dorsay offers practical strategies for cultivating deeper connections in our lives."

> —**Dr. Ruth Gotian,** Thinkers50 #1 emerging management thinker; author of *The Success Factor* and *The Financial Times Guide to Mentoring*; and chief learning officer and associate professor of Education in Anesthesiology, Weill Cornell Medicine

"I'm obsessed with helping my innovation students cultivate excellence. I've seen that the most successful ones are deeply connected to themselves, their work, and the external purpose of their efforts. Connection is a big deal! Dr. Adam Dorsay has written a user-friendly, powerful book on cultivating connection in a customized manner. This book will empower you to find your own way to connect and, ultimately, become more successful whatever your path. Read it, reread it, and enjoy the ride!"

> —**Jeremy Utley,** adjunct professor of Creativity and Design Thinking at Stanford University; coauthor of the Thinkers50 shortlisted *Ideaflow*

"No matter who we are, we all share something in common: we want to experience connection. Yet each of us pursues it in different ways. As a veteran psychologist, Dr. Dorsay has helped thousands of people in their quests to restore or create deep bonds that make for a more meaningful life. This book can help any reader figure out a formula that works for them. Highly recommended!"

> —**Olivia Fox Cabane,** host of *The Autistic Advantage* podcast and author of *The Charisma Myth*

"In a time of rampant loneliness and disconnection, Adam Dorsay provides us with a road map for healing in our modern times: the power of connection. Weaving deeply personal stories with cutting-edge research, *Super Psyched* is one of my favorite books of the year. This is a must-read book for anyone looking to improve their lives and become happier!"

—**Jonah Paquette, PsyD,** author of *Awestruck*, *Happily Even After*, and *The Happiness Toolbox*

"So much of what plagues us is related to the absence of connection. Dr. Adam Dorsay writes in a way that is so relatable about the crucial topic of connection in its various forms and can assist the reader toward their version of connection. Without question, this measure can mean the difference between a fulfilling life and one that is unfulfilling. I highly recommend this book to people in all stages of life. The applications are vast, and for a few hours of a very enjoyable read, you will find insights into how to connect in your own way. Get reading!"

—**Michele Borba, EdD,** educational psychologist and bestselling author of *Thrivers* and *UnSelfie*

"Relatable, resilient, and relentlessly upbeat, *Super Psyched* urges us all to transcend the 'appearance-and-accomplishment' mirror-gaze of today's world through fostering deep connections with ourselves, others, the wider community and world, and through spirituality. Dorsay provides a wonderful atlas of ideas to form meaning and connectivity, providing a lived-experience road map for establishing truly 'connected' life habits. Five stars!"

—**Stephen P. Hinshaw, PhD,** distinguished professor of psychology, UC Berkeley; author of *Another Kind of Madness*

"*Super Psyched* makes a compelling case for connection to be at the heart of happiness. Adam Dorsay deftly connects the dots, allowing the reader to understand why and how to connect more skillfully."

—**Frederic Luskin, PhD,** director of the Stanford University Forgiveness Projects and author of *Forgive for Good*

"Connection is at the heart of our well-being. Adam leverages his experiences as a psychologist and an award-winning podcaster to share research-based ways to increase connection in the four basic areas of life. I highly recommend this thoughtful and readable book!"

—**Frank G. Anderson, MD,** author of *Transcending Trauma* and *To Be Loved*

"Dr. Dorsay has somehow managed to pull off the trick of writing a book that not only redefines one of psychology's key pillars but also provides an actionable toolbox for making better connections in your own life—and all presented with the warm, understanding feel of chatting with a best friend. *Super Psyched* will completely transform the way you think about connection and how to harness it to build a happier, more vibrant, and more fulfilling life."

—**Susan Pollak, PhD,** psychologist, author of *Sitting Together* and *Self-Compassion for Parents*, and cofounder and teacher at the Center for Mindfulness and Compassion at Harvard Medical School

"Success in life is predicated on improving connections. *Super Psyched* is a much-needed and comprehensive exploration of the subject. This well-written and engaging text provides readers with essential wisdom and will advance your process of bringing meaning to life."

—**Jeffrey K. Zeig, PhD,** founder and director of the Milton H. Erickson Foundation and author of *The Habit of a Happy Life*

"Adam Dorsay's *Super Psyched,* a title that coincides with his very popular podcast, is a valuable and easy-to-read exploration of many aspects of human connection. A skilled clinician and interviewer, Dr. Dorsay offers an insightful and timely approach to understanding many aspects of intimacy and self-growth. Adam's consistent interviews with luminaries in many fields support his written presentation. *Super Psyched* (both the podcast and the book) are enjoyable additions to our field."

> —**Jerrold Lee Shapiro, PhD,** professor of Counseling Psychology, Santa Clara University

"Is a feeling of lacking connection to and with others, yourself, and your world all too familiar to you? If so, this book is a must-read. Using sensitivity, humor, and compassion, Adam Dorsay has written an easily accessible book that will help the reader learn ways to establish, deepen, and maintain the connections that energize their lives."

> —**Betty Carmack, EdD,** professor emerita, University of San Francisco School of Nursing and Health Professions

"This book offers something for everyone, regardless of their life journey or current stage of personal development."

> —**Toni Herbine-Blank, MSN, RN,** author of *Intimacy from the Inside Out*

"Drawing on cutting-edge psychology and memorable personal anecdotes, *Super Psyched* offers practical tools and insights to help cultivate deeper connections and unleash your true potential. Whether you're seeking greater happiness, stronger relationships, or a deeper sense of purpose, this book will guide you on a journey to supercharge your life and embrace a new level of joy and fulfillment!"

> —**Carol Novello,** bestselling author of *Mutual Rescue*

"Dr. Adam Dorsay candidly reveals his own lived experiences and seamlessly interweaves them with grounded insights from noted authors and researchers—all coupled with easily applied frameworks that make this read an indispensable guide to leading a fully connected life."

—**Angela Cheng-Cimini,** senior vice president, Talent & CHRO, *Harvard Business Review*

"We all know that connection matters, but it requires uncommon wisdom to articulate why and how best to do it—a combination of psychological, practical, and spiritual wisdom. Adam Dorsay is among the wisest people I've ever known. In *Super Psyched*, he presents a remarkable fusion of science, street smarts, and higher consciousness that cracks the code of connection like no one else has before. You need to read this book."

—**Leidy Klotz,** professor, University of Virginia, and author of *Subtract*

"On the rare occasion when you meet someone who says things that make you stop and think, tells captivating stories, and expresses wisdom, everything seemingly slows down so you can listen carefully. That is what happens when you read this book. I listened. I learned. I was reminded. My life was enriched and expanded. That will be so for each person who opens this book and reads it. As an experienced psychologist, I found endless passages that will matter in my work, my life, and my connections. This is sure to be a seminal book, filled with essential ideas. Read it. Reread it. Listen. Learn. Tell others."

—**Bonnie Bernell, EdD,** licensed psychologist, award-winning author, and recipient of the California Psychological Association's Distinguished Contribution to Psychology Award

"In *Super Psyched*, Adam Dorsay weaves scientific findings, therapeutic observations, and personal experiences together into a powerful set of suggestions for well-being, all written in a way that is characteristically Adam—engaging, lively, optimistic, and fun. This book has so much to recommend it, so do yourself a favor and pick it up. I'm sure that you, like me, will have a smile on your face the entire time you're reading it."

—**Matthew Prull, PhD,** professor, Whitman College

"As a superfan of Adam Dorsay, I'm thrilled to recommend *Super Psyched* to anyone who wants better relationships in their lives. Whether you're exploring the depths of your inner world or trying to enhance your connections with others, this book is a must-read."

—**Britt Frank, LSCSW, SEP,** author of *The Science of Stuck* and *The Getting Unstuck Workbook*

"As a developmental and behavioral pediatrician, I witness every day that connection is critical for happiness. Be present. Take interest. Show love. Dr. Dorsay's book is both an important reminder about the value of—and a guidebook for creating—connection."

—**Damon Korb,** behavioral and developmental pediatrician

"This book is a refreshingly practical, extraordinarily timely guide for the perplexed. In a world where increasing numbers of young people are making heaps of money, particularly in the tech sector, but feeling lost and hollow inside, *Super Psyched* comes as a welcome resource. In a conversational yet highly substantive style, Dorsay's volume is filled with wise and usable advice from his copious experience as a therapist, organizational consultant, and podcaster. But what I liked most about this book is that as a reader, I felt Dorsay's abiding presence in his words, or to put it another way, he personally embodies the connectedness he so compellingly advocates for in his book."

—**Kirk Schneider,** author of *Awakening to Awe* and *Life-Enhancing Anxiety*

www.amplifypublishinggroup.com

Super Psyched: Unleash the Power
of the 4 Types of Connection and Live the Life You Love

For more information, please contact:
Amplify Publishing, an imprint of Amplify Publishing Group
620 Herndon Parkway, Suite 220
Herndon, VA 20170
info@amplifypublishing.com

Library of Congress Control Number: 2024909665

CPSIA Code: PRV0624A

ISBN-13: 979-8-89138-142-1

Printed in the United States

To my beautiful sons, Avin and Bren, who give my life meaning and purpose. You both power me up like rocket engines under my shoes as I move through the world.

And to the love of my life, my primary connection, Aurianne. Words fail to encapsulate all you are, so I'll keep it simple: You are everything to me. I adore you infinitely.

SUPER
PSYCHED

UNLEASH THE POWER OF THE

4 TYPES OF
CONNECTION

AND LIVE THE LIFE YOU LOVE

ADAM DORSAY, PsyD

an imprint of Amplify Publishing Group

CONTENTS

FOREWORD

Among Dr. Adam Dorsay's many wise teachings is that gratitude is one of the keys to happiness. So let me start with some gratitude.

I'm grateful that Adam reached out to me several years ago after reading a book I'd written. I'm grateful he's invited me on his excellent podcast, *SuperPsyched*. I'm grateful we've become friends. And I'm grateful that I got to read this wonderful book he's written and provide a brief foreword.

I know I should probably call him Dr. Dorsay because he has the fancy credentials and well-earned status within the psychology community. But he's such a mensch, so approachable and friendly, I can't help but call him Adam.

The book is all about the importance of connection—connection with friends, connection with yourself, connection with spirituality, and connection with the world. After you read his inspiring story—about how he has struggled with loneliness, ADHD, and dyslexia, and about his charming relationship with his wife—I suspect you will feel a connection to him too.

Now "connection" is a great word, but it's also a bit general and vague. So you might be concerned that the book will be filled with fuzzy therapy-speak. Quite the contrary. Thanks to his years of experience as a clinician, writer, and interviewer, Dr. Dorsay has filled this book with concrete, actionable tools.

I keep a list on my computer of the psychological tools that I find helpful to my mental well-being. I added to that list many, many times while reading *Super Psyched*. I won't list all of my favorite tips here, partly because there's not room and partly because you'll read about them yourself soon. But just to give you a taste:

- The dangers of constantly comparing yourself to others (I loved the story of monkeys and grapes but won't spoil it).
- The importance of putting a name on your fears—as Adam says, in order to tame the dragon, you have to name it.
- Have self-compassion—something that may sound New Agey but has hard scientific evidence and even gets taught to Navy SEALs.
- It's OK not to "win" in the traditional sense—look at Rocky Balboa.
- And Adam's grandfather's advice: If you ever see anyone in the world whose day you can make a little better, you should do it.

I'll end with gratitude once again: Thank you to Adam for this book that improved my mental health. And thanks to you, the reader, for picking it up. I hope you find it as helpful as I do.

—**A. J. Jacobs**,
New York Times bestselling author
of *The Year of Living Biblically*
and *The Year of Living Constitutionally*

PART I
SUPER PSYCHED

CHAPTER 1

CONNECTION IS EVERYTHING

Daniel appeared to have the perfect life. While attending business school at Stanford, he met his wife. Together, they had two children who were "killing it" at school, in their chosen sports, and in other after-school activities. At work, Daniel had ascended to chief marketing officer for one of Silicon Valley's top companies, and he lived in a beautiful home in a great neighborhood.

He told me, "When I'm out walking the dog, I say hi enthusiastically to all my neighbors. They must think I'm the happiest person alive. But they have no idea of how miserable I am."

He unpacked his misery. "I work over seventy hours a week and travel more than thirty percent of the time. I'm rarely home, and when I get home, I'm so exhausted, I'm useless. I hardly see my kids since they're involved in school and every after-school activity under the sun. They have to be—we want them to go to a top-tier school and have the same opportunities my wife and I had."

He also shared that his friends are geographically spread out and he's hardly in touch with them. As for hobbies, he said, "Who has time for those?"

And when I asked him about his relationship with his wife, he said, "We look like a happily married couple. But our relationship is transactional and not emotional. We're like roommates or business partners. There's no tenderness." Then he said, "As for sex"—he looked down at his watch and said snarkily—"today is Tuesday, so that means it's been . . . over three years since our last."

Then he chided, "But my problems are first-world problems, so what the hell am I blathering on about?"

First world or not, Daniel was lacking connection in a host of crucial areas. A big part of our work would be to define connection in his terms, and to figure out ways to find more of it.

Daniel is not alone. While his personal struggle is his own, it relates to all of us. This is because connection is vital for life—just think about what happens when we don't have it.

As infants, we couldn't care for ourselves. While our caregivers could generally read our cues, they couldn't always understand what we needed. The cries and other communications we used to express our needs were sometimes misunderstood. But try as they might, our caregivers couldn't always see us, hear us, and love us in the ways we wanted or needed. We couldn't completely connect.

Throughout childhood, we continued to depend on our caregivers for our survival. We could connect better through communication but often didn't really know what our needs were or have ways to properly convey them. When we tried, we might have been ignored or told our needs were exaggerated. In some cases, our needs might have even triggered our caregivers into anger. But even if we had the best possible caregivers, we still couldn't completely connect.

As we grew, we might have rebelled, but our desire for connection with our caregivers still mattered deeply to us. Many of us remained unable to communicate our needs effectively or to have our needs sufficiently mirrored by our caregivers. As a result, consciously or unconsciously, we told ourselves things like, "I am not going to get what I need, so I might as well give up."

This begins the process of us disconnecting from ourselves, from others, from the world, and, for many of us, spiritually. It starts in infancy and continues as we grow. Without attention and correction, that disconnection increases over the course of our lives.

But once we recognize the disconnection, we can find paths to reconnect with those disconnected parts. This book aims to support you in this process, even if you have no idea where to begin.

* * *

As a therapist for over a decade to many of Silicon Valley's big players and some of the most conventionally successful people on the planet, I've had a front-row seat to the rise of a mental health epidemic.

Overall, people are more financially successful than ever. And yet, these same people are unhappy. Loneliness is rampant. Smartphones and streaming devices have had some benefits but also some major costs. Social media has caused unprecedented levels of comparison between influencers, with their advertised false selves, and consumers who want to keep up with these images.

In the midst of so much technological and financial flourishing, people are depressed and anxious at levels that former generations could not have imagined. People are investing their off-work time in ways that are not regenerative. People who appear to be happy and successful often describe themselves in private as unhappy and unsuccessful.

Maya—for example—was a high-earning VP of sales in her early forties. Since she was a girl, she had done everything she thought was "right"— putting in the time at her job, working her way up, and earning more and more each year. She did well for her employers. In exchange, they helped her create a prosperous life for herself and her family.

She came to me with something she did not, at first, know how to express. Finally, she declared, "I absolutely hate my job."

Hated it. She was good at it, but she felt "like a fraud" doing it. She had chosen a path early in life and found it relatively easy, which allowed her to cruise on autopilot. Decades later, she was so deep into her career that she believed she could not pivot and change course. She described just how unsatisfied she was with this major part of her life. She told me, "It's like I'm supposed to be a tennis player, but instead, I'm playing chess. And even though I'm good at it, it's not my game."

Flora was thirty-five and equally unhappy at work. She was a physician, something she had always dreamed of becoming. She had sacrificed "everything" to reach her goal. Now that she had made it, she believed that was *all* she was. She was Flora the Physician. It was her primary identity. Financially, it had given her stability, and she enjoyed the status of her title. But when she was off the clock, all she saw was her work. She felt bereft of any other meaning or focus. She said that in becoming a physician, she had missed out on so much of life. She sat in my office and stared off into space, not understanding how her hard work had led to such an anticlimactic and hollow victory. She wanted more from her life but couldn't imagine what might fill her emptiness.

Janet was a forty-five-year-old high school English teacher. She worked hard to enter the profession, but she was burning out. "I love my subject, and I love my students, but if I am 'off' for just a second, I'll be clowned on by my students and lose credibility . . . I use all of my energy to be at the top of my game every period."

Janet was an introvert and commented further, "When I get home, I don't want to talk to anyone, and by the time the weekend is over, I am still spent but have to summon rocket-fuel-like energy to blast through the week again." She said she had an understanding wife who gave her space to be alone until she was able to engage but that her wife was also becoming tired of the routine. Janet felt stuck.

Amir was a chief financial officer at a tech company, and he was considering retirement. He'd put in the years and had become very successful. But he was unsettled over the fact that he had never taken a company through an IPO (initial public offering, which opens investment in the company up to public investors) as CFO. He'd been part of a few successful start-ups but never while being CFO. His neighbors and golf buddies had had inconceivable successes with start-ups while playing key roles.

Amir was financially savvy enough to know he could easily retire, leave money to his children, and still enjoy life. He had an adoring wife, and she was itching for him to retire so that they could travel and have the post-kids-at-home fun they'd always dreamed of. Yet he felt stuck and empty. He believed the only way to fill that emptiness was with an IPO like the ones his fellow C-level golf buddies had experienced.

Connor was a veteran police officer. He had come from a long family line of police officers and said his job felt like a calling. He had the utmost respect for the job and for and from his peers. He could be relied on to do work that no one else wanted to do. Yet he said it was very hard being a cop these days due to the public's perception of the job. "This is not the job I had thought I would have when I was in the academy." Things were tough at home, too. His wife complained that he was too hard on the kids. "I'm a way more chill father than mine was with me, but my wife thinks I need to dial it back. On some level, I feel more at home at work than I do at home."

To conceal their identities, the people I've described in this section are composites, as are all the people I will describe working with. The people who enter my office are frequently in the top positions at their Fortune 500 companies. They are wealthy. They drive expensive cars. Some have their own Wikipedia page. They are interesting, captivating, driven individuals who draw attention in any type of room—from a gala event to an international conference to a neighborhood backyard barbecue.

And yet they describe themselves as being deeply unhappy.

Despite their undeniable success and good fortune, they feel distant from the things that truly matter to them. And as smart as they are, they tend not to know why. They have even said it seems like they've been sold a bill of goods—like a joke has been played on them.

Listening to someone who pulled up in a Lamborghini tell me that they don't know how to hug their kids because they were never hugged themselves makes me wonder: Why spend all that time and energy to pay for something that—while pretty cool, I'll admit—does not make you happy?

The Daniels, Mayas, Floras, Janets, Amirs, and Connors of the world are everywhere. You may be one of them or identify with parts of their stories.

But what does all of this mean? And how does it relate to each one of us regardless of where we stand on the financial or career hierarchy?

This book aims to answer these questions as well.

* * *

My time in the therapist's chair hasn't just been with the wealthy and successful. I have also spent many hours with adolescent gang members, immigrants who are survivors of torture, and elderly individuals in a geriatric hospital. Many of them report the same tough-to-articulate sense of discontentment.

As you may have guessed by now, my one-word antidote to this sense of lack of fulfillment in life is *connection*. Life is about connection—deep connection with ourselves, others, and the world. And it's something our society at large is sorely lacking.

Research shows that a third of US adults forty-five years and older feel lonely and about a quarter of adults sixty-five and older are socially isolated.[1] A little over 10 percent of teens and young adults are fully disconnected from real-world social life, meaning they are not in school or working.[2]

COVID did not make things easier. According to the Stress in America series put out by the American Psychological Association,[3] these numbers have increased dramatically because of the pandemic and forced us all further into what Wharton organizational psychologist and mega-bestselling author Adam Grant described as a constant state of languishing ("a sense of stagnation and emptiness").[4]

Many of the people I work with suffer from what is called "alexithymia." Alexithymia is a psychological phenomenon sometimes referred to as "emotional blindness" that occurs when a person has difficulty recognizing, expressing, or describing their emotions. It leads to all kinds of other disconnections from oneself, others, and the world, including low self-esteem,[5] low levels of imagination,[6] low levels of affection toward others,[7] and a general lack of interest in forming relationships with others.[8]

A lot of what I do with the people I work with is to help them identify *what* they are feeling and how to best express these feelings. This may sound unappealing to some readers. However, it's been my experience that it's easier for most to do than they fear it will be. Furthermore, I've seen that people tend to enjoy the process as well as the outcomes, and their relationships usually improve with this skill. For those who experience alexithymia, improving the identification and expression of feelings is a crucial starting point. We cannot truly feel connected to ourselves, others, and the world without it.

We mental health practitioners have a large reference book called the *DSM 5-TR*, or *Diagnostic and Statistical Manual of Mental Disorders*. The book lists all mental disorders, from anxiety disorders to mood disorders to every other known mental health diagnosis.

If you open this book detailing the collective problems of the human experience and read through it line by line, you'll notice something: many diagnoses in the DSM contain a form of disconnection. Depression can bring disconnection from the present due to ruminating on the past. Anxiety can bring disconnection from the present as a result of worrying about the future. Trauma can disconnect us from the present when flashbacks and memories take us to the past. Trauma can also bring on dissociation, what can be described as a "mental escape" when physical escape is not possible or when a person is so emotionally overwhelmed that they cannot cope any longer. These dissociative states can linger indefinitely. As for serious mental illness, like psychosis, it can be characterized by a disconnection or a "break" from reality itself.

And yet, despite its absence, connection is generally not well-defined or talked about as a goal in and of itself.

The Four Types of Connection

I believe most people think about connection in terms of conversations with their favorite family members or friends, a date night with their significant other, or a phone call or video chat with a long-lost friend.

General definitions of connection tend to be limited as well. For example, Wikipedia defines connection as "when two things are put together." This can either be a "real" connection like a chain linking two objects, or you can use the word in a figurative way. You might talk about a train connection between two cities and mean the train system running between them.

These are great and important definitions of connection. But the universe of connection encompasses much, much more.

I define connection pretty broadly. This is the definition I'll use throughout this book:

> *Connection is an internal emotional response. It is life force.*
>
> *It can be the quality of a relationship between two or more people or groups. But it also includes how a person relates to themselves in an authentic sense.*
>
> *Connection is often physical, but it can also be conceptual or symbolic—describing it as "magnetic" or "electric" captures this range of sensibilities. It can include how we relate to art or work or some form of activity. True connection enables vitality and/or safety. It can be what we refer to as love in its many forms. It can include how we relate to nature, and for some, it can be an expression of a relationship with a higher power.*
>
> *It is central to human life and the natural world.*
>
> *A few real-life examples of connection as I define it include: When we talk about something or someone we love and our face lights up. Or when we make a statement we know, deep down, is true. Or when we are engaged in an activity that energizes us even as we exert mental or physical energy. Or when we experience the beauty of a place like*

Yosemite or the Grand Canyon and the amazement we feel opens our bodies and minds to something far greater than ourselves.

There's a spectrum of need for every connection we'll cover in this book. An example of this is my dad, who could go his whole life without petting an animal; my need to connect with animals is so strong, I can barely last a day. I know religious people from all faiths who need to feel a strong connection to God; others I know feel nothing of the sort. Regarding a significant other, my relationship with my wife is the most important in my life, but I know others who have expressed no desire or need for a significant other at all.

It turns out, we all need a different connection prescription. For instance, you've probably heard there's a recommended dietary allowance for vitamin C that supposedly we should all take. But that number isn't really the same for all of us. It's based on an average. In reality, each person's vitamin C requirement falls in a different place along a spectrum. It depends on your body.

Similarly, if I were to impose my connection needs onto my wife or my children, insisting this was the only way to connect, they'd rightfully resent me because it wouldn't fulfill them. Think about someone in your own life who might have different connection needs from you: perhaps that person *needs* to run every day to feel connected with themselves, while you may personally hate running.

Instead of addressing our connection needs directly, we often find ways to self-medicate and distract ourselves from the pain and despair of disconnection. We tend to do this by using technology, substances, "retail therapy," or other analgesics. These may feel good in the moment, but they don't address our deeper needs directly, and if this is our only go-to, things get worse. Instead of seeking meaning through art, we play Candy Crush. Instead of finding purpose in our work, we doomscroll through social media during the workday. In the evening, instead of strengthening our relationship with our significant other, we may crack open a bottle of something with alcohol. And with a 24-7 shopping mall on our phones, we may engage in an all-encompassing research project on the next best thing to buy.

In other words, to treat the pain we feel from our lack of connection, we disconnect further. This disconnection habit tends to create a snowball effect over time. Unwittingly, we push life away. But if we're ever going to find meaning or happiness, we need to understand that what we are doing isn't working. That beer may hit the spot in the moment. That one-more-episode in the darkness of our bedroom may help us fall asleep. That quick phone game while our kid runs around the playground may help us pass the time. That extra hour of work may get us closer to a promotion. Yet when we take a step back and look, what does all of this really get us?

I want to be clear: I absolutely love doing these things, and there are times and places for these activities. I am not recommending becoming a monk (unless that's your chosen path). This book's approach is not about giving things up but rather knowing what gives us a deep sense of fulfillment and using that information to become intentional about our choices. It is about prioritizing what makes living worthwhile. If that is a beer after work or a quick Wordle after your kids have had their third tantrum of the day, then I say, "Hell yes!"

I've organized the rest of this book around what I believe are crucial connection opportunities for *most people*. These are similar to the vitamin C recommendations in that they work for everyone on average. But unlike vitamin C, which everyone needs some amount of, some of these connections you might need none of. Ultimately, that is for you to decide.

Whatever you choose, the hope is you're more connected today than you were yesterday and will become more connected tomorrow than you were today.

The structure of this book is based on these four different types of connection:

- **Connecting to Yourself:** We connect to ourselves by cultivating a deep, authentic understanding of who we are, what we love doing, and what gives us energy. This means increasing our connection to our feelings, our thoughts, our longings, and our sense of purpose. It means knowing what gets us up in the morning. It means knowing what we *really* want and need. And it means knowing what revitalizes us. These can include understanding our innate interests, our desires, our mental health needs, and our physical needs. This is our birthright and the starting point for all other connections.

- **Connecting to Others:** We connect to others by being genuinely engaged in an exchange of energy with the people in our lives. These people include our significant others, our families, our children (if we have them), our friends, and for pet people, our pets. They can also include the so-called "extras" in the movies of our lives such as colleagues, neighbors, doctors, and other acquaintances.

- **Connecting to the World:** Imagine three concentric circles. Connecting to ourselves is the innermost circle. The next circle symbolizes connecting to others. And the third circle signifies connecting to the world. These connections to the world include, but are not limited to, how we relate to our work, to nature, and to art. Connecting to the world can include social causes that are important to us and can also include connections to our ancestry and culture.

- **Connecting to Something Greater:** This book takes no theological position but recognizes that connection for many people involves the spiritual or a relationship to a higher power. This form of connection is very personal and may show up in various contexts. It tends to be experienced from within and can move in an outward direction within a community, nature, one's family, or in a multitude of other ways. Because the possibilities are vast, this form of connection warrants its own section.

I recommend you choose one to three actions from each form of connection that can make you feel more alive. It could be building pillow forts with your kids. It could be crafting that perfect cup of coffee. It could be tantric sex with your partner. It could be geeking out on training your dog. It could be finding the best hiking spots. I can't tell you what it is because it's so personal and I'm not you. But I am asking that you go headfirst into whatever you choose.

For example, my client Mindy was a new mom and a serious live music fan. She expressed grief about not getting to see live music performances as she had before motherhood. To fill the space of this missing piece in her life, she began a regular ritual of dimming the lights, playing recordings of live music, and dancing.

That was enough for her until she could attend live shows more frequently. Finding this form of connection to herself improved this part of her life dramatically.

I recommend you follow Mindy's example by finding your own meaningful activities. I hope this book inspires your thinking and provides insight that will lead to greater courage and behavior change. Or perhaps the sequence will be the opposite: your courageous behavior change will inspire thinking and insight.

Super Psyched: Being Fully Alive

Ferris Bueller was right: life moves pretty fast. So was Paulo Coelho when he said, "One day you will wake up and there will be no more time to do the things you have always dreamed of. Do them now."

The best question I can come up with to address these ideas is this: *What does it take to be most alive while we are living?* In response, I went for the phrase—*super psyched*.

My definition of super psyched is being truly alive. But it absolutely does *not* mean being happy and "up" all the time. This book isn't peddling toxic positivity. That's unrealistic, and as the word "toxic" implies, it would be a reckless and unhealthy target. If there's a single target this book aims at, it is to discover how to feel truly alive *while* we're alive.

Super psyched also means being connected to our psyches, to each other, and to the world. It means feeling vital with our aliveness and in full color, whether we're happy, sad, excited, joyous, brokenhearted, or in awe.

It includes what the great Viennese psychiatrist Viktor Frankl called "tragic optimism" in his landmark book *Man's Search for Meaning*: "the ability to maintain hope and find meaning in life, despite its inescapable pain, loss, and suffering."[9] We can appreciate life by knowing more about it in all of its shades. By knowing the dark, we can better know the light when it shows up. By knowing the bitter cold, we have a more powerful reference point to experience warmth.

Having these ideas front of mind allows us to be connected to ourselves: connected to what makes us truly *us* and appreciative of those things that make others who they are. Doing this requires being conscious and intentional. To be truly connected means to choose thoughtfully what to connect with and, just as importantly, what to disconnect from.

I frequently think about a point Harvard Professor Daniel Gilbert raised in his book *Stumbling on Happiness*. He says that we humans are the only animals that can imagine a future. But despite this distinguishing and miraculous ability, we are very bad at predicting what will make us happy.[10] With that in mind, many of us may be hesitant to engage in such prediction in the first place. But research in positive psychology has provided an excellent road map to help us. The research consistently shows that our opportunities for happiness are dramatically increased through practices like mindfulness, gratitude, flow, and other paths to connection.[11, 12, 13] In addition, we humans are such social creatures that even small amounts of social interaction, like talking a bit with the cashier at the grocery store, can lead to increased levels of happiness.[14]

The paths endorsed by the positive psychology research described above will be covered throughout this book.

We'll also unpack what makes us feel more connected to ourselves, others, the world, and spirituality through data, anecdotes, and advice. Some ideas covered in this book may be familiar. But there's often a difference between common sense and common practice—a chasm between what we know and what we do. This means going beyond merely knowing that we need to connect; it means doing something about it.

In many ways, this is more of a "where to" than a "how to" book. It's a "where to" in that it doesn't present a simple solution or a recipe. Instead, this book is more like an atlas with a greater focus on outlining resources *where* we can look to find greater connection. Regardless, if we are willing to be open and honest with ourselves as well, each of us may find a life of greater connection. Each person's takeaways and to-do lists will be unique.

This is particularly true because each of us has our own connection formula—a set of activities that recharge our life force and allow us to feel truly alive. The purpose of this book is to help you discover yours. I imagine the connection formula for each of Earth's eight billion inhabitants is unique. This means that no book, let alone this one, could possibly be a one-size-fits-all guide.

But if you are willing to seek the connection formula that fuels you and to work toward creating it, I can offer you the required tools for assembly and enjoyment of the benefits.

I have seen it happen so many times before. You can make that change too.

But before we get into *how*, we need to understand a bit better *what* keeps us from living a super psyched life. That's what this next chapter is about.

CHAPTER 2

WHY WE'RE SO DISCONNECTED

Now that we've established what this book is about, allow me to introduce myself more formally. I'm Adam Dorsay, a Silicon Valley–based psychologist who came to the profession later in life. Prior to becoming a psychologist, I worked corporate jobs that I didn't love but had come to believe were my only option. For many reasons, like the clients I cited in the previous chapter, I couldn't imagine that pursuing my true career passion was a possibility.

Much of this disconnection with myself was traceable to my childhood. As a child, I struggled a lot. I was a neuroatypical and socially awkward boy who lacked confidence. I also struggled mightily to make connections with others. I remember one time, at a new school for second grade, I called each boy in my class one by one to come over to play. No one said yes. I received over a dozen rejections, and it was a painful experience. My mom still talks about it. I felt so alone at the time, yet I'm sure I'm not alone in having this type of story.

In adulthood, I grew out of my social awkwardness and made great friends, but I still lacked several important connections to myself, others, and the world. In particular, it took a long time to find myself professionally. Due to my ADHD, dyslexia, and ridiculously poor confidence,

I'd dropped out of a PhD program in my twenties. By my thirties, I had allowed myself to believe that my chance to have a vocation of my choosing had passed.

I remember all too well the suffering I experienced moving from job to job with no hope of ever realizing my true ambitions. Thankfully, I was able to create interpersonal connections in my work that led me to a happier, more fulfilled life. We'll return to my journey toward connection throughout this book because I imagine there are elements of the story that hold truths for many people—and may be helpful to you.

Looking back, I always knew I wanted to be a psychologist. Even when I played bass in a garage band in high school, that desire showed up. When I tried out for the band, I wanted to be the guitarist, but I didn't make the cut. Still, my joyful disposition caused them to keep me around, and they let me play bass. I was so grateful to be there, and my happiness rippled out to the band, which we named Café of Regret.

Yes, it was the eighties, and Tears for Fears–type depressive band names were fashionable.

Everything we did together blew me away, from the practices in a garage to playing house party gigs. Dave, our beast of a drummer, would be the first to call me EnthusiAdam. I soon noticed I'd become the unofficial band psychologist. The other three musicians were extremely talented, and I'm not being self-effacing when I say that I was definitely not at their level; I was good enough to keep the good music from sounding bad. My real contribution was my ability to tune in to the group's connection needs.

My first meaningful suggestion to the band was to nix practicing in a line like a group performing live on stage. Instead, I advised that we practice in a circle so that we could see each other. This amplified our cohesiveness. Being able to connect with each other through our facial expressions and body language brought us closer together and improved our music.

I also did everything I could to keep us hyped while making sure we got along like a solid team.

Feeling the sonic waves from the music we played together put me into a state of transcendence. Time flew by. I wished the practices and performances would never end. But it was not just that—it was everything. The guitar connecting with the bass and drums, the keyboards weaving through, and the lyrics creating a totality that sounded beautiful. As an eighteen-year-old, it was the most alive I'd ever felt. I didn't have this language at the time, but being in that band was deeply fulfilling, and the half-life of the experience left me feeling stoked for days.

A common metaphor for this type of experience is "filling our cup," which describes the return on investment of expending emotional, mental, and physical energy. We are all doing things all the time: some of these things drain our cups, and some fill them. Everyone's cup is different: for some of us, going to the grocery store drains our cup and we'd much rather have our food delivered. Others may find going to the grocery store super-rejuvenating. Having a conversation with our partner may fill our cup, but if we're in a toxic relationship, sitting down to chat with our partner is the *last* thing we want to do. Driving on a Sunday afternoon may be the most incredible experience of our week—or we may be someone who would rather watch paint dry than go for a drive.

Many years past my garage-band days, I still make the effort to fill my cup daily in some meaningful way. And with good reason: being alive is a statistical improbability. I mean, think about it—how likely is it that any of us was born? What are the chances that our parents and all of our ancestors met, procreated, survived, and passed their genes at just the right moment so that we could be here? The answer: infinitesimally small. Estimates of this unlikelihood have ranged from 1 in 400 trillion to 1 in 10 to the 2.685 millionth power. The numbers run the gamut, but to put it in perspective, we are more likely to win the Super Lotto than to have been born.

Since we've won this Super Lotto called life, what's our goal?

I would argue that the goal is connection. In my podcast interviews with over two hundred guests, I've spoken with experts from diverse areas—authors, scientists, athletes, artists, therapists, and experts on a broad range of topics. Regardless of field, a common denominator emerged from the overwhelming majority: the value of *connection*, specifically the four types of connection explored in this book.

Having listened to others for many hours as a psychotherapist, in addition to reading extensively on the human condition, I've come to the conclusion that this single criterion, *connection*, is the most predictive variable of how we're doing. It's central to living a good life.

Disconnectors

I was once asked to copresent at a continuing medical education course for a group of physicians discussing how fatigue can lead to medical errors.

As you might imagine, the audience was a highly intelligent and focused bunch, and my role was to offer ways to support their mental health. I knew that—being a non-MD speaking to physicians—I needed to get their attention. I decided to talk first about a big obstacle to rejuvenation: time invested poorly during off hours. This is something many of us do during our time off. It's as if we're trapped by our habits when we're off the clock. I referred to these common traps simply as *disconnectors*. Disconnectors refer to a category of thoughts and behaviors that prevent or disrupt connection.

Here's what I shared: Fatigue can be exacerbated by poor time investment and mindless multitasking during our off-hours. Every action—even when it feels like we're on autopilot—is a *choice* we make about how we spend our time. I provided a comical but not unrealistic scenario: Imagine it's Saturday. We wake up, binge-watch a show while texting or looking at social media, folding laundry, petting the dog, and answering emails and texts—all while making and drinking our coffee. By multitasking, we are not experiencing any of those things fully. As a result, we miss out on the benefits offered by any one of them. When they are done individually, we can find joy in each. Doing them all at once, on the other hand, can lead to fatigue. When we return to work on Monday, we're still tired, wondering "What happened to the weekend?"

Disconnectors can be a constant drain from our cup, and they show up in many ways. Imagine a hole in your cup where energy is slowly dripping into the world of social media, work, doomscrolling, and the other elements of our lives. Nothing is replenishing the cup, leaving us with less and less energy to do what we need to do and want to do, let alone to enjoy ourselves while we do it. This makes it challenging to be super psyched about anything.

The effects of these habits contribute to us becoming less able to handle the stresses of the day-to-day. These practices become more deeply reinforced the deeper and longer we go down these habitual paths. As the quote variously attributed to Gandhi, Lao Tzu, Ralph Waldo Emerson, and other brilliant thinkers goes, "Carefully watch your thoughts, for they become your words. Manage and watch your words, for they will become your actions. Consider and judge your actions, for they have become your habits. Acknowledge and watch your habits, for they shall become your values. Understand and embrace your values, for they become your destiny."

Research shows that sending and receiving a high number of emails and social media messages, along with increased internet multitasking, leads to increased stress and can have indirect effects on burnout, depression, and anxiety.[1] People still choose to do all these things at once. They do so, at least in part, because of "fear of missing out" (FOMO) and to keep up with their friends.[2] We spend tons of time stressing out about what's happening without us. With our social brains, we can be guided by FOMO more than by connecting with the people and activities that really matter to us.

And yet we are less likely to benefit from our choices if we are not intentional about them. When we are not making an intentional choice, we are on autopilot and digging deeper into the disconnectors of our daily habits. Automatizing our daily habits is important to keep things moving efficiently. However, when being on autopilot interferes with our ability to develop meaningful connections, it can become a problem.

So at the end of the day, instead of feeling refreshed because we have made choices for ourselves based on our connection needs, we may feel drained and exhausted. These disconnectors are nonrejuvenating. We're simply doing what's easy. Our brains are wired to go with what's easy, and disconnectors tend to be easy.

In my presentation, I shared that being stuck with these disconnectors during our off-hours could increase the risk of returning to work tired and burnt-out. I encouraged the audience to be more intentional about their days off and how they used their breaks. I gave them well-researched methods from positive psychology research to find "flow" in their work; some of this came from the data gleaned by the Values in Action (VIA) inventory, which you'll read about later in this book. I also suggested ways to enhance the depth of their relationships through exercises like gratitude letters, an exercise I'll explain in chapter 8. I recommended they take their breaks someplace besides their office or breakroom and avoid mindlessly scrolling through their phone or bingeing TV. A workout, a walk outside, or even a short nap can be more rejuvenating.

We might spend a lot of time with our disconnectors, but here's the good news: we *can* change our habits! Scientists have found that our brains have a high amount of plasticity,[3] which means that we can learn new things and even teach so-called "old dogs new tricks" in ways that were previously thought impossible. Neuroscience has revealed that "neurons that fire together, wire together." They grow, rewire, and continue to do so throughout life, allowing for all kinds of new possibilities . . . allowing us to become more of who we want to become. So take heart—it's not too late. Even if we have been clocking time with our disconnectors for years, we can change course and find new paths that are more aligned with what we want and need. We can figure out who we are and pursue what we really want.

I worked with a brilliant biotech professional, Brendan, who at forty-two found his job less fulfilling than he'd hoped. "I worked so hard to earn my doctorate, and this is what I get for it," he said, alluding to the anticlimactic nature of attaining his position. His day was full, he had a long commute, and he felt deflated after work. As a result, he developed a nightly routine that he described as mindless: smoke weed, watch *Looney Tunes* reruns, go to bed. Rinse and repeat daily.

This would not have been a problem if he didn't believe he was wasting away on weed and cartoons. He was stuck, depressed, and said he had "the dad bod of dad bods."

"And I'm not even a dad," he added.

Brendan said he could feel himself "rotting," and he felt a sense of guilt that he wasn't doing anything that really mattered to him. He said he needed some way to know that he'd done *something* of value. Drawing on research on what makes us feel sustainably fulfilled, I developed an easy-to-remember acronym to help him determine if an activity filled his cup. Simply stated, we can ask ourselves, does the activity "FEED" us? In other words, are the following criteria met?

Flow: Does the activity challenge us and cause us to improve our skills? Do we lose ourselves in the activity?

Educate: Does the activity cause us to learn?

Energize: Do we feel invigorated even when we exert energy on the activity?

Depth: Does the activity provide us with a sense of meaning and purpose?

It took time to identify his FEED activities. But when Brendan identified gardening as one example and took action, he looked forward to each day he got his hands dirty. Initially, he allocated about thirty minutes a day for his new activity. After a month, he was gardening for over an hour each day and studying gardening and horticulture at night. Eventually, his cannabis and cartoon routine took the back seat, and he did those only occasionally. His desire to make his green thumb greener took priority.

This small change boosted his mood and his self-regard. Surprisingly— to support his love of gardening—he went to bed early and woke up early in the morning. By 6:00 a.m. he was outside gardening, rain or shine. He even went to the gym after work to increase his strength to support his outdoor hobby. A byproduct of this, he said, was an increase in his energy, intelligence, and ability to garden. It also enhanced his mood and helped him get into shape to the point that his physique was what he called "*just a dad bod.*"

By FEEDing himself, Brendan found himself in a virtuous circle. He loved gardening, and as he engaged in the other activities that supported his hobby, a more authentic version of Brendan began to emerge. He is proud of his beautiful and ever-improving backyard space, and he loves entertaining there as well, giving him the added benefit of connection with others.

Chasing Distractors

When Ted began seeing me, he was a young man going into his senior year of college. On the surface, he was a self-described frat bro. He spent a lot of time with his frat buddies, drinking, going to parties, and hanging out. In his words, they were all focused on one thing: "hooking up." Each weekend, they'd go out to a party, possibly hook up, and share stories the next day.

Ted liked his friends and he liked the camaraderie of being in the fraternity, but he reported that something was off. He did not have the enthusiasm that his fraternity brothers had for their weekends. He was not super psyched. We worked to separate who he was from the noise of his life—those external voices of his fraternity brothers that didn't reflect *his* truth. We concluded we needed to find out what allowed him to feel a strong connection to himself and to others around him.

What we discovered—which surprised him but may not surprise you— was that he did not want to hook up. Instead, he wanted a long-term relationship. Specifically, he longed for someone who shared his love for nature, someone with whom he could explore the great outdoors.

Ted had been habitually chasing something he did not want due to FOMO. Why did he do this? Why do we all do this in our own ways to ourselves? If we aren't motivated by true desires, what are we motivated by?

Ted, like all of us, was chasing *distractors* that he thought would make him happy. Distractors as I discuss them here can be anything in our life that we think will make us happy but won't. Distractors can be beer commercials that promise our doors will be knocked down by beautiful women or the idea that some high-cost luxury will give us long-term happiness.

Ted had been told that hooking up would make him happy. It didn't. In the same way, many people are told that focusing primarily on their jobs will make them happy. For some people, this may be true. For others, it's a serious distractor.

Dr. Janna Koretz, a Boston-based psychologist who was a guest on my *SuperPsyched* podcast, has written about the concept of "enmeshment" as it relates to work for the *Harvard Business Review*. As she defines it, enmeshment occurs when "the boundaries between people become blurred, and individual identities lose importance." She makes a case that this can occur with one's job. In this case, the boundaries between you and your job become blurred: You *are* your job.[4] Similarly, in Ted's case, he *was* his frat.

This loss of identity keeps us from having a healthy sense of self. And when we sprinkle in the very human trait of FOMO, we get another distractor. Patrick McGuiness, another *SuperPsyched* guest, was the person who coined the acronym FOMO. It is deeply embedded in our genes and has been passed down by our ancestors. It's likely that FOMO protected us by keeping us in the tribe. Not participating with the tribe could lead to expulsion and near-certain death. Patrick has even cheekily described us as FOMO Sapiens on his podcast.

FOMO elicits anxiety when we imagine missing out on the experiences of others. It can lead us to participate in activities we don't want to participate in rather than keeping us attuned to what *we* actually want to do. This puts the distractors on steroids. Distractors can cloud our thinking and keep us from knowing our true needs and desires. If we hate the job or the group we've overidentified with but allow FOMO to drive our decisions, we can end up feeling profoundly disconnected from ourselves.

We are also wired to conform—to "go along to get along." Just as is the case with FOMO, we're genetically programmed to conform for survival. These days it remains important for us to conform *at times*. For example, in a work setting, we may prefer to recharge alone during our lunch hour. Yet periodically overriding that need and *choosing* to join colleagues for lunch may be important for group cohesiveness. That is to say, overall these conformity needs for survival are less pressing today. What is important is that we're aware of our drive to conform and that we make it a conscious choice rather than a reflexive behavior.

Further, these unconscious decisions can lead us to what I call the "consent and resent" cycle, another prominent distractor. The consent and resent cycle comes from a reflex to "be nice" and avoid discord. This reflex to remain in harmony is often stronger than our willingness to risk conflict and be true to ourselves. In these moments, we fail to recognize the long-term consequences of saying yes. It can happen with our intimate people or even with a pushy sales rep. In the moment, it can feel harder to say no even though saying yes could lead to days, months, or even years of regret. These distractors connect to our biological programming to conform, so we need to be aware of this drive.[5]

We've all done it. And when we do, we feel angry at the person we said yes to and angry at ourselves. Worse still, we can become less trusting of our feelings, eroding our connection with ourselves.

Nancy Levin shared her hard-earned wisdom on my podcast. Nancy describes herself as a former people pleaser but has become a self-described "boundary badass," and she is the author of a well-regarded book on boundaries. Nancy said that no one can cross our boundaries without us letting them; she also revealed that her new favorite word was "no." I agree and believe that sometimes the biggest "yes" we can give ourselves is a "no" to someone else. My wife even chimed in after hearing the interview by saying, "*You* need to do this more."

Turns out, I'm also a people-pleaser.

We don't need to be passive, and we don't need to be hostile or aggressive either. The best method is simply to be assertive when needed. That means being clear, concise, and kind when we deliver a "no." This serves both us and the other person because they will not feel the resentment we carry when we say yes and really mean no.

Nancy stated that without this authentic, assertive form of relating, there can be no real intimacy.

There are also many distractors from societal mores that deceptively lead us to act without considering our own needs and desires. These distractors are all around us, every day, whether we're aware of them or not. Perhaps a well-intentioned adult figure told us to behave a certain way based on their understanding of the world, which had no basis in ours. Relatedly, we often hear gender-based dictates like "Boys don't cry" or "Girls should be pretty," and these can set us up for a life of chasing gendered distractors: becoming a tough dude who hides emotion or a girl trying to fit into a societal stereotype of beauty. Even song lyrics and movies purport to teach us what it looks like to be in love. Unfortunately, they're often based on external qualities that don't lead to authentic love, rather than internal, character-based, sustainable qualities in each partner. Of course we need to feel attracted. But how many of us in our romantic pursuits have had a primary objective of finding a mythic Margot Robbie or Ryan Gosling?

Or, consider this: for those of us who've watched *The Bachelor* or *The Bachelorette* on TV, we've seen large numbers of competitors vying for the love of one person. Hey, don't laugh! It's a real social psychology experiment, and our psyches are not so different from those of the contestants. The show features men and women pining over the prize of the final rose and a marriage proposal from the star of the show. Yet, do the contestants actually *love* the bachelor or bachelorette as much as they profess? Might competition, FOMO, social comparison, fear of rejection, a sense of powerlessness, or other distractors at play obscure the judgment of the contestants? With all of these distractors, are they able to connect deeply with what's true for them? While the show has produced some great long-term relationships, the statistics don't lie: most couples dissolve their union after the show ends.[6]

These distractors can lead us to poor decision-making that incurs pain. They push us to do things that we *think* will make us happy but instead harm us.

Decades after an incident, a young man named Liam came to me for therapy and shared a memory. It was the day before starting high school, and his mother introduced him to a former principal who she thought could help him prepare for his first day. Liam entered the room and was greeted with "Son, are you at the top of the heap or the bottom of the heap?" Liam was taken by the man's powerful status and appearance. He knew he wasn't at the top, so the only logical conclusion was that he was at the bottom. This binary question led Liam to a harmful view of himself that stayed with him for years and took him a long time to unlearn.

Similarly, beauty standards for women can feel oppressive. When we finish shopping at the supermarket, the checkout counters are full of magazines promoting the rich and beautiful, creating unrealistic standards and leaving us feeling inadequate. Women may ask themselves a variation of "How do I compare to the images in front of me?" We know those images are not true images. We know they are graphically enhanced. Yet they influence our self-perceptions. As a result, women (and their significant others) may engage in social comparison and feel substandard.

In sum, I've identified three primary sources of our distractors: our cognitive biases, our comparisons to others, and our fears. If we can understand these three sources of distractors, we can break out of their traps and find connection with what really matters to us.

Biases Mislead Us

Our brains are incredibly powerful. They are the most complex structures in the known universe. They are also very old-fashioned, especially by modern technology standards. When did you get your last smartphone? And what version is it? The iPhone has been around for less than two decades, and as of this writing, it has more than a dozen upgrades and at least thirty-four iterations. In stark contrast, over the last 35,000 to

100,000 years, our brain structure has had only one model. And, get this, *no upgrades*. But our surroundings have vastly changed—especially over the last century. I mean, especially over the last fifty years. Oops, scratch that, over the last *decade*.

Hey, can I call a manager? My brain needs an upgrade—it can't handle its surroundings!

Our brains have evolved to keep us alive and make sure that we keep breathing, eating, and knowing what to do when we feel threatened. They act as prediction machines, doing everything they can to help us avoid that thing called death.

Keeping us alive is a lot of work, so the brain has also worked to become as energy-conserving as possible. As it evolved, it developed a series of cognitive shortcuts that help us to reach fast and (usually) accurate-enough conclusions about problems that have allowed us to survive and to procreate. But these shortcuts have the unfortunate side effect of causing mistakes when we are dealing with harder questions and problems of modern-day thinking. Five thousand years ago, we weren't confronted with many of the tough questions we have today, so the shortcuts we had at that time were a real asset. Today, they can present problems instead of solving them.

These shortcuts are unconscious and called "cognitive biases." They help us think more efficiently, and help us make sense of the world, but they can be misleading and can cause us to chase unhelpful distractors. They facilitate speed but do not necessarily create the long-term outcomes we want in our lives. We need to be aware of these biases so that we can name them and tame them rather than allow *them* to claim us and drive us into an undesired future.

Our brain's drive to keep us alive can keep us on constant watch for threats in our day-to-day lives. Our brain is always on the lookout for things that we imagine will hurt us, and it's focused on helping us avoid them. Which makes sense—if there's any possibility that something could hurt us or even kill us, why even chance it?

This causes pessimism, or more scientifically, the negativity bias. This is a bias that leads our brain to think something's bad when it's not, or us to remember what was bad about an experience rather than focusing on the good. An easy way to remember the negativity bias is to think of Teflon and Velcro: The good stuff slides right off like Teflon. But the bad stuff? It sticks like Velcro. When pro athletes say, "Losing hurts more than winning feels good," that's the negativity bias. When we go on vacation and one hundred great things happened but one bad thing also happened, what do we remember most? The bad thing. That's the negativity bias.

What's that sound of rustling leaves? A lion? A squirrel? Let's assume it's a lion because if we're wrong, we're dead. That means no more bloodline for future versions of us—our genes are gone.

This constant vigilance against threats is a major cognitive bias, but there are hundreds of others. Confirmation bias is an important one that you may have heard of. As described by psychologist Peter Wason, we favor information that confirms or strengthens our beliefs. Once we believe something, it's really hard to convince us otherwise . . . even when we're dead wrong.[7] Simply put, we seek information to confirm we're right so that we can feel good about our beliefs and what we've done.

Let's go back to our example of the frat boy, Ted. He experienced confirmation bias that kept him chasing distractors. He'd wake up next to a woman he'd hooked up with after a night of partying. He'd feel crappy about himself but didn't know why. He'd say to himself, "That bad feeling must be a hangover. Everything is fine. Look at how hot she is."

But his desire to confirm his current lifestyle created distance from himself. He didn't allow himself to question it or to connect with what he needed to be happy. Instead, he settled for what he believed "should" have made him happy. The next weekend, he would do the same thing. Rinse and repeat. Ted's brain believed it was protecting him from regret, but instead, it kept him on a hamster wheel, leaving him in a state of perpetual discontent.

Recency bias is another big one. We tend to favor or focus on what's *recent*, potentially to the exclusion of what is *true*. We give more weight to an argument we heard just yesterday rather than the one from last week, even though last week's may have been more on point. Over that week, the information faded from our memory and became less accessible. This bias makes it easier for us to make decisions and spend less energy on remembering; it also frees up energy to act, even if the decision is wrong.

Recency bias keeps Ted in a cycle of hanging out with his frat bros every weekend. He remembers what he recently did and says to himself, "Well, I guess that was fun," so he does it again. But he doesn't remember how much fun he had camping last summer and fails to consider that he would enjoy camping now.

★ ★ ★

Biases can bring on unnecessary pain. For example, sometimes we may interpret an ambiguous situation as negative or threatening, like if a friend walks by without acknowledging us and we assume our friend must be angry with us (without other supporting evidence). This is called interpretation bias. Research finds that those who frequently fall for interpretation bias have higher levels of anxiety.[8] This makes sense: if your brain is constantly misinterpreting things and following distractors, over time it can lead to or amplify anxiety.

One way we can deal with these cognitive biases that is simple, though not easy, is mindfulness. Simply put, mindfulness is being aware of *what's going on while it is going on,* or to quote mindfulness teacher James Baraz, "Mindfulness is simply being aware of what is happening right now, without wishing it were different; enjoying the pleasant without holding on when it changes (which it will); being with the unpleasant without fearing it will always be this way (which it won't)."[9]

Now we know: just be where you are. Be aware. Pay attention and notice. Notice your thoughts without judgment. These tips are easy to describe but harder to put into practice. They require repetition and patience with yourself. Mindfulness becomes a self-perpetuating cycle. When you become mindful of your thoughts and aware of the biases that define your life, you can decide what to do with them. You can then identify what makes you feel connected to yourself, others, the world, and spirituality (the latter if you're so inclined).

Being mindful makes you feel more connected. And feeling connected makes you naturally more mindful. The virtuous cycle of rejuvenation thus continues.

The Age of Comparison

I remember walking through the halls in high school assuming everyone had it more together than I did. The athletes, the cheerleaders, even the geeky kids—I believed they all knew themselves and what they wanted. I thought they were comfortable in their skin. I believed only I was the awkward one, the outsider, and, literally, the only one who didn't have it all figured out.

Years later, I went to my high school reunion and saw many people with whom I hadn't conversed since I was eighteen. They represented many cliques, and I talked with someone from each. Being EnthusiAdam, I had to get in there and connect with people from all walks of life. As we caught up, I learned something: what I had believed—that everyone had it together in high school except for me—turned out to be a nearly comical illusion. I learned everyone had struggled in their own way. Some told me they had parents who were alcoholics, some said they had been depressed just like I had been, and many said they had been overwhelmed with what to do after graduation. They were coping, and I discovered we were all in the same boat: faking it to hide just how terrified we were.

I walked away from that reunion with new insight. Our social brains are wired to take in messages about others' perceptions of us. It reminded me of a quote attributed to sociologist Charles Cooley, one that summed up everything I heard at the reunion. It may require reading it twice, and here's how it goes: "Today, I'm not what I think I am. I'm not what you think I am. I am what I think you think I am."

These days, thanks to all the enticing social media apps on our phones, we're constantly walking down versions of those high-school halls, comparing ourselves to everyone—not just in our school but across the entire world.

There is no shortage of comparisons to be made: it seems like everyone else is richer and better-looking. Everyone seems to be having more fun. Everyone's got it all figured out. On TV, we see glamorous homes filled with glamorous people talking about their glamorous lives. On Instagram, we have influencers showing us how amazing they are at working *and* parenting.

We also see not only our friend's incredible Hawaiian vacation, which may make us happy for them, but also photos from a guy we met at a conference. He's on a hiking trip with his family, having what we imagine must be the most beautiful experience with a gorgeous partner. We conclude they are having the best sex ever and that they are also superior parents to children who never misbehave. This leaves us feeling diminished and inflates our real and imagined inadequacies.

This is the modern-day social disease of comparison. Social comparison, like other cognitive biases, is rooted in our evolution.[10] By our nature, we compare ourselves to others around us. This makes sense. We needed to know our placement in the social hierarchy in order to survive and procreate. Now we evaluate and define ourselves by how we stack up to friends and leaders. "Are we at the top of the heap or at the bottom of the heap?" When we believe we don't stack up well, we feel miserable.

★ ★ ★

The drive for social comparison runs deep in our genes. To understand this better, consider the cucumber-fed versus the grape-fed monkeys. You can see this experiment on YouTube, and here's how it works: Scientists conducted an experiment on monkeys to bring out their inherently comparative nature.[11] Although the experiment was designed to demonstrate how other species relate to moral behavior, fairness, and justice, it also reveals a lot about social comparison as it relates to us humans. They had two monkeys who could see each other in conjoining cages and initially fed them both cucumbers.

Monkeys like cucumbers, but they don't *love* cucumbers. They *love* grapes. So after some time, the scientists kept feeding one monkey cucumbers while the visible neighboring monkey got a massive upgrade of grapes. The cucumber-fed monkey took one look at the grape-fed monkey and freaked out. He saw the mediocre cucumbers he was being fed and became furious when he saw his neighbor enjoying a five-star meal of delicious grapes. Outraged, he started to throw the cucumbers at the scientists in what looked like a serious protest.

In other words, before there was another option, the cucumbers were fine. But when the grapes were introduced, cucumbers became unappealing.

While the study shines a light on justice and injustice in primates, it also shines a light on how social comparison can warp our perspective on our own lives and lead us to chase distractors. A person can be pleased with the home she bought after saving up for years, but that pleasure evaporates as soon as she watches HGTV. Suddenly, on *House Hunters*, she sees someone younger and more attractive who bought a house five times as expensive. What does she do? She starts thinking about her version of the grapes and ignoring the perfectly fine cucumbers that had made her happy until a few moments ago.

In response to our growing sense of inadequacy, many of us change our behaviors and our desires to match what others have. We don't connect with the people and things that would enrich us internally; we seek out what others tell us will prove our value externally. We put everything into getting grapes, whether or not we actually want them.

And this touches on the other unhealthy aspect of modern-day social comparisons. It isn't just that we're watching everyone else; we're also assuming or at least hoping that everyone is watching *us*. This makes sense: we humans have an innate desire to be seen. That's why when we post on social media, we hope to get likes. We want to feel relevant. We want to be seen, and we want to have the sense that we have social value.

We live our lives as if we're producing our own *Truman Show*, starring and directed by *us* . . . since we think only about what others might be thinking of us. And we consistently ask ourselves, "How do I rank on the social hierarchy?"

But comparing ourselves to others is a distractor. At its best, it can only lead to a temporary boost. At its worst, it can cause misery. Instead, I propose that we focus primarily on *ourselves relative to ourselves*—that is, who we are now compared to who we were in the past. It makes little difference how we compare to the person we envy down the street or to that hotshot colleague on our team. What is important is how we compare to the person we were yesterday or last week or last year. Are we becoming more of who we want to become?

There's a surfing metaphor that sums up how we relate to ourselves rather than others; it is articulated by *Black Cake* author Charmaine Wilkenson, who wrote, "Some people think that surfing is a relationship with the sea . . . but surfing is really a relationship between you and yourself. The sea is going to do whatever it wants."

Charmaine nailed it. Again, in terms of comparison, it should be between us and ourselves. That's where our focus needs to be.

Living in Fear

Like our cognitive biases, our brains are wired for fear. Fear can keep us safe, and there are real things to fear. I will not be writing about those. Instead, I will be writing mostly about imaginary fears. There's a primitive part deep inside our brain called the amygdala that monitors how we experience the world. One of its important jobs is to help us process our most primal emotions, like fear. And real or imagined, fear is one such basic emotion.

Fear is processed in the lower portion of the brain, making it a great model for survival. It served our ancestors well in the cave, and today it can serve those who are trapped in war zones and other dangerous environments. Alane Freund is an expert on highly sensitive people (HSPs). She shared on my podcast that HSPs are deeply attuned to stimuli that may trigger fear and anxiety. Yet, from an evolutionary perspective, HSPs may have saved the human race with their finely tuned nervous systems. They were the first to notice a storm coming, to be on the lookout for predators, and to call "fire" at the first hint of smoke. And these days, HSPs can exhibit all kinds of strengths, including creativity, empathy, and well over a dozen others.

But this heightened sense of danger often comes at a very high cost for those of us who live in a safer, more secure modern world. In particular, it means fear plays an outsized role in our lives even when our survival is not actually at risk. Making a difficult phone call, giving that public address, or taking a chance and writing a book (I know from experience) raises cortisol levels, increases stress, and produces a fight-or-flight response. This occurs even when nothing we are experiencing is actually dangerous as it relates to our survival. To cite a familiar idiom, we are making a mountain out of a molehill, fearing things that can do us no harm.

These factors relate back to the centrality of connection in our lives. For, ironically, we can also fear things that can do us a lot of good, like various forms of connection.

My client Steve had a good friend named Miguel. They met in med school and became fast friends. After graduation, it was hard to stay in touch. This was before Facebook and email. Things like this would happen—if you did not live close to someone, there was a good chance you'd lose touch.

Steve cherished his friendship with Miguel. As Steve got older, he thought fondly of the time they spent together. He always wanted to reach back out to Miguel with a phone call or a letter, but he never did. He was afraid to. He worried about what Miguel was doing now and how Miguel's life might compare to his own. Steve even wondered whether Miguel thought of their friendship as fondly as he did.

Not long ago, Steve learned that Miguel had died. He had allowed his fear of connection with others to limit communication. His chance to rekindle their connection was lost forever.

Steve got in touch with Miguel's widow and learned that Miguel regularly thought of Steve but failed to reach out for similar reasons.

Fear does not necessarily lead us to chase distractors, but it often prevents us from going after the connections we desire in our lives. Fear of connection takes many forms, including fear of rejection, fear of failure, fear of asking for help, fear of making phone calls, and fear of the unfamiliar. Confronting these fears, understanding them, and removing their power over us can help us move toward the greater connection we need.

So if you're afraid to do something that really can't hurt you, remember, you're physically safe! Pick up the phone, write that email, get the process started. We have all heard the famous Lao Tzu quote "A journey of a thousand miles begins with a single step." This brilliant, twenty-five-hundred-year-old quote is only useful if you put it into play in your life. And the more you make beginning that journey a knee-jerk habit and override the noise, the easier it will become to attain a life of real connections.

Fear of Rejection

"What if the person on the other end of the line rejects me? What if they've moved on, and they realize I haven't?" Many of us have allowed these fears to keep us from picking up our phones and making the call. I've been there. We all have. We want to connect or reconnect with someone, but that fear of rejection pops into our heads and interferes.

Like all of these distractors, this form of fear is understandable and likely has historical underpinnings. In the prehistoric world, being rejected from a tribe could lead to death. But today, rejection won't kill us. And while functional MRIs show that the pain of rejection hits the same brain receptors as physical pain, we have the power *to change the meaning* of the pain signal. If I reach out to an old friend and get rejected or the call doesn't go so well, it will hurt. However, I can *choose* that it also means:

1. I took a positive, safe, and reasonable risk.
2. I learned that my old friend and I are not currently well matched.
3. It may be time for me to find local friends or renew relationships with other people.

In fact, the rejection can ultimately serve as data, data that can make us stronger and far more rejection-tolerant.

Steve's challenge with Miguel is a common one for my clients. They are hoping to reach out to a past friend, a lost love, or a new connection. When they overcome this fear and push forward, the interaction tends to be very positive. Often, they find the friendship is as strong as ever or the new person is as eager to pursue connection as they are. Even when things don't work, knowing they can survive the perceived rejection and move on is empowering. At other times, it's less about rejection and more about the individuals being in different places, unavailable, or wanting different things. Yet reaching out can be cathartic regardless.

In these cases, we often find that the people who supported us and loved us in the past still want the very best for us whether or not they'll be a part of our future. If we can take a moment, breathe, and focus on our desired outcome, we may find the reinvigoration that comes with a new connection to someone. It can be scary, but the more we do scary stuff and understand the landscape of fear, the more the fear diminishes.

Wouldn't you rather try and fail than do nothing and regret the consequences?

I have never heard anyone say no to that question.

Fear of Failure

Sometimes, we're just afraid we'll suck at something. This is the fear that keeps us as newbies from trying just about anything because we know we'll look kind of silly when we first try. It's the same fear that keeps many of us from dancing in front of others.

Our fear of failure is an offshoot of shame, which, according to social psychologist Daniel Sznycer, developed "to prevent us from damaging our social relationships, or to motivate us to repair them if we do."[12] In other words, we feel shame over behavior that could harm our connections.

If we want to connect to anyone or anything, we must come to terms with the fact that failure is merely an entry fee we pay on the way to getting to that point of connection. Although we are averse to failure for a good reason, it will help us if we can see it for what it is: data. As Dorie Clark, a professor, author, and one of the world's leading business thinkers, reminded me on my podcast, failure is data. Of all the phrases I've ever heard about failure, this may be my favorite. Think of being wrong as data. Failure tells us what not to repeat and what to try next.

And that's not a bad return on investment for failure.

Or if you're afraid of mistakes, consider what Stanford Graduate School of Business lecturer Matt Abrahams said on my podcast: "Mistakes are just *missed takes*."

Or consider the funniest version of all time, from Guy Kawasaki, a man who worked alongside Steve Jobs at Apple and was one of the people who helped launch the original Macintosh. When asked on my podcast about learning to surf at sixty, he said, "You gotta make ass." What is "make ass"? I asked. Turns out, it is a Hawaiian expression essentially meaning "make an ass out of yourself in order to learn."

This is all to say, failure is such an important concept to wrap our minds around. Michael Jordan once explained, "I've missed more than nine thousand shots in my career. I've lost almost three hundred games. Twenty-six times, I've been trusted to take the game-winning shot and missed. I've failed over and over and over again in my life. And that is why I succeed."

★ ★ ★

Let's check out the opposite of our fear of failure by pivoting to our *fear of success*. A favorite quote of mine, from Marianne Williamson, relates perfectly to this: "Our deepest fear is not that we are inadequate. Our deepest fear is that we are powerful beyond measure. It is our light, not our darkness, that most frightens us. We ask ourselves, 'Who am I to be brilliant, gorgeous, talented, fabulous?'"

Or, as Steven Pressfield, author of multiple books including *Do the Work*, writes, "Our greatest fear is our fear of success. When we are succeeding—that is, when we have overcome our self-doubt and self-sabotage, when we are advancing in our craft and evolving to a higher level—that's when panic strikes. . . When we experience panic, it means we're about to cross a threshold. We're poised on the doorstep of a higher plane."

Other nagging fears of success include: As we succeed, will we still have our friends? If we succeed, how long will our success last? Will we get knocked back to where we were before our success? What will people think of us then? And can we tolerate having the spotlight on us? What if we embarrass ourselves while the spotlight is on us? What if people throw shade or hate our way when we put out our best stuff?

These self-sabotaging questions can be distractors that deter us from even starting on our desired paths.

But enough about our fear of success. Let's get back to our fear of failure.

I believe it is our own internal battles with failure that have led to so many of us resonating with the first *Rocky* film's story. Spoiler alert: The movie ends with Rocky ostensibly losing to Apollo Creed. When I saw it as a child, I hated the first Rocky film because I wanted him to win, and that was all I cared about or understood as a nine-year-old. But watching it as an adult, I came to realize the intention of the classic film: within that failure is his triumph. Throughout the movie, he's dismissed as being unworthy of the fight. Everyone sees him as a loser and wonders why he even tries. The fact that he gives it his all, performs that iconic training montage, and decides he's going to fight all twelve rounds is a personal victory even if the judges hold up Apollo's arm at the end.

Rocky is the real victor because he went the distance, courageously showed up with every ounce of his being, and refused to let a fear of failure hold him back.

That's how we can approach connection. We will not always win, but by giving our all in the ring of our choosing, we walk away winners by showing up and overriding our resistance to enter in the first place.

Fear of Asking for Help

Still, Rocky doesn't reach that fight against Apollo on his own. Throughout the movie, he needs help. He needs the support of his trainer, and he needs the support of the woman he loves, Adriana Pennino. Whatever our objectives in life, we all need help along the way. But in our American culture, we're taught to fear asking for it. We're often told we should be rugged individualists who take care of ourselves through every circumstance. As a result, we often fear reaching out for assistance.

But that fear is misplaced. It's true that our country benefited from its share of rugged individualists, but the success of its founding was built on mutual assistance. It took a community of people building on one another's ideas and an army that worked together to win independence. Our country came together over mugs of cider in the spirit of fellowship. After signing the Declaration of Independence, Benjamin Franklin is believed to have said, "We must all hang together, or . . . we shall all hang separately."[13]

In a poetic sense, we needed to demonstrate a healthy *interdependence* to gain independence.

While we may not live in small tribes anymore, we all still must work together to build and maintain our communities *and* our individual lives. We are social creatures, and we need each other; no one really makes it on their own.

I often think about Joseph Campbell's idea of the hero's journey, a timeless pattern used by storytellers. It was the pattern that was used to create *Star Wars*. It is so timeless it can even be traced to Homer's *Iliad*. A part of the timeless pattern is that the hero has both a mentor and allies. As with fiction, any real-life hero's journey features helpful and supportive characters without whom the journey could have ended badly.

There's nothing to fear in needing others. It's how we're built, and when we resist it, we can become lonely, depressed, and sick. We all do better by owning up to and embracing that need.

Fear of the Unfamiliar

There's a saying that our brain will always choose a familiar hell over an unfamiliar heaven. In other words, we'd rather continue suffering in known ways than take a chance on the unknown, even if we suspect it would be better for us.

Many of us love doing new things, but even for those of us who do, there tend to be limits; we love our well-known comfort zones, and we have a natural fear of stepping outside of them. This makes plenty of evolutionary sense. Going beyond the boundaries of known territory can put us at risk. It stimulates our amygdala, our brain's fear center. Invoking the recesses of our ancestral memories, we don't know what to expect. We don't know if there are dangerous animals or rival tribes who might attack us. We conclude that it's better to stay in a location we know with the people we know, doing the things we know.

Even if it all sucks.

But in the modern world, where the unknown tends to be more uncomfortable than dangerous, this fear keeps us from trying new things. We stick to routines that offer us no support or joy simply because they are familiar. We avoid new foods, new people, and new activities . . . only because they're new, unfamiliar, and, therefore, unknown.

What if instead we made it our business to try the new? Sure, there is sense in sticking with some reliable routines that work. But what if we each committed to swinging out of our routines for a particular percentage of the time? A simple example might be going to known restaurants 50 percent of the time and trying new places for the other 50 percent. Or we could generate some campy but mind-expanding rituals like deciding to embrace a Wacky Wednesdays playlist that features all new music. Or we might decide the fourth Friday of the month is Foreign Film Friday, a day to experience a new foreign film.

Any of these could serve as exercises to stretch into the unknown. Author and podcast guest Will Schwalbe described his practice of going out once a week to an event that specifically does not interest him. What has he discovered? Indeed, some events are boring. But he has also found that he's interested in far more than he'd imagined.

We might even take a tip from Alex Trebek, host of *Jeopardy!*, who said to A. J. Jacobs, "I'm curious about everything, even things I don't care about."

I'm sure there have been unexpected gems in your life that you wouldn't have found if you hadn't challenged yourself. Keep challenging yourself to go beyond the things that are familiar.

Viral Thoughts

One of my clients, Zach, was an author who had published a highly successful book and had signed a contract with his publisher to produce a second. He told me he felt tremendous pressure because his publisher had high expectations. He'd also been told his second book would be the one through which he'd prove himself as an important new voice. Unfortunately, he was facing extreme writer's block—for five years—and he said he couldn't get the book done. He was considering quitting writing and getting a "normal job" instead.

One day he came to me with what he thought was the issue: he said he "lacked character" and was unable to just suck it up and get the book done. I silently disagreed with his harsh self-assessment. I knew Zach's story well, and so I had evidence that he possessed plenty of what he referred to as "character."

I asked him where the idea of his lack of character came from. We dug deeper and realized that it came from the voice of a childhood neighbor, Mr. Johnson. Mr. Johnson was a successful, well-regarded, but cranky man who lived in the same cul-de-sac as Zach. Mr. Johnson openly resented Zach and his neighborhood friends and regularly told them that they "lacked character" because they engaged in activities that were different from what Mr. Johnson did in his childhood. Mr. Johnson was an Eagle Scout, had a job at the age of fourteen, and later served in the navy. As for Zach, he engaged in activities that teens normally did in his generation—they rode BMX bikes off jumps, skateboarded aggressively near houses of neighbors (like Mr.

Johnson), all the while blasting AC/DC and Van Halen on the boom box.

But Zach cared deeply about his community elder's assessment—even if he'd seemed rebellious as a teen.

Without Zach noticing it, Mr. Johnson's assessment had burrowed into his self-identity, and it was as if he'd caught a virus. Zach had downplayed the significance of writing a successful book by saying he was a "one-hit wonder" who, as Andy Warhol would say, had had his five minutes of fame. He believed the real proof of who he was would come through his being successful twice. He said the first book came naturally but—in his mind—the second required character he didn't possess. We worked on this and realized that he was in fact experiencing a situational depression that was exacerbating his writer's block. The echoes of Mr. Johnson's voice and Zach's depression were co-occurring and serving as a false advertisement on repeat in Zach's mind, telling him he had a character flaw, leaving him stuck. He was eventually able to disconnect from this untrue, unhelpful disconnector through our work.

Working together, Zach and I were able to identify a character virtue that could be useful to his problem: his curiosity. He was naturally curious, so we leveraged his curiosity to help him slow down his thinking and identify what was really going on and how to find a path out. Over time, he was able to disconnect himself from the belief that he lacked character. After doing so, he was able to complete his book—and with great success.

Once we identify these unconscious entities known as our disconnectors and distractors, we can attend to them. Then we can free up space for greater connection with what is real and what we care about.

In that spirit, before we get into the next chapter, I'd like to close with one of my all-time favorite quotes from Carl Jung. It sums up the lion's share of what we've looked at in this chapter: "Until you make the unconscious conscious, it will direct your life and you will call it fate."

CHAPTER 3

GETTING CONNECTED

Frank, a forty-eight-year-old attorney, entered my office, and even before sitting on the couch, he said, "You're gonna love this—I found out my wife is screwing her personal trainer."

I felt for him. He was in a world of hurt and anger. They had what might have seemed like a storybook relationship, but it was anything but. They had met in law school and were married for over twenty years. They were both highly successful attorneys, and both had worked very hard to achieve their professional success. But their dynamic had a sharp edge due to an element of competition that bled into the relationship.

I asked him what effect he thought that had on them as a couple.

"Probably not a good one," he said with a laugh. "It's hard when the person you love the most isn't really cheering for you and you're not really cheering for her—but you act like you are."

I asked him to share his thoughts about their relationship, how the two of them might have gotten into their situation, including contributions he may have made to it. Initially, he blamed the affair entirely on his wife. At this point, they were living separately, which was hard on them both, and she desperately wanted to reconcile. When I asked him if he thought that was possible, he said the odds were less than 1 percent.

One day, though, he shocked me by saying, "When you first asked me if I might have any role in what led up to the affair, I kind of wanted to say, 'Screw you' and walk out of your office. But then I sat with the question, and I realized that this might have been more my fault than I was willing to admit."

I asked him to fill me in. Ever the good lawyer, Frank stated his case: "When I come home from work, I don't kiss her. I'm kind of a cliché: I crack open a beer, go to the TV and channel surf between sports and news, and I even bring my meal over to the couch. I tell her that it's the only way I can relax after a stressful day.

"And many weekends a year, I'm off on 'guy trips' to Vegas, Cabo, New Orleans, with my high school and college buddies. I looked through my calendar over the last three years. I was shocked to notice that I hardly took her out on the weekends, let alone for a date night or a couple's weekend.

"We coparent well, but between our competitive styles, my obsession with work, and not giving her any time during my nonworking time, she's lost me."

With Frank's initial level of defensiveness, I was surprised by his willingness to consider his own role in his wife's affair. Frank elegantly articulated a case in which his wife, Fiona, not feeling the love and connection of her husband, had strayed to another man. Fiona and Frank didn't foster the ability to speak to each other with vulnerability because, he said, there was "too much competition and a need to appear strong."

Over the next several months, they explored this realization in couples therapy with a colleague of mine. With a signed release from Frank and Fiona, I was able to coordinate care and consult their therapist as I treated Frank individually.

Today, after a lot of hard work, humility, and a spectacular commitment to growth, their relationship is intact and strong. They no longer compete with each other; that competition has been replaced by mutual championing. Frank knows his wife's love language (quality time), and he can connect with her deeply. It's not perfect, of course, and neither of them wishes that the affair happened. But to borrow an idea from relationship expert Esther Perel, the affair shined a light on what was missing in Frank and Fiona's connection. They both came to see how the affair took shape and what to do to prevent it from happening again.

And stay connected.

Finding Your Connection

As we discussed in chapter 1, connection happens in four ways: with yourself, with others, with the world, and, for many, with spiritually. Finding connection in each of these areas can help "fill your cup." Ideally, you already have some meaningful ways to connect in all of those areas, but starting with just one of these areas, with intention, can help.

Frank and Fiona independently thought they'd been filling their own cups for years. However, after therapy, both came to realize that it had been an illusion; they hadn't been coming close. They also became aware that they weren't filling each other's cups. Through thoughtful and sometimes painful conversations, they identified what had led to the affair. They also figured out what they needed from their relationship in order to lead a more fulfilled and connected life together and individually.

Frank acknowledged his dismissiveness toward Fiona's needs, and the couple created a realistic plan to make a change. Frank also recognized that in order to fill Fiona's cup, he needed to fill his first. To do this, he went beyond his "go-to" of sitting in front of the TV and often went out on his bike or for a run instead to clear his head after a stressful day. To fill her cup, he also became willing to get creative, spending time with Fiona in ways that mattered to her. To ensure that he and Fiona had their quality time—while he still caught his games—he recorded about 50 percent and said being "live with Fiona" was more important than watching those games live.

He came to realize he was giving his attention and presence to his beloved team and not his beloved wife; he was not the husband he'd wanted to be. When Fiona shared her need for "quality time" with Frank, they set up a monthly date night and a quarterly weekend away.

In addition, they both expressed a desire for greater and more regular family connection, so they established a family dinner routine with their three children.

And they had more frequent and higher-quality sex than they'd had before the affair.

This helped them feel connected to each other. It also helped them feel more connected to their own needs. They were able to identify hobbies and other activities that helped them feel connected to the world around them. Fiona started getting more involved in her children's school, which helped her feel a sustained sense of purpose outside of work while also being more involved with her kids' lives.

I learned through Frank that Fiona described her new world as a virtuous cycle: Her cup was fuller. She was more aligned with her values as they related to family and as they related to her relationship, as well as in the areas of her life that deeply mattered to her. She said it was as though a connection circuit was emerging, synergistically impacting and strengthening all of her important connections.

* * *

The goal of connection is to become more intentional about what we are doing and immersing ourselves in the present moment. This is the experience of "flow," as popularized by psychologist Mihaly Csikszentmihalyi, who defines it as "a state of concentration so focused that it amounts to absolute absorption in an activity."[1]

This kind of immersion is helpful in many ways and can lead to a state of bliss. It's as if you connect so deeply with what you're doing that you become one with the thing you're doing—writing, reading, talking to your friend, playing basketball. After being in flow, people report a loss of time and a feeling of transcendence.

I'm sure you've experienced this, being in the zone, merged, and in flow to such an extent that you do a thing for two hours but feel like only thirty minutes have passed.

In many cases, we erroneously seek flow in the wrong places, leading to disconnectors or distractions. But getting into that flow state generally requires intention since, in the way I think of it, it comes from challenge and meaning overlapping. It requires skill. It's not just pleasurable or hedonistic. In Csikszentmihalyi's far more authoritative words, flow is "the melting together of action and consciousness; the state of finding a balance between a skill and how challenging that task is."[2]

This is what I hope we experience from our connections to ourselves, others, and the world. Finding these connections generally requires the process of slowing down our thinking and being intentional about what we want and the connections that are authentically important to us. By doing this, we can lead ourselves to a path of flow, which is a telltale sign we're deeply connected—generally with ourselves and what we're doing—but possibly in other ways too. Ironic, and very much on point, are the words of Eminem when he sings "Lose Yourself." Flow can be a combination of deep connection to ourselves and other entities while experiencing a simultaneous loss of self.

Sometimes the state of flow can also lead to a state of exhaustion. These deep connection activities require some energy, sometimes a lot of it. Think of Michael Jordan and the famous "Flu Game," in which he played in the NBA finals while he was very sick. In the documentary *The Last Dance*, he described himself as being in a flow state during that time, but he was also completely drained by the end.

It helps to have a diversified portfolio of connection activities that can fill our cups. The challenge and meaning of a podcast interview puts me into such a flow state that I lose track of time. The same is true of a deep conversation with anyone in my family. Watching great stuff on TV is also one of my favorite things to do, and I'm not going to give it up. But unlike my podcast or family-based activities, TV gives me a false sense of connection. It's what the science refers to as hedonic. It's *pleasurable* but does not cause flow. In fact, I've heard it referred to as fake or faux flow. I'm immersed, it's enjoyable, but no skill is required here. Still, I love it and do it. Hedonism has its place, and I believe we need proper doses of it, just not at the expense of flow-based activity.

Frank and Fiona's relationship continues to require the maintenance that all relationships need. Perhaps even more because so much harm was done before they decided to make an intentional step toward reconciliation. But they made a choice to come back together and rebuild their connection. And they renew that choice of connection each time they override their previous nonconnection habits. It's as if the relationship itself strengthens—like it's doing a push-up—each time they recommit to connect.

How can we all take these same steps toward rebuilding a connection with ourselves, others, and the world?

Cutting Yourself Off

To build or rebuild connection with ourselves, others, and the world requires an intentional commitment to attaining what we want. This is true of changing careers, pursuing a hobby, entering a romantic relationship, or deciding to have kids. If we want something, we need a plan. As the author of *The Little Prince*, Antoine de Saint-Exupéry, said, "a goal without a plan is just a dream."

There is always a cost to making a plan. Making a plan means making a decision, choosing one option, and discarding others. The words "decision" and "incision" come from the same linguistic root. When we make a decision, we essentially make an incision by cutting off other options so we can focus on the one that we want to pursue.

Some options are more permanently "cut off" than others—after all, we can change jobs or switch hobbies far more easily than we can walk away from our family—but there's always a set of roads that we must pass to find the road we really want. And no matter how much we dream otherwise, none of us can do everything. Taking one job means leaving all the other potential jobs behind—at least for a time. Monica on *Friends* lamented that marrying Chandler meant she was closing doors to anyone new. And having a child means we won't have as much free time or freedom as we used to.

For this reason, decisions can be scary. Often, we freeze in the face of decision, struggling with "analysis paralysis," spending so long considering our choices that we never make any choice. As psychologist Barry Schwartz, who authored *The Paradox of Choice*, once told me during a podcast interview, "Life is easier with fewer choices." Having many alternatives may lead to an optimal or better decision, but it can also lead to no decision at all. As Theodore Roosevelt once said, "In any moment of decision, the best thing you can do is the right thing, the next best thing is the wrong thing, and the worst thing you can do is nothing."

Or I'll paraphrase what Guy Kawasaki said on my podcast: Don't spend all your time focusing on making the right decision. *Focus on making the decision right.*

In this sense, constraints can help us. They can limit our options enough so that we can more easily make decisions. On the face of it, this seems like a bad thing because it means some options are off the table. But constraints can be the source of tremendous creativity and a path to the good stuff.

Counterintuitive, I know! If your professor gave you an assignment asking you to write a thousand words on "any topic," you might freeze up. You could choose anything—and you'd likely spend hours just figuring out what you wanted to write about.

But if the professor assigned you to choose between writing about your love of your favorite breakfast food or your love of your favorite dinner food, it probably wouldn't take you that long to choose. You'd pick one, get to writing, finish your hedonistic essay, and, as a bonus, you'd probably have a good idea about what to eat later!

Connection is as broad a subject as that first essay, one with no limits. Your whole life is filled with connections. I hope you're convinced by now how important it is to attend to those connections. But where to start? With family? With work? With spirituality?

The easiest solution would be to start nowhere at all—to abandon connection and get back to social media or streaming videos . . . essentially doing what Teddy Roosevelt warned against. But instead, let's start with fewer choices. We can do that by creating an inventory of our connections.

By identifying areas where we are strong and need less attention versus areas where we need to pay more attention to our unique and personal connection needs, we can limit our choices and make it far easier to decide where to start.

Name It to Tame It and Claim It

Beyond the value of limiting your options, there's real power in simply naming what is missing in our lives.

Zach Gottlieb, a high school student, activist, and artist, pointed this out to me. He was only sixteen when I spoke to him on my podcast, but he was wise beyond his years. One of the greatest insights he shared during our chat was that *we can't change what we don't talk about.* The dude is sixteen, and he understands this! Where was he when I was in high school? And he realizes the thing that many adults live their entire lives ignoring: we often struggle to identify, talk about, and deal with the things we most need to change.

Zach's comment made me think of the great children's book *There's No Such Thing as a Dragon* (by brilliant author and illustrator Jack Kent). In it, a young boy named Billy wakes up with a baby dragon in his room. Billy tells his mom about it, but she insists that dragons don't exist, and his dad agrees. The more his parents deny and refuse to identify the existence of the dragon, the bigger it grows—until it takes over the whole house and wreaks all kinds of havoc. It's only when the parents acknowledge that the dragon is real and talk about it that it begins to shrink, eventually returning to the size of a kitten and becoming harmless.

Knowing there's a dragon without acknowledging it doesn't work. The dragon's going to grow until it pushes us out of our houses. But people do it all the time. The dragon seems too large and too scary for us to acknowledge. So we compartmentalize. We deny. That is a great short-term strategy for lots of things—it allows us to ignore the pain of a horrible breakup and get through the workday or get out of bed the next day—but it doesn't resolve the issue long term.

That's true when you have a problem that needs to be dealt with, and that's true when your car's dashboards says "check oil." That's also true with your missing connections.

If your mechanic said, "Just ignore your car's check-oil light because it'll fix itself," you'd fire that mechanic on the spot. If you followed the mechanic's terrible advice, eventually the car would break down and probably at an inopportune moment.

If we try to just keep going and deny our dragons, they keep growing— and the damage they can cause increases.

We don't have to just live with this emptiness or dissatisfaction. We can find what is bothering us, give it a name, and work on improving it. If we admit there are dragons, we can name them, tame them, and move forward.

Our Most Limited Currency

Or we could just pretend that the dragon isn't there a little longer and think, "I'll deal with it someday." That's often our go-to solution. When we face serious and difficult decisions, the easiest immediate option is always to delay and numb out. We'll think about it next week. After all, the problem will still be there next month.

Given an infinitely long road, we'll kick the cans down it forever.

The thing is, we don't have an infinitely long road. Every day, we have a little less road left. Time is our most nonrenewable resource. You can lose money and gain it back. You can lose your health, and generally, you can get that back too. But once we lose time, there's no getting it back. We only have so much of it, and how much we have left on the battery of life doesn't show up on a screen like it does on our smartphones.

As the old song goes, "It's later than you think." At some point, we run out of road and our chance to live better, happier, and more connected is gone forever.

This happened to me with one of my most beloved mentors, Martin Doerner. Martin helped me immensely in my early professional journey. After I started my family, though, we lost touch. He didn't want to drive forty miles down to see me, and I believed I didn't have the time to go see him. The infrequent visits and occasional calls eventually ended entirely. There were no hard feelings, but I sensed that neither of us *believed we had the time* to reach out. I didn't know then how little time we had left. During our period of silence, Martin grew ill. I received notification of his death from a mutual friend. I was heartbroken. Time ran out before either of us could make a better decision.

I had fallen into the trap of assuming the road was infinitely long. But we must be willing to invest time in what matters. I'm a fan of the saying "A stitch in time saves nine," and I love how psychologist Amos Tversky once articulated a variation: "You waste years by not being able to waste hours."[3]

Had I been willing to "waste" figuratively just a few hours to drive out to see Martin, I would not have *actually* wasted years of regret over not seeing him.

I think about Martin literally every day. What I wouldn't give to be able to go back in time and drive forty minutes to see him one more time—he was one of the funniest, most interesting, most generous people I've ever met.

It's so easy to forget that the clock is ticking for all of us and for all of our connections. If we want to live a more meaningful, joyful life, we have to focus *today* on connecting to the things that really matter to us.

Your Connection Inventory

This is your moment to narrow your connection choices and name what is important. Then you can tame the list and make it your own. The rest of the book will focus on laying out in more detail the potential elements of your individual connection formula. But everything will refer back here, where you begin the journey toward the connections that you sense will have the biggest impact on your life.

To aid us in this process, I was given permission to adapt the best list of activities I've seen. It was published in the *DBT Skills Workbook* by psychologist Dr. Matt McKay and his team.[4] This list is superb. Yet of course, no list is totally comprehensive, so please add your own meaningful activities to it if they are missing.

As you review this list, grade each activity on a scale from −5 to +5, moving from connection activities you would like to decrease in your life—those are negative—to those you most need—those are positive. And zero is neutral—those activities you feel you have just the right amount of or don't feel you need at all. This scale will allow you to differentiate between what you have, what you need, what you need less of, and the degrees of their importance.

This ranking is important as you seek to inventory your connection needs and prioritize your options. Once you've completed the survey, tally up the total for each category. Those with the highest positive scores are the areas most deserving of your focus. If you need to draw attention away from other areas that may be distractors, you can look at areas with the lowest negative score. And the areas that fall close to zero can be safely ignored for the time being.

This survey will help you figure out what fills your cup and what does not. What is a distractor and what is not. What rejuvenates you and what keeps you stuck with those disconnectors. This survey helps you ask my favorite cup-filling questions: Are these things that feed me? Or do they bleed me?

Only you will know the answers.

_____ Talk to a friend on the telephone.

_____ Go out and visit a friend.

_____ Invite a friend to come to your home.

_____ Organize a party.

_____ Exercise.

_____ Lift weights.

_____ Do yoga, tai chi, or Pilates.

_____ Stretch your muscles.

_____ Go for a long walk in a park or someplace else that's peaceful.

_____ Go jog.

_____ Ride your bike.

_____ Go for a swim.

_____ Go hiking.

_____ Do something exciting, like surfing, rock climbing, skiing, skydiving, motorcycle riding, or kayaking, or go learn how to do one of those things.

_____ Go to your local playground and join a game being played or watch a game.

_____ Get a massage.

_____ Get out of your house, even if you just sit outside.

_____ Go for a drive in your car or go for a ride on public transportation.

_____ Plan a trip to a place you've never been before.

_____ Sleep or take a nap.

_____ Eat chocolate or something else you really like.

_____ Eat your favorite ice cream.

_____ Cook your favorite dish or meal.

_____ Cook a recipe that you've never tried before.

_____ Take a cooking class.

_____ Go out for something to eat.

_____ Go outside and play with your pet.

_____ Go borrow a friend's dog and take it to the park.

_____ Give your pet a bath.

_____ Go outside and watch the birds and other animals.

_____ Watch a funny movie.

_____ Go to the movie theater and watch whatever's playing.

_____   Watch television.

_____   Listen to the radio.

_____   Go to a sporting event, like a baseball or football game.

_____   Play a game with a friend.

_____   Play solitaire.

_____   Play video games.

_____   Create your own website.

_____   Join an internet dating service.

_____   Sell something you don't want.

_____   Go shopping.

_____   Do a puzzle.

_____   Call a crisis or suicide hotline and talk to someone.

_____   Get a haircut.

_____   Go to a spa.

_____   Go to a library.

_____   Go to a bookstore and read.

_____   Go to your favorite cafe for coffee or tea.

_____   Visit a museum or local art gallery.

_____   Go to the mall or the park and watch other people.

_____   Pray or meditate.

_____   Go to your church, synagogue, temple, or other place of worship.

_____   Join a group at your place of worship.

_____   Write a letter to God.

_____   Call a family member you haven't spoken to in a long time.

_____   Learn a new language.

_____   Sing, or learn how to sing.

_____ Play a musical instrument, or learn how to play one.

_____ Write a song.

_____ Listen to some upbeat, happy music.

_____ Turn on some loud music and dance.

_____ Memorize lines from your favorite movie, play, or song.

_____ Make a movie or video with your smartphone.

_____ Take photographs.

_____ Join a public-speaking group and write a speech.

_____ Participate in a local theater group.

_____ Sing in a local choir.

_____ Join a club.

_____ Plant a garden.

_____ Work outside.

_____ Knit, crochet, or sew—or learn how to.

_____ Make a scrapbook with pictures.

_____ Paint your nails.

_____ Change your hair color.

_____ Take a bubble bath or shower.

_____ Work on your car, truck, motorcycle, or bicycle.

_____ Sign up for a class that excites you at a local college, adult school, or online.

_____ Read your favorite book, magazine, paper, or poem.

_____ Read a trashy celebrity magazine.

_____ Write a letter to a friend or family member.

_____ Write things you like about yourself.

_____ Write a poem, story, movie, or play about what happened to you today.

_____ Draw a picture.

_____ Paint a picture with a brush or your fingers.

_____ Masturbate.

_____ Have sex with someone you care about.

_____ Make a list of the people you admire and want to be like—it can be anyone, real or fictional, throughout history.

_____ Write a story about the craziest, funniest, or sexiest thing that has ever happened to you.

_____ Make a list of ten celebrities you would like to be friends with and describe why.

_____ Make a list of ten celebrities you would like to have sex with and describe why.

_____ Write a letter to someone who has made your life better and tell them why. (You don't have to send the letter if you don't want to.)

This is a big list, but it's not meant to overwhelm you! Consider your inventory like the old Netflix DVD queue. You prioritize the ones you need to experience immediately, with some others there for when you have a little time on your hands. Remember, this exercise is intended to help you identify what is most important to you for greater connection and to go deep in those areas. It is not, however, a list to complete in its entirety. And, to reiterate, feel free to add anything meaningful to you that is not on this list.

The Messiness of Learning

I'm a big fan of witnessing creativity in all its forms. It's one of my areas of necessary connection. But while I love going to movies, live shows, or museums, I rarely get a chance to see how art is made.

One time, I was invited to a great artist's studio. I went in not really knowing what to expect, but what I saw was so far from what I had experienced as the artist's final product that I was shocked.

What I saw was disgusting.

It felt like I was in a delivery room in a hospital after a cartoonish, over-the-top-horror-movie-version of a delivery. It was dirty and messy. It was smelly. There was paint everywhere, which was expected. What wasn't expected was that trash was strewn about next to a couple of half-eaten sandwiches and a few old coffee cups with what looked like fetid and aged liquids.

I held my thoughts and was polite to the artist, but the whole time I was there, I kept thinking, "How is *this* a place of great art?"

When I left, still thinking about it, I realized, "Of *course* this is a place of great art." It made a world of sense that it was the kind of place where great art was born. That was why it reminded me of a delivery room or even a compost area near a garden. That's the only type of place that great art can come from. It's the equivalent of smelly manure fertilizer, which offers rich nutrients to grow beautiful flowers.

I love experimental artists like David Byrne and Kate Bush. They come out with some powerful stuff. Even if you aren't familiar with their work, you'd probably recognize Bush's "Running Up That Hill," recently revived on *Stranger Things*, or Byrne in his giant suit singing "Once in a Lifetime," which remains the "same as it ever was," iconic even after all these decades. But what we didn't get to see was the necessary mess, the mistakes and frustrations, along the way to these masterpieces.

And as in that artist's studio, our process of learning what makes us feel connected to ourselves, others, and the world might get messy. We are going to have to fail along the way. And failing sucks. But remember, failure is just data.

* * *

To get to our desired connections, we will find ourselves moving along the "four stages of learning" (sometimes called the "four stages of competence," popularized by many amazing thinkers, including Martin Broadwell). I like to think of the four stages in this way:

- **Unconscious incompetence:** We're total newbies and know nothing about the skill we're trying to perform.
- **Conscious incompetence:** We know about the skill but also now know the full extent to which we don't know how to perform the skill.
- **Conscious competence:** We've done it several times and now know how to do the skill we're trying to perform, but it takes all of our mental energy.
- **Unconscious competence:** We've done the skill so many times we can do it without thinking. It's in our muscle memories. We're basically Jedis who have mastered the skill, and it's automatic.

This movement from unconscious incompetence to unconscious competence describes the process of rewiring the fast-processing part of our brains (fast thinking) toward greater connection.

Let's think about this in terms of the book in your hands. Before opening *Super Psyched*, we might not have known that we needed greater connection. Now we know we need it (conscious incompetence) and that this book will help us become consciously competent. But it's going to take practice and application of what this book offers to get us to the last stage—unconscious competence.

This will involve some messy failure as we ascend to unconscious competence . . . but it will be worth it.

To move forward, we need to play in the messy spaces of being wrong.

The process of "ready, aim, fire" usually helps us hit a target. But "ready, fire, aim" also works if we are learning something new, as long as it doesn't endanger us. We do not always have to hit the target exactly. We can learn how to get there through missing a few times and adjusting based on the feedback, also known as data.

If we want to learn ballroom dancing, let's not fall in love with the image of ourselves as the next pro on *Dancing with the Stars*. Instead, let's fall in love with the feeling of being in flow while we are dancing. This means focusing on how we feel inside rather than how we may appear to others on the outside. We were not trained this way. But we can learn new methods that will be more helpful in getting us to a deeper state of authentic connection.

Let's Get Super Psyched!

The rest of this book is going to help you put your personal connection formula into action. Each chapter will cover a different topic relating to connection. I'll offer some "Connection Mastery" exercises to help you personalize and put into practice what each chapter has covered. Please go deeper into the chapters that resonate with you, and do not push yourself to take on things you think "should" fill your cup. Rather, go with what you believe actually *will* fill your cup.

However you decide to approach the rest of this book, I wish you happy travels as we explore the world of potential connections before you.

I'm super psyched to begin this process with you!

PART II
CONNECTING TO YOURSELF

CHAPTER 4

CONNECTING TO WHO YOU ARE

Although I didn't earn the nickname until high school, I was EthusiAdam the moment I was born. According to my mother, I came out of the womb ready to connect. In my first few months, every time she pushed me in my stroller, I was eager to make eye contact with every person who walked past. My reflex to connect with others just intensified from there.

Throughout my life, this natural inclination has drawn me toward a profession of helping others. When I was considering a career, I was totally overwhelmed and lost. Like many people, I spoke to a vocational counselor, and to help figure out my profession, I took the Strong Interest Inventory. The three top positions that came up were clergy, teacher, and social worker, all of which share components with the job I have now as a therapist. I tend to connect with people who are also seeking connection in others. My best friend from college, Aaron, is a psychologist. So is my wife, Aurianne.

From the outside, it was always clear what direction my life *should* take. In my adolescence, when I experienced depression and anxiety, I sought treatment with my therapist, Dr. Gordon Cohen. By sheer coincidence, I went to summer camp with his nephew, Marc, and while at camp, when I was just thirteen, I said to Marc, "I would love to do what your uncle does." Dr. Cohen had helped me. I wanted to help others. What better way to connect with people than by sitting with them for an intentional amount of time, digging deep into their thoughts, feelings, and longings, and then finding ways to improve their lives working alongside them?

★ ★ ★

While there were signs from an early age of what I *should* do, my distractors and fears got in the way. My path to psychology was anything but straight. For years, I felt incapable of achieving my dream. Dealing with dyslexia, undiagnosed ADHD, and a powerful belief that I wasn't smart, I struggled in school. I had a lot of trouble paying attention, and I couldn't focus inside the classroom during lectures or outside the classroom when I attempted to study. I was nearly twenty when I first read an assigned book cover to cover.

Through extreme effort—and some powerful mentoring—I managed to get my undergraduate degree and even entered a doctoral program in psychology. But considering all the hurdles in the doctoral program, I decided I couldn't do it. I dropped out of the program and gave up my dream. I decided I would make money at work and find meaning elsewhere.

Switching away from psychology was not catastrophic for my life. In fact, I was able to be quite successful in my plan B: Corporate Guy. I traveled. I met my wife. I made friends. By the time I was in my mid-thirties, I had a child, a nice house, and a good life. In most respects, I was happy and fulfilled—but that dream I had as a kid wouldn't leave. The fact that I'd missed my chance to do what I believed I was meant to do gnawed at me.

Aurianne kept telling me to go back to school. She pleaded with me. "I don't care what it takes. I just want a happy husband."

I would tell her, "I made my bed; I need to sleep in it," thinking I was being virtuous, manly, and accountable for what I believed were my bad choices.

That was my mantra. However, I wasn't being accountable; I was punishing myself. I was denying who I was and what I needed. I refused to open my mind to the various solutions because they appeared inconvenient.

I trained and became certified as a coach, hoping that would offer enough of what I was looking for to make me content, knowing it would take less time than being trained as a psychologist. Coaching would also allow me to keep working in sales as I built my practice. I absolutely loved (and continue to love) coaching. But studying and training to become a coach felt like an appetizer to a big, delicious meal; it only made me want to dive in headfirst and become a therapist. I wanted to be a therapist the way a dog wants to go for a walk—it was deep within my nature.

In the end, stopping short of becoming a psychologist was never going to work. By depriving myself of the connection I needed, I was making myself and *the people I cared about most* miserable. It wasn't selfish to pursue what I needed and to go back to school—I needed that connection for myself, yes, but I also needed it for all my significant others.

Finally, my buddy Aaron and wife, Aurianne, both convinced me. I went back to school. And, well, you know what happened after that: I finished school and started my practice, putting me on the path to writing this book you are now reading.

Know Thyself

When my father-in-law, Alvin Jacobs, was dying, he shared a great deal of wisdom. He told me to rely on the classics. If something has been considered true and valuable and has survived for dozens of generations, it's probably true and valuable for you too, he'd say. In the history of well-worn advice on the search for connection, one of the greatest of the golden oldies is "know thyself." That comes from Socrates, a founder of Western thought. These words are so powerful because at their root, they speak to a very basic truth, one that Socrates knew well: we can't get very far if we don't first understand ourselves. Years later, Shakespeare would echo this point in *Hamlet*, advising, "To thine own self be true."

Toni Herbine-Blank is a renowned couples therapist and the creator of a model for couples therapy called Intimacy from the Inside Out. When she guested on my podcast, she said that before we can be intimate with others, we have to be intimate with ourselves. We need to know who we are because *we* are our own primary tool of connection.

Knowing who you are is where being super psyched starts. Everything goes outward from there.

A rough fact of life is that we are all born alone and we die alone. Major bummer, I know. You are the only one who's there for your whole journey. You are your only constant companion. And it's better to take that journey knowing yourself well.

Knowing ourselves allows us to build healthy connections *beyond* ourselves. And, for the record, increasing this connection to ourselves is *not selfish*! The self is the foundation for everything we do.

Whatever our connection activities include, whether volunteering or spending time with our kids or writing a novel, being able to connect with ourselves is foundational. When that foundation is cracked, it limits our ability to build anything on top of it. When we build on a cracked foundation, the cracks may widen, negatively impacting us and the people around us.

Who are you? And what do you want? They seem like simple questions. But finding the answers can be harder than you think. This chapter will walk you through ways to discover, on your own, who you are, so you can learn what you need and what you want.

Tools for Learning about Yourself

During the time I lived in Japan, I was in good shape. I had great "cosmetic" muscles—meaning I *looked* strong. In those days, I sometimes engaged in arm wrestling with friends. One evening, a super-slim young martial artist named Tetsu challenged me. Looking at the two of us, the idea he'd win seemed laughable.

As we locked hands, though, I found to my surprise that his arm was like solid steel (and in a wacky irony, *tetsu* can be read to mean "iron" in

Japanese!). He didn't look it, but Tetsu was internally jacked. No matter what I did, I could not move his arm. I had the "bigger" muscles, but his arm wouldn't move an inch. Tetsu destroyed me, but as a true Japanese gentleman, he was very gracious in his victory.

I believe a reason Tetsu could so easily overpower me was his deep awareness of himself, what he would have referred to in Japanese as *ki*, or the energy that flowed through him (known as *qi* or *chi* in Chinese). He had such supreme mastery of his energy that my superficial strength was inferior to his deeper strength. He had taken the tools that he had—his body, however slight—and learned how to master those tools to achieve his goal, which, at that moment, was kicking my butt.

Another point relating to this phenomenon is a moment from Dr. Christina Heilman's keynote at the 2019 California Psychological Association. Chris instructed the attendees to stand up and find a partner. One person in the dyad was to put their arms straight out and make a statement that was positive about themselves. The other person was instructed to push down on their partner's arms as the statement was made. Generally, when the positive statement was made, the arms were strong. Next, the same person was told to say something that was negative about themselves. Can you imagine what happened next? Within seconds, the entire room erupted in laughter.

Our arms were not nearly as strong when our statements were negative.

Then something powerful: Christina told me that same response could occur when we say or think a *true versus a false statement about ourselves.* I've used this exercise in my practice, and the results have been consistent: the person's arms tend to be far stronger when a true statement is made.

This is the power of authentic connection as it relates to self-knowledge—our first stop on the connection tour. What is your primary motivator? What gets you moving and makes activities and connections enjoyable? What gives you the strength and resolve to be your strongest, regardless of your physique?

If you don't have answers to those questions yet, that's OK. You may even have some resistance to the idea that you're special or have strengths.

But you are, and you do. And it's worth taking some time to seek out those strengths.

We as individuals are comprised of many aspects and characteristics that define our *selves*: thoughts, feelings, behaviors, beliefs, a soul, an inner voice, among others. This book will not attempt to define who we are from that vantage point. Entire books have been devoted to this subject, many of which have done an outstanding job.

Instead, I'll leave it to each of us to answer the following questions, which will assist us in defining what "self" means in the context of this book:

- When have I felt most alive?
- When have I felt strong in my body?
- When have I had conviction about my beliefs?
- When have I felt my heart open up?
- When have I been most loving?
- When have I felt most loved?
- When have I been most focused?
- When have I experienced clarity in my thoughts?
- When have I stretched my mind to understand something new?
- When have I felt authentically me?

Connect with a felt sense or an image in response to each of these questions. These are the "selves" I am referring to.

There are multiple ways to begin this search for self-understanding. As Tetsu demonstrated, martial arts are certainly one avenue, as is meditation. Others prefer therapy or journaling. Some seek understanding through deep conversations with loved ones or long, contemplative walks.

Whatever your current methods for self-connection are, know them and maintain them. Sometimes, taking a ten-minute shower or listening to your favorite song is enough to recenter yourself.

* * *

One of my favorite tools is the Values in Action (VIA) Inventory of Strengths, a superb offering from the world of positive psychology.

In 1998, University of Pennsylvania professor and psychologist Martin Seligman was elected president of the American Psychological Association. After stepping into the role, he was unsure what his platform would be. He wanted to make an impact and not just be a figurehead of the organization. Puzzling over this, he went out to weed his garden, a place of rejuvenation and thinking for him. Wrestling in the dirt with those weeds, he began sweating and swearing as he worked. At the time, his daughter was outdoors with him. As kids tend to do, she got herself upset over one thing or another, and she started to whine.

"Stop whining," he snapped.

"I'll stop whining," she countered, "when *you* stop being such a grouch."

As he says in his book *The Hope Circuit*, Seligman had nothing to say to that. He was shocked. How could he lead the American Psychological Association when he couldn't even be in control of his own mood? Instead of being present with his feelings, he let them define him, causing him to snap at his daughter.

He realized that there was a blind spot in modern therapy. Clinical psychologists had become very good at identifying problems, reducing those problems, and getting our patients to a neutral state, often neutralizing distress or pain. But we didn't have anything in the clinical toolbox to get us north of neutral, to a state of feeling happy or fulfilled, that could serve as a positive target for our outcomes.

That led him to the study of happiness and the discipline of positive psychology. His aim was to create a framework that might offer guidance for making life more engaging, meaningful, and joyful. Not surprisingly, this discipline has found that material things give us limited happiness. We believe, for example, that a new car will make us happy. But on average, material things do not create sustainable happiness. Instead, intangibles like connections do.

Seligman and fellow psychologist Christopher Peterson created a multi-disciplinary team of social scientists to develop a list of values (also called character strengths) that have existed throughout time, across religions and cultures. People could look at this list of timeless values, figure out their top five, find ways to tap into at least one of them, and make their lives more fulfilling.[1]

Soon, a systematic way of figuring out one's values and character strengths was born: the VIA Survey of Character Strengths, a questionnaire that helps you discover your top-five value strengths (the website for the questionnaire is listed at the end of the chapter). These are virtues like curiosity, kindness, leadership, humor, and self-control. You can rely on these virtues to guide nearly all of your actions. By concentrating on these strengths, you can find the best ways to leverage them to fill your cup and increase your enthusiasm for life. Doing so will make your work more fulfilling, your connection with others easier, and your life more enjoyable in general.

The VIA survey is a tool I consider necessary for everyone to identify their strengths and how to put them into use. In very little time, you can come to know a lot about yourself and what you need to reinforce each of your connections. I have a neighbor who is a full-time dad. He loves being a dad. The VIA identified his greatest strength as love, and he embodies the value of love in everything he does—love for his kids, love for repairing his home, and big doses of love for his spouse. He is able to provide strong support for her career because of his love for her and his children. Pretty much everything he does for his family he does through the lens of love. This value creates a virtuous cycle for him.

Two of my strengths are curiosity and love of learning, which I use every day in my career as a psychologist. This love of learning propels me to hone my craft and to understand how people in my office see the world. Other strengths of mine include kindness, gratitude, and perseverance. Each of these, too, has an important place in my life and energizes me when I put it into practice.

Knowing our strengths and values is a powerful first step in attaining greater connection; these elements drive us toward the connections we seek.

Accept Your Whole Self

As we learn about ourselves, it can be hard to accept parts of who we are: not just our weaknesses and limitations but even our talents and strengths. I've always loved a quote that is attributed to Einstein: "Everyone is a genius. But if you judge a fish by its ability to climb a tree, it will live its whole life believing that it is stupid."

This was certainly my experience. Until I learned what my weak points were in education—namely, that I had ADHD and dyslexia—I was certain that I was stupid. I kept trying to climb trees (when I should have been swimming) until I figured out I needed to swim.

We all have our weaker points. When taking the VIA survey, we learn not just where we are strongest but also which strengths are least prominent in us. And though it's far less helpful to concentrate on our weak points—since we get a bigger return when we focus on improving our strengths—it's useful to identify them and to know how they may affect our lives and our needs for connection.

We all have challenges. For me, one of them was my inability to learn and my difficulty with follow-through. We often learn about these less-than-wonderful aspects of ourselves from feedback in our relationships. For many of us, it could be a lack of confidence, a short temper, or something else we don't like about ourselves. We all have elements of our conscious and unconscious selves that we wish weren't there.

Carl Jung called these rejected parts of ourselves "the shadow," and many of us might recognize this concept from Darth Vader in *Star Wars*. In the series, a man named Anakin Skywalker was unable to identify and manage his anger, fear, and desperation. In other words, he was unable to manage his shadow. Anakin famously became Darth Vader, the ultimate villain. Perhaps a reason for the huge popularity of *Star Wars* is that we feel a deep connection with the struggles of the characters. The series contains universal, timeless themes including positive examples of managing our shadows. A stark comparison to how Anakin managed his struggle shows up in his son, Luke, who was the hero of the series. Like his father, Luke struggled with fear, anger, and desperation. Unlike his father, Luke was able to channel these emotions by knowing and managing his shadow. Doing so allowed him to become a fiercer warrior for good.

The light side / dark side example from *Star Wars* may be a cliché, yet it gives us a helpful way to think about these concepts. Sometimes, our dark side needs to be expressed so we can get it out into the light. According to Jung, this is the paradox: "One does not become enlightened by imagining figures of light, but by making the darkness conscious."[2]

Even though I am EnthusiAdam, I have plenty of dark days. Like all of us, I don't enjoy those days. But when I'm at my best, I try to be curious and learn what I can from them.

Being super psyched doesn't mean being "always happy." Instead, it means being "super" connected to our *psyches* and knowing all of our parts, including the darker ones. Without this knowledge, these parts are more likely to control us or get us into trouble. Imagine those parts presenting themselves at the worst possible time. Not a pleasant image! Yet ignoring our dark side keeps us from being able to choose how we use our emotions and behaviors. Ignoring our dark side causes us to lose control, say something we can't unsay, or do something we can't undo, and possibly lose the trust of others and ourselves.

So what do we do with the energy of our shadows? We can find ways to rechannel that energy toward something productive. For example, we can use our anger on a physical task like a do-it-yourself (DIY) project. When we feel a little bit out of control, focusing on a tangible, controllable task can put the focus on the external, giving the internal some time to stabilize. As a bonus, we may knock some stuff off our to-do list!

I wholly agree with Winston Churchill, who said, "Never let a good crisis go to waste."

To sum up, if we want a more connected life for ourselves, we have to know our shadow and make efforts to choose how it shows up in our lives. We can channel it into art, exercise, writing, or other places where it can contribute to, not diminish, our lives.

The Gospel of Tomas contains this timeless and salient quote: "If you bring forth what is within you, what you bring forth will save you. If you do not bring forth what is within you, what you do not bring forth will destroy you."

A Journey to Connection

I first mentioned that I wanted to be a therapist at thirteen, to Dr. Cohen's nephew Marc. I didn't become one until decades later. It took me exactly thirty years from uttering those words to Marc to get my psychologist license and establish one of the foundational connections in my life: my profession.

Newly licensed, I finally got my own office as a forty-three-year-old. Here's the kicker: my office was just down the street from Dr. Cohen's. Even as I write this, I'm still shocked by this coincidence. It was a long journey that concluded back where I had started. But I did complete it, for myself, for my family, and for the people I would come to serve.

That same opportunity is there for you. The better you know yourself, your strengths, and your shadow, the better you can approach the connections you need to feel fulfilled in your life.

CONNECTION FORMULA EXERCISE

Take the VIA Inventory at www.viacharacter.org and learn about your character strengths. After completing the inventory, take stock of your top five strengths. Choose one of them. Put that strength into daily use. Find novel ways to implement various expressions of that strength. Notice how it feels. Did you experience more flow in your day? My guess is that your answer will be a solid *yes*.

CHAPTER 5

CONNECTING TO WHAT YOU NEED

I work with highly seasoned executives. But despite their admirable strengths, they almost always become flummoxed when I ask, "What do you hope to get from our work?"

These are highly educated professionals and executives who have climbed to the top of the corporate ladder, and yet they don't know what they want or need.

And I relate to them. Like many with ADHD, I was a late bloomer. Those with this condition are often up to three years behind their neuro-typical peers.[1] That's a huge gap to cover, and until my adulthood, I was sure that the gap was my fault. What other explanation could there be as to why I couldn't cut it but my relatives had?

Eventually, I managed to overcome my early setbacks. And I don't think it would have been possible for me to do so if I hadn't addressed my mental health needs first.

My efforts to come to terms with ADHD and dyslexia took me many years and consistent effort. But it all began with finding a mentor who could guide me toward who I could become. That mentor was Professor Allen Greenberger. I had just finished my first semester of college, and let's just say it did not go well. I had acquired a 2.2 GPA. Before that semester, I'd never read anything longer than a CliffsNotes booklet. This was the habit that allowed me to pass classes in high school. I felt bad about taking this shortcut, but anything longer or more complicated seemed completely out of my reach. Eventually, though, my unrecognized disability finally caught up with me, and I could no longer fake it in college.

I couldn't seem to make any progress on reading, no matter what I picked up. I would often sit in the library for hours only to discover that I'd barely made it through a single paragraph. I'd spent the whole time reading and rereading the same sentence, just trying to understand it. This experience was infuriating and demoralizing. I couldn't figure out what caused me to struggle like that and determined I was stupid, lazy, or both. I felt entirely hopeless about my future.

My buddy and roommate David thought Dr. Greenberger could help me with these struggles. I was a bit starstruck and intimidated at the mere thought of talking to the professor. He was known to be especially brilliant, and he was the most popular professor on campus. Each day, there was a line of students outside his door, seeking his wisdom and guidance.

But one Friday afternoon, I joined that line. By the time I got in to see him, it was nearly evening.

Sitting down, I took a deep breath. "Professor Greenberger, I'm thinking of dropping out of college. I don't think I have what it takes, and I don't think I am valuing the opportunity of being in college."

"What will you do instead?" he asked.

"I could become a waiter," I suggested. I expected him to immediately dissuade me.

Instead, he nodded. "Yeah, that sounds like a good idea."

My mouth dropped open, and I protested, "But I can't do that!"

"Why not?" he asked.

"Because I'm better than that!" I huffed.

"No, you're not," he said bluntly.

I let that sink in. He was right. I wasn't just being hard on myself. I was being judgmental toward a whole industry. What made me think I was "better" than someone who waited tables? And yet if I didn't want to be a waiter instead of going to college, what was I going to do about it?

After a moment, he looked at his watch. "Listen," he said, "it's Friday and it's late. If you want to continue this conversation, come back on Monday at ten."

Over the weekend, I had an epiphany. So I came back on Monday at ten to share it. This time, it was his turn to be stunned.

"Dr. Greenberger, I figured out my problem and I have the solution," I told him after I sat down.

"OK. Let's hear it."

I said, "I got through high school without reading a book. I just read CliffsNotes. My problem is, I can't really read. What I'd like to do is read one book a week that you assign to me. I'd prefer the book not be available in CliffsNotes. I want to make sure I can't cut corners so I *have* to read it. And you'll drill and grill me for one hour each week on the book, and we'll discuss it. It'll be an independent study for a portion of a class credit."

Professor Greenberger said, "That may be the strangest thing a student has said to me in twenty years . . . but I'm in." He pulled a book off his shelf, *The Woman in the Dunes*, by the Japanese existentialist author Kōbō Abe. "Read this and come back and see me next Tuesday at ten a.m."

That week initiated one of the most transformative few months of my life. Every week, I'd get a new book, go to the now-defunct Benji's Coffee Shop, self-medicate on tons of caffeine through endless refills of mediocre but effective coffee, and read as much as I could in one sitting. Every three-hundred-page book would take me around thirty hours to complete, but I did manage to read all of Dr. Greenberger's assigned books cover to cover. And I didn't just read them. I took pages and pages of notes. For the first time in my life, I palpably felt my brain turn on. It was as if I were painfully but gainfully carving new neural pathways with each read. Slowly, I discovered that I loved books. I loved reading. I loved *thinking*.

That independent study was only worth one-third of a class in terms of units. But by the end of the semester, I had completed the best class I would ever take and received one of the greatest gifts ever. *I could read and think*. One of the great joys of my life had been unlocked. And although I was still many years away from managing my ADHD, reading and thinking were the links to the future I never believed I could have.

Connection Requires Health

Next time you're sick, check in with your body and see how hard it is to connect to anything outside yourself. Sickness turns us inward. We focus on our pain, stuffy noses, or fatigue. We often feel isolated. In such a state, connection is nearly impossible. One of my all-time favorite ideas, in the words of the English pediatrician and psychoanalyst Donald Winnicott, was conveyed and paraphrased to me by a colleague, Dr. Hugh Grubb. These are the wise words:

A good sign of mental health is the ability to share yourself and receive another.

When we're ill, so many resources are going inward to conserve energy and heal, making it hard to share or receive. And this same phenomenon occurs with mental health issues like anxiety and depression. When we are depressed, we ruminate, and when we're anxious, we worry. We get stuck in our heads. It can be a lot harder to connect to ourselves or with others. In those moments, a huge portion of our mental energy and resources goes to the thoughts and feelings we can't get out of our heads.

If we want to connect outside ourselves, we have to first attend to our health needs. This is why when on a plane, we are told to put on our oxygen mask first before we help those around us. If we aren't breathing well, we can't help others breathe.

We all have physical and mental health needs that we must prioritize. Of course, those needs look different for each of us. Everything is on a spectrum, and so are we and our needs. To make an automotive comparison, a Ferrari, a Prius, and a Ford F-150 truck, like us, all have different needs. Among their many differences, each requires different maintenance schedules and each works best on different road conditions. If we want them to take us where we need to go, we need to tune into those needs.

It's the same with our bodies and our minds. If we want them to take us toward the connections we need in our lives, we'll need to give them a personalized tune-up first.

The last chapter focused on the basic first step of the connection process: connecting to ourselves and our distinct characteristics. This chapter is going to focus on the next step to greater connection: connecting to what we need. We all have physical needs, emotional needs, and the need for self-compassion.

These can't be ignored.

Connecting to Physical Needs

"Mr. Duffy lived a short distance from his body." That's how James Joyce describes Mr. Duffy, a man who was numb to life and divorced from all valuable connections—including a connection to his body.

We all act like Mr. Duffy sometimes.

We tend to feel this type of disconnection most acutely in times of stress. Often, our bodies can feel separate from us, like something we lug around begrudgingly. But our bodies are not luggage. They are central to how we experience and connect to the world, and they demand our attention and care.

It's hard to overstate this demand. And the Hierarchy of Needs, developed by Abraham Maslow, helps us understand what properly attending to our bodies might look like. It is a famous framework for thinking about human needs and motivations. You may remember it from your high school or college Intro to Psychology class. There have been several versions of this hierarchy visualized as a pyramid, with various stages of growth: physiological needs such as water, food, and shelter as the foundation, safety and security as the next stage, love and belonging after that, and esteem and self-actualization at the top of the pyramid.

You need to meet the first two elements of the pyramid before you can move on to love and belonging, let alone esteem needs or self-actualization. With that in mind, it's all the more important that we listen to our bodies' individual needs before approaching subsequent levels on the pyramid.

We all have a winning formula to keep our body operating at its best. Honoring your answers to the following questions can make a notable difference in how well your body performs for you:

- How much sleep do I need?
- What foods provide me with the best fuel?
- How much hydration do I need? And how can I make that hydration easily accessible?
- How much and what kind of exercise powers me up?
- What relaxation or meditation methods work for me? And which ones are user-friendly enough to implement regularly?
- What other practices will power my body? How can I make them as easy as possible to implement?

Once you know what your body needs and you are responding to those needs, new connections can appear—seemingly on their own. This is the virtuous cycle of connection. For example, getting a gym membership is a great opportunity not just to take care of your health but also to connect with others getting in shape. You can take up jogging and invite your significant other or a friend to join you. On the other hand, joining a yoga, Zumba, or spin class can connect you with people who become new friends.

Connecting to Mental Health Needs

According to Mount Sinai Health System's website, the average person waits three hours after a heart attack to get help.[2] Let's compare that response time to an emotional crisis of the heart: on couples therapist John Gottman's website, it says that most unhappy couples wait six years to start counseling.[3]

Sadly, a reason for this delay may be the perceived taboo of receiving mental health treatment of any kind. Thankfully, various athletes are sharing their mental health struggles and their success with treatment. We can't perform at our best if our emotions or anxieties are inhibiting us. As *New York Times* best-selling author and therapist Lori Gottlieb said on my podcast, our mental health *is* our health.

Further, our mental health and physical health are deeply intertwined. There are promising studies that show strong cardiovascular exercise can be as helpful to our mental health as psychotropic medications for reducing the incapacitating effects of depression and anxiety.[4]

Often, healing involves therapy and/or medication. There will be readers who are hesitant about one or both, but I want to be clear that either can be helpful and often, a combination of the two can do wonders. A good fit with a therapist alone can make all the difference for many people. Meta studies have shown the effectiveness of therapy, and they're positively encouraging.[5] And studies show the right psychotropic medication can be a valuable tool that helps millions return to healthier, more joyful, and more connected lives.[6]

For some of us, medication can be temporary—like a knee brace—providing extra support while therapy and skill-building help strengthen the muscles. This was a key part of my journey in treating my own ADHD. For about five years, I took medication daily to treat my condition while I did the heavy lifting of therapy. I attended trainings and read books on how to develop better time management and focusing skills. I put these new skills into practice and patiently visualized the person I wanted to become: a focused and reliable person who could be the husband, father, and professional I deeply wanted to be. I referred to this practice, in jest, as my self-imposed Navy SEALs training.

I believe all of these resources were necessary. Not making use of all of them would have prevented me from connecting with my authentic self. I needed to shave away what wasn't consistent with who I wanted to be and build what was.

These days, I rarely use medication. I only take it when I need support for extremely mentally challenging tasks. I am now able to concentrate and function by using the habits I created during my self-imposed training. For many of us, though, medication is a lifelong commitment, like wearing eyeglasses or treating a chronic condition like diabetes.

★ ★ ★

It is true that many psychological disorders—anxiety, depression, schizophrenia, bipolar disorder, PTSD, and so on—can harm our ability to connect. But it's also true that our habits and activities can harm our mental health in less obvious ways. Scott, a person with whom I worked, was a high-level software engineer. He was addicted to the news. He identified as a hard-core doomscroller.

One day, he entered my office and said, "I can't sleep. I can't focus on work, and I'm way behind on a bunch of projects. My kids and my wife keep telling me I seem like I'm somewhere else when we're together."

We talked about what was going on, and it didn't take long to figure out the answer. "All I can think about is the news," he said. His outrage, fear, and sense of helplessness kept him from connecting with virtually everything that mattered to him.

Despite being a natural news junkie, he's made a concerted effort to limit his exposure to the news. There are costs: he says he's not as well informed on the day-to-day events of the world as he used to be. But he emphatically reported that the benefits have far outweighed the costs. He is more present at work, at home, and with his thoughts.

We took a look at the phenomenon of highly sensitive people together in chapter 2 of this book. Their heightened awareness also means they are likely to be more affected by their environments. After we reviewed the characteristics, it was clear, albeit surprising, to Scott that he was a highly sensitive person. There's a 1 in 5 chance that any one of us is, and it is not a pathology.[7]

Like Scott, who needs to monitor his reflex to take in copious amounts of news, we all need to protect ourselves from what renders our Superman useless around our own versions of Kryptonite.

Self-Compassion

An important part of attending to our needs is being kinder to ourselves by learning to demonstrate self-compassion. Dr. Christopher Germer is a psychologist and lecturer at Harvard Medical School who appeared as a guest on my podcast. He's also the world's leading expert on clinical applications of self-compassion and explained we often speak to ourselves in harsh ways that we'd never use with anyone else. He said something else: if we spoke to others the way we speak to ourselves, it would likely kill the relationship.

Put another way, if we want more robust health and connection in our lives, we need to start treating ourselves with the kindness we reserve for others. Many of us erroneously believe that being harsh with ourselves is virtuous. But it's not.

This is backed by research. Germer and Dr. Kristin Neff, a pioneering researcher on the topic, have done extensive work on the topic of self-compassion. They have found that all types of physical and mental improvement can come from treating ourselves with compassion.[8]

Germer has pointed out that it's so good for us, it can improve a spectacular range of physical or psychological outcomes.

The power of self-compassion isn't just used by psychologists either. Coach Steve Kerr blew my mind on my podcast. Steve is one of the greatest figures of all time in the NBA. He played professional basketball alongside Michael Jordan on the Chicago Bulls and has coached Steph Curry and the Golden State Warriors to extreme success. As of this writing, he is one of the winningest people in NBA history, with five championship rings as a player and four as a coach. He shocked me when he told me that he places compassion among his four core values for winning.

Further, self-compassion is not New-Agey. The Navy SEALs use it because it gets more positive results better and faster, according to Germer. So if we want to win, we have a better chance when we are clearly on our own sides and acting as our own supportive coaches cheering ourselves on.

We struggle to accept this point because self-compassion often runs against the instincts we've developed from our social programming. In America, we are taught that self-flagellation is practically a virtue. We may think of self-compassion as something that gives us a "get out of jail free" card for anything or an act of self-indulgence.

Yet far from being a "get out of jail free" card or self-indulgent, it is actually an act of protection against toxic self-harm. When we practice self-compassion, we can access strength from within ourselves.

Let's take a moment to think of the opposite: When we are in the midst of adversity, will we respond better if the voice inside of our head is cruel? In the face of stress and pressure, what's the voice we need?

We need the voice of kindness. We need a voice that is on our side: a voice that allows us to be the strong—even rugged—person we need for ourselves. And, of course, this voice allows us to be the same strong person for the important people in our lives.

You may already know the value of compassion when it goes outward and the power it can have in someone else's life. Just think about how you responded the last time a friend felt bad about themselves. Did you tell them to just "get over it"? And if you did, did that work? I doubt it. Instead, I imagine you showered them with enough compassion to help them fight off that attack of shame or disappointment.

And I'm asking you to do the same for yourself.

Cultivating Self-Compassion

Neuroscientists estimate that we have thousands of thoughts per day. The funny thing is that most of our thoughts on a given day are not new; most are useless repeats from yesterday and long before, like our brain's version of junk mail or spam. More discouraging, the thoughts most of us have about ourselves are overwhelmingly negative.

To develop strong, stable, happy relationships, John Gottman describes a "magic ratio" that helps maintain contentment and satisfaction in a relationship.[9] This magic ratio is simple but surprising: for every negative interaction or feeling, you need five positive ones to get to a positive state.

No relationship is as central to our happiness as the one we have with ourselves, but many of us think extremely negative thoughts about ourselves. Why wouldn't we take the time to improve our relationship with ourselves just as we would with a partner? To do that, we need a practical strategy to increase self-compassion and start inching toward that magic ratio.

We can begin practicing self-compassion in three steps, as endorsed by Germer and Neff and paraphrased below. They are simple but perhaps not easy. They take time, and they're worth it.

1. **Common Humanity:** Recognize that the suffering and setbacks we experience are universal. We humans are *all* on a tough journey, and we're *all* making similar mistakes and experiencing similar feelings along the way. It helps to remind ourselves that *we are not alone*. We aren't especially weak or sad or stupid. Our feelings

are just part of being human. And the feeling of "I'm alone" makes things so much worse. We social animals tend to heal better with company, real or imagined. Recognizing our common humanity allows us to know we are not alone.

2. **Mindfulness:** We must be accurate about what is actually going on to avoid inflating the drama of our situation. And while mindfulness may seem esoteric, as you may recall, *it's being aware of what's going on while it's going on.* That simple. Imagine you are a sportscaster running the play-by-play of your life and emotional state. Most of us aren't running color commentary. To address this, we can label our feelings and the events of our lives as clearly as we understand them using feeling statements: "I feel sad and fearful about my prospects for finding what I'm looking for." "I feel angry at myself for making a poor impression in the interview." "I feel disappointed with myself because I gained so much weight over the last few years."

3. **Self-Kindness:** The third way to self-compassion is talking to ourselves nonjudgmentally, in the way we'd talk to a good friend who just revealed things they're struggling with. We'd likely be kind to them and should follow that example for ourselves.

The overall aim here is to be kind to ourselves, gentle with ourselves, *and real* with ourselves. We aren't telling ourselves fairy tales or excusing our bad behavior. We're leveling with ourselves, but we're being kind and compassionate while doing so. We're approaching our pain from a perspective of love. If we do that, we're more likely to change for the better.

So lean into any of these three or a combination. Speak to yourself as you would a friend instead of being self-critical. This is an opportunity for you to be the beneficiary of the kindness you would ordinarily reserve for others.

The Value of Boundaries

One of the most powerful things we can do is to understand how to create a boundary. Not having boundaries can do us great harm. According to an empirically validated form of therapy called interpersonal psychotherapy, many people who are anxious or depressed find their systems were first strained by a lack of boundaries earlier in life.[10]

Creating boundaries protects us and our health. It sets limits on what we can handle and what we allow in. To summarize my colleague Dr. Susanne Weir, knowing how to say no to another can be a big yes to ourselves. Do we really want to attend that party for someone we barely know and give up a lovely, quiet evening at home that we desperately need? Do we have to pick up the phone for a person who talks our ear off when we're at the end of a long day and need someone to listen to us instead? What if we receive a request that is a big *no* but feel guilty about saying anything but yes? Sometimes we need to suck it up and override our desire for self-preservation. But we need a balance, and that means a capacity to say no. Setting boundaries can make the difference between good and ill health.

In setting boundaries, the point is not to "teach" others a lesson or to make demands of them. Instead, it is to thoughtfully determine our own limits, to communicate those limits clearly, concisely, and kindly, and then to stand guard over them.

I have found it useful to use the "K sound" with the people I serve as a mnemonic device for boundaries: keep them *clear*, *concise*, and *kind*.

It takes commitment to maintain a boundary—and it can include real sacrifice. Dorie Clark shared on my podcast that she turned down a fully paid trip and gig in the Cayman Islands because she realized she didn't have the space in her life for it.

Now that is a firm boundary.

That may not be the right boundary for you—I don't think I could give up a paid gig in paradise! But Dorie knew her limits, and she guarded them carefully, and she was better for it, with no regrets. I imagine that instead of FOMO, she experienced JOMO: the joy of missing out.

As we set boundaries, we also have to accept the boundaries of others and accept that we have no control over how others respond to our boundaries. In a few circumstances, I have seen people lose friends ostensibly due to a response to a boundary. But such scenarios have been very rare in my experience, and the dissolution of those relationships likely had other causes.

Having clear boundaries is a way to take care of ourselves and, ultimately, others.

CONNECTION FORMULA EXERCISE

Take a video of yourself having a conversation on the phone with someone. Alternatively, take a video of yourself giving a presentation. (You can use your computer's video app for either.) If on the phone, it can be particularly rich to try this when you're speaking with a family member or friend. In either case, the recording will be one-sided, focused only on you and how you present. Note your blind spots and habits but do so as if you were your own best friend and wanted to offer supportive feedback. Notice anything you don't like that is changeable, like your tone of voice, your facial expression, or other verbal and nonverbal expressions. Many of us are particularly self-critical when hearing ourselves or seeing ourselves, but keep in mind that others are likely less critical of us. So be extra gentle with yourself. This is a great opportunity to practice self-compassion in any combination of the three ways described in this chapter.

CHAPTER 6

CONNECTING TO WHAT YOU WANT

Let's revisit my client Zach, the author who was stuck with writer's block. He had a misguided but deeply ingrained belief that "lack of character" kept him from success. We decided to work on his connection to who he was and who he wanted to be. He was a restrained, conflict-averse guy who struggled to assert himself. These traits held him back from following the steps I outlined in the last chapter: setting boundaries, taking care of his physical and mental needs, and cultivating self-compassion. A stated goal of treatment was that he would be able to better identify how he was feeling and what he needed out of life.

I walked him through an exercise. Because he was a writer, I asked him to write a story with himself as the protagonist. In this story, he'd need to write himself as a passive character, consistent with how he'd been interacting with people. This character was the opposite of the assertive character he wanted to be in real life. And to turn up the amplifier to eleven and make it more intense, his character needed to do everything everyone asked of him.

He wrote the story. Not surprisingly, it read well and was vivid and imaginative. I asked him what he thought of himself as the passive protagonist. He said he felt angry with the character he wrote. He didn't like what he read. But he also recognized the truth in the story. He could see, as an outsider to his own story, that he'd been letting others define him rather than tapping into himself and taking on what he wanted.

Then I asked him to write a second chapter of the story, one where the same character (Zach himself) was assertive about his needs. In this chapter, he had felt the pain of not speaking up and, instead, decided to override his habitual style and speak up about what he wanted and what he needed. In this version, he maintained boundaries. He was to have self-compassion. And he was to articulate his boundaries through the guidelines of the mnemonic of K sounds: clear, concise, and kind.

When he returned the next week with this version of himself, his mood was vastly improved. Zach liked his character much better. He had identified who he wanted to be. And he committed to faking it until he became it.

In real life, over time, Zach succeeded in becoming the second, more assertive version of himself. He made gains but also experienced predictable setbacks, and ultimately, I witnessed him gain a sense of mastery in becoming assertive.

This story illustrates at least two things: One, we can increase our connections to ourselves when we know what we want and when we are able to ask for it clearly, concisely, and kindly. Two, we can change who we are. Zach did not immediately become the person he wanted to be. It took him time and practice. But the act of merely writing it out moved him closer to his goal more quickly. It helped him see far more clearly and feel deep within himself where he was stuck versus what this new version of himself would look like. It compelled him to feel into the discomfort of how he was doing things in the present and to think through doing and propel himself to do whatever it took to get him to this level of assertiveness.

We know from research in cognitive behavioral therapy (CBT) that behavior can be a powerful driver of change. While you can *think* about who you want to be and what you want, you can also *act* your way to this new state of being. In my experience, we often get more and faster results from action rather than from just thinking. Insights alone don't create a good life. Instead, I endorse doing the courageous thing and gaining those insights later.

One of the best ways I know to achieve this is to "Fake it till you make it." Or better still, "Fake it until you *become* it." Or, my very favorite, "*Act as if.*" In other words, pretend it's already true, which is what I did with Zach.

The exercise I did with Zach was a little trick to help him move from thinking to action. We know from Motivational Interviewing—a great method for behavior change—that we listen to no one more than we listen to ourselves.[1] Dr. Stephen Rollnick, a cocreator of the approach, shared on my podcast that it's the discomfort or dissonance we feel about ourselves that drives the change. And Zach, feeling the dissonance, asked himself, "Who am I now? Who do I want to be? And how do I not become the guy in the first chapter but, instead, become the guy from the second?"

By writing yourself as the hero, you externalize what is internal. You see yourself as if through the eyes of another, even though it's still actually you who's viewing you. And in doing so, you prepare to self-correct and engage your truer voice and behaviors.

In this chapter, I hope to help you identify that truer voice. We have covered the basics of connection with yourself: identifying who you are and what you need. Now we get to take one step up: connecting with what you want.

Get in Touch with Your Desires

I love barbecuing, grilling, and smoking food. For me, it's not just about the delicious meals. It's about the very act itself. It's the smells coming off the grill that bring forth warm, happy associations with past outdoor events and time well spent with those I love. To me, it represents a form of positive energy that makes me feel alive—a connection back to a sort of prehistoric type of cooking over a fire to provide an amazing meal for my family.

I've felt this way about grilling for as long as I can remember. For years, I'd walk by the grills on display in one store or another and tell myself, "Someday, I'll get one of these. I'll cook for my family, and it will be awesome. I can't wait to smell, feel, and experience that magic with the people who matter to me."

I didn't grow up with a grill in the home. No one ever taught me how to be a "grill guy." I didn't even know where to start. I had no idea whether I should get a charcoal or pellet or propane grill. I didn't have any recipes to follow. I knew no techniques. And so, for years, I put the purchase off.

Then, one day, I couldn't take it anymore. I *wanted* a grill. I *needed* a grill. I wanted it so badly, in fact, I didn't care about the learning curve, so I got one.

My life—and, by extension, my family's life—is better for it. I love being a grill guy. Buying a grill or a smoker is a small thing, but it has vastly improved my quality of life. It's a cherished connection that always recharges me.

This is the nature of our *desires*—a word I like for the intensity it suggests. Small or large, when they are healthful and contribute to who we want to become, our desires have the potential to vastly increase our happiness and fulfillment. Desires can be huge—a dream career, the person we want to marry—or they can be smaller and seemingly inconsequential. They can also be clear and obvious or completely unconscious. The only thing that ties them all together is that they can add real value to our lives and tell us more about who we are. Not who we want to be. Not who we are pretending to be.

Who we are.

To help bring those types of desires to the surface, I am a fan of creating bucket lists. You've heard of this list, the one that lays out all the things you want to do before you kick the bucket. It's a list of desires you need to check off to feel you've lived a complete life. You don't have to be old to draw one up, and you're never too old to start. I created one in my twenties. And on that list, I placed items like traveling to several countries, biking five-hundred-plus miles on the California AIDS Ride, making my own wine, and parachuting out of a plane. I also listed my desire to own a grill. While I haven't jumped from a plane yet, I've done a lot of the others . . . and still have a lot more to do.

The list offers no guarantee that anything on it will make you happy or improve your connections. We've all done something that we thought would make us happy or bought something that we felt certain, at the time, would make our lives better, only for it to sit in a corner for years and gather dust. Most of us have also dated someone we thought we had a deep desire for only to discover we really didn't connect well. Sometimes, desires don't work out. But very often, they do. And the only way to know if it's a success or a dud is to try it.

Think of the example of a swimming dog who's never seen water—the only way to bring out the inner swimmer is to expose that dog to water.

By creating a thoughtful list, we're more likely to target the things we can get super psyched about—and those are things we're more likely to be motivated to pursue and enjoy when we attain them.

As you draw up your list, consider a common, self-limiting trap: the "I'm not the sort of person who . . ." trap. This idea was presented to me by a brilliant person in tech, and I love the act of breaking out of the "I'm not the sort of person who . . ." trap. Far too often, we know what we want but deny ourselves the opportunity to pursue it because we place limits on ourselves.

Often these limits are based upon old beliefs that restrain us or no longer serve us. We all can act like the character in Zach's first story chapter: the person we think we are or who we've allowed ourselves to be. But we need to act like the person in the second chapter: the person we want to be.

We tell ourselves that we "aren't the sort of person" who travels or joins dating websites or learns another language. We've been told we aren't musical, so why bother picking up a guitar? We believe we aren't social, so why bother even applying for the sales job we want?

Maintaining these limiting beliefs can harmfully narrow our lives. Let's opt out now.

* * *

I recommend approaching your desires from a place of challenging yourself. Don't avoid getting uncomfortable; in fact, seek out discomfort. Channel your inner A. J. Jacobs. A. J. is easily one of my all-time favorite people and a frequent guest on my podcast. And one of the reasons I find him infinitely interesting and inspiring is that he seems willing to try just about anything. Over the course of a thirty-year writing career, he's authored books about reading the entire thirty-two-thousand-page *Encyclopedia Britannica* in a year (*The Know-It-All*), evaluating every major health fad (*Drop Dead Healthy*), and discovering what it would be like to follow all the laws in the Bible (*The Year of Living Biblically*).

In one book, *Thanks a Thousand*, he tracked down and thanked over one thousand people who played a part in producing the cup of coffee he was enjoying in the morning. We're talking about the growers of the bean, the makers of the equipment used to cultivate it, the guy who created the wooden boxes it traveled in, and 990 others. He thanked each of them. In another, *It's All Relative*, he tried to track down every relative, no matter how distant, in order to have the world's biggest family reunion.

He's become the guy ready to try anything. Yet he's human, so I imagine he's had the thought "I'm not the sort of person who . . ." and has done the work of overriding it. It appears there are few ideas so weird or out-there that he wouldn't at least consider giving them a go.

And that's one of the most valuable lessons to take from connecting with what you desire. Whatever is on your bucket list, don't discount it because it's outside your normal experience. In fact, that may be all the more reason to pursue it.

Quiet the Imaginary Audience

One of the main reasons we try to avoid the things that are outside our everyday experience is because we are afraid we'll look bad. We might want to learn to dance, but we know we'll look awkward at first and fear the judgment of those who see us in our beginning efforts.

Fear of other people's judgment is part of how we are wired. We can never fully escape it; it's deeply wired in us, but we can recognize that much of it is overblown. In fact, it's so overblown that often we feel shame for things that no one ever sees.

A common phenomenon that emerges in early adolescence and increases our self-consciousness is what's called the *imaginary audience*. It's a psychological phenomenon that has various potential effects on us, including dissuading us from expressing our individuality. But we are social creatures, so, for many of us, it can show up throughout life. It's the voice that makes us feel embarrassed even when we're alone. We may imagine people staring down at us from on high, judging our efforts in a negative light.

This imaginary audience can be a potent force in influencing our behavior, sometimes for good, sometimes not. It can even influence our health. I once knew a doctor who had a serious medical condition. He was afraid to use hypnotherapy because he worried about what his peers would think—even though there was no way they would ever find out. He had to consciously convince himself of this fact before he would pursue a treatment that could relieve his pain.

Fortunately, he pursued it, and he's grateful he did because it helped.

It should go without saying—but I'm going to write it all the same—if no one can see you doing something, it's up to you to override the jeers of your imaginary audience.

Even when other people actually *can* see us, they probably aren't paying attention to us. A glance in our direction is no more than a glance. They forget about us the moment we're out of their line of sight, and they generally go back to the thoughts in their own heads. And even if they do think about us, we shouldn't assume their thoughts are all negative; they may admire us and what we're doing. There are many people who would like to take up jogging but worry they'll look goofy like Phoebe from *Friends* when she tried to jog. They never leave the house for fear of being judged by strangers.

Don't allow yourself to be imprisoned in this way and squander time during which you could be doing something awesome! The thoughts of others are as likely to be positive ("Look at that guy go!") as negative. And most likely, no one is thinking about what you're doing at all.

What really matters, at the end of the day, is what *you* think. That's what should be occupying the high rent of your penthouse suite, also known as your brain.

No Guilty Pleasure

I once went to a concert put on by the person I believe was the greatest singer ever: George Michael. Feel free to laugh; I don't mind. I'll defend the late, great George Michael all day long, and I'm so glad he was finally inducted into the Rock and Roll Hall of Fame. But there was a time when I used to turn the volume down and roll the windows up whenever George was playing in my car.

By 2008, when I stood in the concert audience, I was well past that, and I'm so glad I was. George Michael died in 2016. But because I embraced my love for his music and got over my ridiculous worry of appearing dorky, I got to see him live. I went to that concert and had the time of my life. He delivered big. I may have been one of the only straight guys there who wasn't there because of his girlfriend, but I danced hard and loved it.

As long as you're not hurting anyone, including yourself, there's no such thing as a guilty pleasure. The idea is flawed because it gives too much value to the opinions *others* have of the things *we* like. When we order coffee, wine, or beer, we may feel doubt about what we like because we've been told it's not what we *should* like. We let our friends' TV preferences dictate what shows we can feel good about enjoying. But none of these people are living our lives.

Shawn Steiman has a doctorate in coffee studies from the University of Hawaii and is the coauthor of one of the most comprehensive books on coffee. He said on my podcast, very simply, "You like what you like."

This idea was corroborated by the leading researcher on olfaction (smell), Dr. Rachel Herz of Brown University Medical School. She wrote two books I love, *Why You Eat What You Eat* and *That's Disgusting*. She said during an interview on my podcast that if you find something truly disgusting in a taste, you will probably never come to like it.

I'm not suggesting we shouldn't grow our tastes if possible. There are some things to which we don't have as strongly negative reactions, and for those, we can develop a taste, appreciation, or even love. But we have a right to enjoy what we enjoy. Our enjoyment of entertainment and activities—so long as they don't hurt us or anyone else—should always be more important. There's nothing to feel "guilty" about.

This goes for rejecting what others want for us as well. We shouldn't feel guilty for wanting to take our own path. One of my patients, Lakshmi, is twenty-five. She had been accepted into one of the most prestigious graduate school programs in the world—a program that offered her a clear path to a high income and an impressive reputation. The only problem was that *she didn't want to go.* It was what her family wanted but not what she wanted for her life.

She was indecisive about attending and deferred her acceptance. After a few weeks, at dinner with family, her grandfather asked her when she was going to get her life together and accept her place in the program. With immense courage, she let him know that his priorities were different from hers.

She ultimately chose her own way, pursuing a master's in a so-called "impractical" field of study. And as of her last report, she is very happy about her choice, and I believe she'll find a practical way to use it!

That level of courage is quite rare. We often take direction from others standing on the sidelines of our lives. And this leads to a phenomenon I see all the time in my office: people in their forties and fifties who are at the top of their careers only to wake up and realize they're miserable because they followed someone else's vision of the best path for their lives. Can you imagine being super psyched about living someone else's vision of your life?

I sure can't.

You Are Entitled to Joy

Truman was a CEO in his early sixties. His board had voted him out after some internal squabbles, and after a year of looking for a new position, he recognized he wasn't going to find a new job.

The Valley is a small place, he said. People talk, and too many bad things had been said about him and his performance.

He had no idea what he would do if he wasn't a CEO. Truman had come to identify so strongly with his job that he believed he didn't know anything else. In fact, he told me he had been marinating in that identity long before he actually stepped into the role.

"Ever since I was in high school," he said, "I was told I was like a young CEO, and that became my singular focus. I got into Princeton and from there, Stanford Business School, all with one goal in mind: CEO."

For him, CEO was a final destination. A complete sentence. An identity.

My work with Truman took a long time. But over time, he told me about the road not taken: music, writing, photography, community service. These were things he wanted to do but didn't because he was a CEO. He said that even on his off time, he needed to engage in activities to support that role. He liked brewing beer, but he believed CEOs didn't do things like brew beer unless they were selling it. Like me, he played bass in high school and longed to be in a band. He hadn't played beach volleyball since college. He liked barbecuing but couldn't imagine spending time at the grill when he could pay a private chef to make the kind of food he believed was consistent with what a CEO would eat. And although he'd always wanted to serve on the board of a humanitarian nonprofit organization with his hard-earned executive skills, there had been no time.

After many sessions exploring his thoughts, feelings, and options, he decided not to consider new career options. Instead, he decided to retire and began to revisit various abandoned parts of himself. To his delight, it was like starting a new love affair. He decided to focus on what he called his five Bs: brewing, bass, beach volleyball, barbecuing, and board work.

"I can't believe how much I love doing this stuff," he said. "I wake up every day more excited than ever. I didn't want to be fired from my job, but ultimately, I'm grateful for it. If I was still CEO and working, I wouldn't have done all of these amazing things."

You do not need to go through what Truman went through to find your "five Bs." You do not need to worry about what you "can" or "can't" do based on your identity. You don't have to wait for someone to fire you from your job, for your marriage to end, for your kids to leave home, or for . . . whatever it is.

You don't even need his bank account. Zero in on the joy that the items on your bucket list would bring you, recognize those activities as your birthright, and do something from that list.

We'd all be better served if we could cultivate a healthy sense of entitlement. We are entitled to ask for what we want. We are entitled to strive for what we want. Of course, we aren't always entitled to *get* what we want. We have no right to violate others, demand that others date us, or demand they give us the job we want, for instance. But we do have a right to want something for ourselves and to do what we can to get it.

In fact, that entitlement to our joy is key to all of our connections. We deserve to live fulfilling lives sustained by connections that matter to us. Whatever the nature of those connections—whether romantic, friendly, occupational, spiritual, or anything else—we are entitled to reach out for them. We have a right to seek the things we desire: the people, the activities, and the grills.

CONNECTION FORMULA EXERCISE

Take Zach's lead and write a two-chapter story about yourself, the first about how you are currently behaving in ways that don't serve you. And in the second chapter, write about yourself behaving in ways that *do* serve you. Notice the feelings that arise as you write and read each chapter. Think about your options, and find strategic ways to move toward your desired version of yourself in chapter two. You may want to start slowly, moving forward little by little. Or, if it feels right for you, consider taking a bigger swing toward that second version of yourself. Consider what you can do to live that new story. Be courageous and move forward.

PART III

CONNECTING TO OTHERS

CHAPTER 7

CONNECTING TO A SIGNIFICANT OTHER

I met Auri, my wife, when I was eight years old. We attended the same religious school. Neither of us was interested in the other. We were in third grade and in that "girls/boys are gross" phase.

At some point in high school, I realized I was attracted to this girl I'd known most of my life. I wrote something very flirtatious in her yearbook, but I was so completely off her radar she didn't even notice I was trying. After graduation, I assumed I'd never see her again.

But sometimes, life gives us another shot at a missed opportunity. I got mine seven years later in the Bangkok International Airport. I was walking through an empty corridor at 7:00 a.m. on the way to Kathmandu to visit my friend Aaron, who was in Nepal at the time. As I plodded along the empty corridor to my gate, I saw a lone beautiful woman smiling at me as she was walking toward me. I didn't recognize her, but attention from a beautiful female felt great.

"Adam, it's me, Auri, from high school!"

I couldn't believe it. Meeting Auri again—and on the other side of the planet. This was definitely unlike any other chance meeting I'd ever had.

"What are you doing in Bangkok?" I asked.

"I'm off to Calcutta. I'm going to work with Mother Teresa."

Lo and behold, like me, she was also working on a doctorate in psychology. It was just one more thing that drew me to her. We chatted for only ten minutes, but I felt something strong inside myself. If I have a type, it's *her*. She was everything I was looking for. But I had to catch a flight, and so did she. We parted, and again I assumed that was it.

But it wasn't. Nine years later, in March 2002, I was volunteering for a youth group at my childhood synagogue. It was "mitzvah day," which roughly means "a day of doing good deeds." It is kind of funny to note that it was an event that had been created by my mother, and I brought my youth group of fifth- and sixth-grade kids to an activity for this event. That year, we were making greeting cards for children in hospice care.

The woman in charge of the activity asked me to go down the hall to get paper towels and water for the project. The moment I stepped out of the room, I saw Auri. This time, I recognized her first, and, unlike in the previous meeting, she didn't recognize me.

I walked by her, tapping her on the shoulder, and said, "Hi!" As she recognized me, her eyes lit up.

And this time, we talked and I got her number.

That night, I left her a voicemail and told her I wanted to hang out.

But I didn't hear from her for two days. When she finally did call back, she seemed far less excited.

In her message, she sounded professional and distant. I can still hear her voice saying:

"Adam, I got your voicemail. If you'd like to talk, I have some time from six to six thirty p.m. Thursday or nine thirty to ten a.m. Friday."

I called her, saying I'd take the thirty-minute slot on Thursday.

She was extremely punctual. Six on the dot, she called. The first words out of her mouth were "Congratulations on your engagement."

I was floored. "Engagement? Auri, I am not now, nor have I ever been, engaged. I'm single."

In an instant, the tension broke. It turned out she had heard a rumor that I had proposed to someone. No wonder she had tried to keep her distance. I decided to make sure that there was no other confusion. I'd been attracted to Aurianne since high school, and it was time to make my intentions clear. On that call, I told her that I was interested in more than friendship, that I was looking for something serious.

We set up a date. To get to her residence, it took ninety minutes, and my back was sweating and tightening up the whole way. Getting out of the car, stretching my back, I thought to myself, "If this woman isn't who I think she is, I'm not making this drive again."

Apparently, my first words to her were "OK, I'm here. Now tell me everything about you." Not a date opener I would ever advise, but it accurately reflected my desire to know if I'd be making the drive again.

In spite of my ill-advised opening, we had an awesome nine-hour date, and we moved slowly. By the end, I was ready for another date. Lucky for me, she felt the same way. After I left, Auri called her best friend, Renee, and said, "I've met my husband—or at least the prototype."

Moving Beyond Yourself

My relationship with Auri—to whom I now refer by her full name, Aurianne—has been the foundation for much of the happiness in my life. Together, we bought a house and started our family. She encouraged and supported me to return to psychology. We share friends, adventures, and new experiences. And we take care of each other in hard times. I'm forever grateful to have her in my life.

I'm not alone in this situation. For most people, a spouse, a significant other, or a partner is the most important relationship in their lives.

I think Freud got it mostly correct when he said, "Love and work . . . work and love, that's all there is." Love, as the word is intended in this book, has multiple implications, including friends and other places we apply our love. And, of course, one of those is our primary relationship. Those are the central pillars of connection that sustain most of us in most of what we do. And no pillar is as fundamental for *most* people as their long-term romantic relationship.

But as with most things, long-term romance is not for everyone. There is a growing number of people who decide to remain single or to express themselves differently in relationships, and they, too, have meaningful and full lives. While this chapter is dedicated to people who wish to be in a romantic relationship, I want it known that I fully respect how each person chooses what's right for *them*. Although I can't speak to the love needs of all readers, it is my hope that this chapter will convey useful information to many people.

As with everything in this book, please use anything relevant to you and discard the rest.

Despite the potential for so much joy within our primary relationship, we all know that it's not all fun and games, and certainly not all the time. A relationship with a spouse or partner can go south quickly if we do not regularly attend to the needs of the relationship.

The last few chapters helped you connect with yourself to lay a solid foundation for the other connections in your life. Now we move on to how you connect with others. We start with the connection to your significant other.

Feeling Accepted

When Aurianne and I crossed paths that last time, we both knew what we wanted from a relationship. In fact, I was extremely clear. On our first call, I told Aurianne that I was looking for a relationship that could lead to marriage. I was in my early thirties. I wanted something real and sustainable. I was ready for marriage.

Aurianne was in the same boat.

Because I knew what I was looking for, I could be transparent and up-front with her. That set our relationship on a much stronger footing from the start.

The same wasn't true for Mario, someone I once worked with who struggled with erectile dysfunction, also known as ED. He was in his late twenties and had been to every doctor he could think of. He received a full urological and blood panel. Nothing came back suggesting a medical cause. He'd begun using Viagra, but he found that at times, even that didn't work.

He was young and in great physical shape. He wasn't depressed to the point that it appeared to reduce his libido. "What the hell is going on?" he desperately asked me.

"I have a hypothesis," I told him. "Since you've had a complete array of medical tests, your ED might not be physical."

But Mario dismissed me immediately. "You have *no* idea how attractive these women are," he protested. "There's got to be something wrong with my *body*."

Then he met someone he really liked—he said she was special. He had been able to get hard with Viagra. But a month later, even with the blue pill, he went flaccid. Instead of finding an excuse, he told her the truth. He told her how long he'd been struggling and how upsetting it had been.

He expected rejection. Instead, she got playful. He was shocked and felt loved, accepted, and, for the first time, safe.

He arrived at the following session with this insight: "Both my head and my heart wouldn't let my penis do its thing until I felt a strong connection. I finally felt truly safe and accepted for all of me. My relationship had to be beyond the physical."

This was a crucial moment for Mario. *True connection offers vitality and safety.*

We continued to work for over a year, and his erectile issue resolved without any other interventions. After careful consideration, he proposed, and they got married. He continues to have check-ins with me from time to time, and he reports that he still hasn't needed a single pill. It's been nearly a decade, and he marvels at how healing and rejuvenating his relationship has been.

Themes and variations of this happen a lot with my clients, especially the heterosexual males I see. They may be fearless bulls in the boardroom, but they're Bambis in the bedroom. They can close a multimillion-dollar venture capital round and show up for tense board meetings with no problem, but they report feeling scared to be vulnerable with their wives. They say they do not know how to be open and honest with them. This drives them to my office, where we explore what's really going on and how to understand their thoughts, feelings, and fears in relation to their partners. By exploring these internal states in a safe space, we can process the vulnerabilities and find ways to connect more authentically. The men report that they inevitably feel more connected to their spouses afterward.

Choose Wisely

If my private practice were a game of *Family Feud*, the number-one answer on the board for why my clients seek therapy would be "My Relationship." (Number two, incidentally, would be "My Job," which we'll get to shortly.) This is all the more reason to follow the advice of author H. Jackson Brown Jr.: "Choose your life's mate carefully. From this one decision will come 90 percent of all your happiness or misery."[1]

Of course, our hearts need to be heard in our love decisions. Yet in my clinical experience, many people have not used their brains sufficiently to weigh in on this crucial decision. We need to leverage the best of both sources for this life-changing decision.

This may seem obvious. But people often come to my office saying, "When it came time to choose my spouse, they seemed to be a close-enough match." Upon further exploration, they came to understand that they married based on *potential*. The person they married wasn't a great fit, but they believed or at least hoped that the person would change.

If you're seeking a partner, I recommend creating a list based on the characteristics that work for you. This list will consist of the traits of your potential partner. They're not based upon a promise, belief, or hope; these are actual, observable, and consistent traits. Tap into your memory and think about what has and what has not worked for you in past relationships.

Before having the good fortune of remeeting Aurianne, I wrote out such a list and divided descriptions into three categories: *Must-Haves*, *Very Important*, and *Would Be Nice*.

Some of the Must-Haves included:

- Putting the relationship first
- Taking care of her health
- Being "psychologically minded"
- Being a good travel companion
- Loving pets
- Similar values on spending and saving
- Being a nonsmoker

As a sidenote, a lot of people ask me what *psychologically minded* means. To me, it means having the capacity to empathize with others and to understand emotions. It also means a person who has a hunger for growth.

As harsh as this might sound, these Must-Haves were the nonnegotiables. There was no room to debate a Must-Have. Any woman I met, no matter how amazing, needed to check *all* of these boxes in order to be someone I could consider. In the absence of any one of them, we might have gotten along very well, but I knew in the long run, we'd hit a relationship wall.

The Very Important items were more negotiable. Here I included:

- A love of music (with our tastes at least somewhat overlapping)
- A general political alignment (with a capacity to debate in a civil manner)

While these were important, they would not sink our ship in the marriage. Musical tastes and political views are unlikely to be totally overlapping, but either can be like nails on a chalkboard if they're totally out of line.

In the last category, Would Be Nice, I had general wishes that weren't even close to deal-breakers. Generally, they included superficial attributes that "would be nice" but didn't really matter. For example, I love *The Lord of the Rings*, and while it would have been nice for my future spouse to share that enthusiasm, I knew I'd be OK if she didn't.

Once again, luck was on my side with Aurianne. She hit everything on the Must-Have and Very Important lists. She didn't necessarily like all the same music, but our tastes were compatible. A miss on the Would Be Nice list was that she didn't like *The Lord of the Rings*—and on her end, I didn't want to go to a bluegrass festival with her. But these were not deal-breakers. We were immensely compatible in all the necessary ways. The only way I knew this was by leaning into my historical experience and knowing what data points mattered from my life. Thankfully, by that time, I knew for sure.

Importantly, this isn't a one-way street. I encourage you to pull for the same thoughtfulness from the person you are interested in. Part of choosing wisely is making sure the other person accepts the whole you. Often, when we date, we try to hide our less attractive qualities, hoping we can get by without those being noticed. But that can lead to unexpected disappointments, anxiety that those qualities will be discovered, and conflict down the road if we don't take time to be more forthcoming.

* * *

Another concept that assists good connections is *efficiency*.

I know. What an odd term to use in describing a romantic relationship. But it's important that you and your romantic partner make an efficient system. Things work best when you're both heading in the same direction. For sustainable connection, it's crucial to have aligned agendas, for example: Wanting to get married (or not). Wanting kids (or not). Agreement on child rearing (if children will be present). It's also helpful when you both want to live in similar locations and environments and/or desire similar communities and levels of engagement with your community. And it also helps to have similar views on finances and spending.

All of these components are necessary for a maintainable relationship. Just thinking our partners are hot is not! Hotness alone cools over time. But efficiency may be the unsung hero of hotness. When efficiency shows up through a massive overlap of values and needs, it can keep our relationships thriving.

Because differences are inevitable, you will have to find ways to stay connected through those differences. And simply put, efficient systems, even in the world of romance, work better than inefficient systems.

Argue Productively

Believe it or not, even arguing can be efficient. When Aurianne and I were getting ready to move in together, we ran into a problem. Our homes were an hour and a half away from each other. We both had jobs and friends in our own towns.

Aurianne had a very efficient solution, and she put it like this: "Unless we're both happy, neither of us is happy."

That aim was a vast improvement on the old axiom "happy wife, happy life." Such thinking is, in the first place, misogynistic, implying that the wife must be placated. But it's also wrong. It's a formula for a future of "consent and resent." If the wife's spouse gives into everything and the resentment builds forever, it creates a ticking time bomb for both members of the couple.

A good relationship seeks an efficient means to resolve differences in which both people come out better and sustainably at peace with the result.

My preferred definition of conflict is the perception or reality that "if you get what you want, then I can't get what I want." Understandably, conflicts can be scary for some, and many people are conflict-averse. Many of us come from homes where conflict resolution was not well modeled. However, the skills are learnable, and resolving conflict can facilitate greater closeness.

This may require that you and your partner do what my podcast guest A. J. Jacobs describes as seeing the problem as a puzzle that needs to be solved together. A. J. has also said, "Get curious, not furious." Both of these ideas lead to better management of conflict.

So here's a related puzzle, one that suggests getting curious and not furious. It's a thought experiment that I often use at conflict resolution workshops. It starts with an orange. Two people want the orange. But there's a problem: there's only one orange, with no possibility of a second orange. What should be done? Some of the most common answers I get at the workshops are "Cut the orange in half!" or "Flip a coin for the orange."

But does each person get what they want with those solutions? They don't. That is, until they talk extensively about *why* they want what they want and consider flexible ways to get those needs met. In this example, after talking, they discover one person wants the orange to make orange juice and the other wants it to make marmalade: one wants only the meat of the orange for the juice, and the other only wants the rind for the marmalade.

By conversing about their interests and being flexible, they find creative means to solve for their differing needs.

Arguments always involve some element of emotion, and often, we struggle to be fair and compassionate toward the person we are arguing with. But that doesn't mean we can't improve.

Even with two doctorates in psychology between us and decades of argument practice in the family, my wife and I still disagree from time to time and, therefore, argue. And not always efficiently. I'm human, and I've had many bloopers with the accompanying thought "Hmmm . . . not my finest moment as a husband." I'm sure Aurianne has had her version of that experience as well.

As did Debra, a PR professional who is an outstanding communicator. She's well-paid for her communication, and top firms rely on her ability to do just that. Yet, at home, with her husband and two kids, her strong suit is challenged.

She came in one Monday after a late night of arguing with her husband. She said, "There was nothing good that came from our conversation. I think we both lost the argument."

It turned out they were both exhausted after a busy weekend with the kids. They decided to go to bed early to prepare for a busy week ahead for both of them. When her eye mask was on, her husband brought up a loaded topic. It went sideways from there until nearly 2:00 a.m. They were icy and disconnected when they left for work that morning.

Drs. Harville Hendrix and Helen LaKelly Hunt shared wisdom on my podcast that would ultimately help Debra. They created a system called Safe Conversations that starts with asking your partner for a date to speak. As Debra's argument demonstrated, timing is everything when initiating an important conversation. There are good times, and there are bad times. A bad time could be when we are *hungry*, *angry*, *lonely*, or *tired*, which we can remember by the acronym HALT, since even the word "halt" suggests we hold back. Debra and her husband were the T in HALT, and it would have been better to have followed Harville and Helen's rule: it's best to meet when we're mutually able to be present, without distractions, and have a sufficient window of time to engage. Setting up a time is crucial to creating a productive and connective space for this type of conversation, and Debra and her husband now do this.

★ ★ ★

Another helpful skill is a high-powered, easy-to-describe technique in communication called the "I statement." This is in stark contrast to its opposite, the "you statement." I'll share both types of statements, but let's start with an example of a couple of "you statements": "You are such a terrible driver! Slow down!" or "You're such a thoughtless spouse—I can't believe you forgot our anniversary again!"

On the other hand, if we frame these hurts around our individual experience, it makes our feelings and needs more likely to be heard. Here are two "I statements" that can be used instead of "you statements": "I feel scared and unsafe when you drive at that speed." Or, for the second, "I feel sad and hurt when you forget our anniversary."

Listen to the differences between the two types of statements. Imagine being on the other end of each. Which feels better to you? I'm guessing that for most of us, it is the "I statement."

"You statements" attack and shame the other. When we're on the receiving end of this message, it increases our body's sense of threat, causing our nervous system to go into high-alert mode. This induces the fight/flight/freeze response because all it hears is "Danger!" Hearing a "you statement" causes the recipient to focus on self-protection rather than being able to receive the message. Making things worse, the "you statement" doesn't get the hurt person what they want: repair. It's kind of like when we were kids and said, "Screw you, I'm going home!" but really hoped the other person would follow us, comfort us, and repair things.

We may think we're settling the score when we blast the other with a "you statement," but the victory may ultimately be hollow. Even though it may feel gratifying in the moment to let it all out, now there are two hurt people instead of one. Worse, here's a sequence I've heard many times from a person who was hurt but unable to skillfully share their hurt:

1. They get hurt.
2. They blast their partner.
3. They have to apologize.
4. Their hurt is never heard.

In stark contrast, "I statements" are nonattacking messages that empower the hurt person since *the hurt person* becomes the focal point of the message. With the "I statement," the hurt person takes responsibility for their feelings. No one can argue or disagree with you when you share your own feelings because *they are your feelings*. "I statements" are less likely to induce the fight/flight/freeze response in the other. Instead, they tend to decrease defensiveness, increase receptivity, and tap into the other's capacity to care. Our nervous system is more likely to go to its "tend and befriend" mode, which might sound like, "My loved one is hurting. How can I help?" Consider it an insurance policy: using an "I statement" when you're hurt will increase the odds that you're heard.

It's a virtuous cycle. The hurt person is empowered and more likely to have their needs met, and the recipient is more likely to fully receive the message.

Often, within these "I statements" there is a request. As world-renowned family therapist and author Terry Real put it on my podcast, "Don't complain about what the person's doing wrong; teach them what right would look like. Every complaint has in the heart of it a potential request."

★ ★ ★

On my podcast, author and psychologist Dr. Molly Howes identified another game-changing relationship booster as she explained that *apologizing well* is an important skill. I took that advice to heart. I shared her steps for a good apology with my client Mario, who implemented it after he had hurt his wife's feelings badly. He had humiliated her by sharing something personal at a party that she did not want shared. He followed Molly's steps in his apology:

1. ***Understand the injury.*** Mario told his wife that he recognized what he'd done and its impact. He did not say, "Well, I didn't intend to hurt you." Instead, he said, "I shared very personal information about you at the party that you did not want shared." He asked her to confirm that he got it right. He'd come close; she added one aspect: it was especially hurtful because the audience was people she didn't know well but had wanted to think well of her. So Mario included the missing piece. Afterward, she told him he got it.

2. ***Express regret.*** Mario said he was sorry for what he had done. He didn't use some variation of "I'm sorry if my actions hurt you." Instead, he said, "I'm so sorry I disregarded your feelings by sharing your personal information. It was not my information to share, and I did it anyway. I am deeply sorry." He also acknowledged the impact of his actions.

3. ***Take responsibility through restitution.*** He asked what he could do to make things better. She said she wanted him to email her

friends apologizing for sharing information she wanted private and to take responsibility for what he'd done.

4. **Establish a plan to never repeat the wrongdoing.** He promised her he would not share private information about her with others without her consent.[2]

She accepted that apology and agreed to move on.

Apologizing well is a crucial skill that can sustain connection between two people, romantic partners or otherwise. Similarly, true acceptance of a heartful apology is also valuable. Often, people lug along a growing pile of resentments as ammunition for the next smackdown, and this always interferes with the deep connection and trust that each person likely longs for.

The act of carrying resentments as ammunition is very inefficient—and very toxic to building closeness and trust over time. This approach, named the "kitchen sink" approach by John Gottman, is when one person "throws everything into the argument but the kitchen sink." So in each argument, that person decides to list out every complaint and mistake of the other person throughout history. It leaves the other person feeling hopeless. They think, "Even if I fix what's in front of me, I'm still in trouble for what's behind me." And how can a couple efficiently move forward together if at least one of them feels that way all the time?

Instead, we have to deal with the past separately and get to a point where we can leave it in the past. Yale School of Management professor and author Dr. Zoe Chance shared a great question on my podcast. It comes from research and is called the "What would it take?" question, which she refers to as the "magic question."[3] I recommend this in a variety of contexts, encouraging couples to ask each other, "What would it take for us to put this behind us?" or as I might reframe it, "What do you need from me for this hurt to heal?"

Often, the answer is as simple as knowing they have been heard and are receiving a promise that this won't happen again.

To truly listen and make such a commitment, we need to recognize that there is no right way or wrong way in most arguments. There's *the way I see it, the way you see it,* and *the way we see it.* Reality is intersubjective, and that means there are three realities: *yours, mine,* and the overlap between the two, *ours.*

As listening expert, author, and popular TED speaker Julian Treasure said on my podcast, "Two people can be right in completely different ways given their perspectives."

Efficiency, ironically, can feel inefficient at times, especially when it comes to listening. We need to slow down to *really hear* the other person. Without that, we get nowhere.

Erich Fromm reminds us, "Love isn't something natural. Rather it requires discipline, concentration, patience, faith, and the overcoming of narcissism. It isn't a feeling, it is a practice."

The applications of the above quote are infinite. And it speaks to how we can find a way through almost anything—together.

Prepare for Adversity

Unsexy idea alert: a couple's ability to make it through the tough stuff is extremely important because the tough stuff comes up a lot in life.

That was a lesson Aurianne and I learned tragically early in our relationship. I proposed to her after just four months. It is the easiest decision I have ever made. Yet I feel a bit self-conscious about the rapidity because my timeline was faster than the one I would usually recommend for the people who see me. Having walked with many people through relationships and marriage, I now have come to advise that they are with someone for four *seasons* so that they can experience the relationship in at least one period of adversity.

As I said, we never want to squander a good crisis. So ask yourself one of the most important questions: "Based upon real evidence, *what is this person like when things go wrong?*"

That's the sort of question you want an answer to before committing to spend the rest of your lives together.

But to be fair, Aurianne and I were already dealing with adversity when we got married. While we were dating, her father was being treated for cancer. We weren't too worried about it, though, because he'd been told by the doctors that he'd die *with* the cancer, not *from* it.

It didn't turn out that way.

In November, just two months before our planned wedding ceremony in January, we found out Aurianne's father's health had taken a turn for the worse—and he wouldn't make it to the wedding. This was a huge blow to Aurianne, and it was also hard for me. Not only did I need to be strong for my fiancée, who was losing her beloved dad, but I also had to face my own grief. Though we'd known each other for only a few months, I'd grown very close to Aurianne's father, Alvin. He was my ideal father-in-law, and he was being prematurely taken from our lives.

We were fast friends. The first time we met, I invited Alvin to a Giants game.

"I haven't been to a baseball game in years!" he exclaimed in absolute joy.

We were like two kids at the baseball game, screaming for the Giants and taunting the Mets. I pranked him by paying to get his name in lights on the scoreboard. The scoreboard read "Happy Birthday, Alvin Jacobs" on a day that was definitely *not* his birthday. Our connection only grew from there. He may have been my father-in-law, but we were instant bros. At one point, he joked with Aurianne that he was envious of her for getting to live with me.

Now Aurianne was losing her father, and I was losing my father-in-law before he and I ever officially got to enjoy the new relationship.

By early December, it was clear he was running out of time. So we decided to change our plans. We got married four weeks earlier than scheduled, in front of his bed with only our immediate family present. During the ceremony, he came into and fell out of consciousness. He died eight days later. Our public and formal wedding became a nonlegal ceremony and, in many ways, both a celebration and a time of mourning.

Some people in our lives advised us against this decision. "If you do this," they said, "it'll put a massive shadow over every anniversary."

And they were right. Every anniversary is tinged with sadness. But it's also a monument to the resiliency of our relationship. We were able to deepen and strengthen our connection during one of the toughest times in our lives together.

Knowing that you and your partner are capable of this kind of team-work helps keep a relationship solid. When the people who see me are in a new relationship and want to take things to the next level, I recommend that they travel together. By doing so, they can see how they coordinate and handle adversity as a unit when things don't go as expected. How do they handle it when the airline wants to charge them extra for their luggage or when the car they rented isn't available or when the hotel room has two single beds instead of a king or when bad weather alters their plans or when one of them gets food poisoning?

These are tough moments at the time, but they can also be a powerful sign of how each of you will respond: Do you come together or apart? And to what degree? How the couple responds can be predictive of the state of the connection amid life's challenges.

Obstacles to Connection

An entire book could be written on this topic. Even stating "obstacles to connection" may have many readers thinking about the myriad of possibilities. Without proper attention, these factors can become corrosive to connection. No matter how long the obstacles have been present in your relationship, naming them and developing a strategy to mitigate their presence can greatly improve your connection. Think of it as weeding a garden. Not fun, but the blooms and growth afterward are always worth the toil in the soil.

This process starts with identifying the obstacles to connection, otherwise known as "thirds."

What's a third? So glad you asked! It's any entity that interferes with connection to your partner. No one phrases it better than Dr. Stan Tatkin, who has talked about thirds on my podcast and more extensively on his website and in his books. He says thirds are anything "that threaten the safety and security of the couple system [and] should be comanaged by partners in a timely fashion so as not to disturb the peace. Thirds can be alcohol, drugs, people, tasks, work, porn, parents, children, friends, exes, pets, or electronics. If one primary partner experiences jealousy, that is certainly a sign of mismanagement by the other."

The solution? He says, "The proper use of a third is to work with it—on it, for it, or against it—together and not separately."

I love that quote, and I appreciate that the fix must be done *together*, not separately. As I mentioned earlier, unless both are happy, neither is happy. Managing thirds must be a cocreation.

For example, a couple can work together to define the parameters of phone use. Together, they can create boundaries to protect the integrity of their connection. In my practice, individuals and couples cite the phone as the most intrusive of all thirds. To bring this point home, one survey revealed that 10 percent of people check their phones *during* sex![4]

To enhance connection, a couple I work with chose to place their phones in a basket when they returned home from work. They turned off notifications and agreed to check their phones at predetermined times.

A guest on my podcast, Tiffany Shlain, described the positive impact of turning off her phone from sundown Friday until sundown Saturday night. She described the meaningful connections that had occurred with her husband and family since implementing this agreement.

Another example: Perhaps before you invite a houseguest over, both parties agree to the parameters of the visit. While some cultural norms might inform the terms of the decision, the decision must work for *each individual*. That means checking in with yourself, checking in with your partner, and asking, "Is this something each of us can agree to?" If not, continue to discuss or counteroffer and stay open-minded about possible solutions.

To be rectified, all thirds—whether they're phones, children, in-laws, work, exes, friends, et cetera—must be identified as intrusive or disruptive to connection. Thirds have their place, but when they consistently interfere with the quality of connection or cause recurring conflict, the couple can work out a strategy or develop guidelines to minimize the intrusions that the thirds impose.

Putting the relationship before thirds can be tricky, and there will likely be relapse. Be patient with yourself and your partner as you manage your thirds. Like Gollum's ring in my beloved *The Lord of the Rings*, some thirds can have a hold on us. That's how they got there in the first place. If they become too tricky to manage, consider seeking support. As novelist Courtney C. Stevens says, "If nothing changes, nothing changes. If you keep doing what you're doing, you're going to keep getting what you're getting. You want change, make some."[5]

It takes repetition, commitment, and courage to drive change. But with repetition and commitment to making your relationship the main thing, courage can be called upon for the sake of a more connected relationship.

Make Time for Reconnection

We are constantly in flux with our connections and disconnections. In our important relationships, our most important contribution is a commitment to the act of connecting and *reconnecting* with our partners.

The importance of connection and reconnection is demonstrated in a raw and unvarnished way in the Still Face Experiment, conducted by Dr. Edward Tronick. While it's ostensibly about a mother-child connection, it relates to all of us. It's a poignant example of what can go wrong when there's a disconnect, and I regularly share the three-minute video of it on YouTube with couples.[6] So far, everyone who has seen it under my care has said it was extremely useful in illustrating what can go wrong when we do not focus on or attune to the one we're with.

In it, we see a mother and her preverbal one-year-old daughter. You can see that the two of them have a loving relationship, as evidenced by their warm facial expressions, their coos, as well as their body language. That is, until the mother gets the prompt to make her face blank and be unresponsive to her daughter's attempts to connect. Immediately, the daughter notices that something is different. The baby does everything she can over the next several seconds (which feel like an eternity to the viewer and almost certainly more so to the baby). Soon, the baby begins to cry and appears very distressed. Seconds later, the mother reconnects and comforts her baby, and very quickly, a repair occurs; the baby appears to return to her original state.

Even as adults, deep down, we all have the same inner workings as the baby. Most of us long for connection, and while we may act out something very different, we're saying some variation of "I'm hurting! Love me. Pay attention to me."

So while we may masquerade with bravado as opposed to the unde-fended example set by the baby, the experiment provides a visceral example of what can happen to couples when they feel unseen or disconnected. The experiment also demonstrates that reconnection is possible.

In that vein, here are three quick tips for reconnection:

1. A hug. A twenty-second hug can reduce stress, reduce blood pressure, and release our body's natural feel-good hormones like oxytocin, serotonin, and dopamine. Frequency of hugs matters, and so does the twenty-second duration.[7] It may be one of the quickest ways to reconnect when things are going well and when things are not.

2. A "do-over." *Webster's* defines this word as "a new attempt or oppor-tunity to do something after a previous attempt has been unsuc-cessful or unsatisfactory." You remember that one from when you were a kid. Something went sideways, and the peacemaker might have said, "Let's have a do-over." Those work in adulthood as well.

3. Turn toward your partner's bid for connection. When a (nonabu-sive) partner is trying to extend an olive branch, connect, or as Dr. John Gottman calls it, "make a bid," it's important to accept the bid. A bid can be something small. Bringing a glass of water. Asking how your day at work went. Or offering a smile. When a partner makes a bid, we can *turn toward* (accept) it, *turn away* from (ignore) it, or *turn against* it (reject it in an argumentative way).

Bottom line: the more we turn toward the bid, the more our trust goes up. Sustainable and fulfilling relationships are highly correlated with our ability to accept our partner's bid for connection. Couples who do this have a higher likelihood of increased trust, deeper emotional connection, and improved sex lives. Gottman found that when couples break up, it's less frequently because of big fights or infidelity. More often, it's a result of the resentment and distance that build up over time when partners continually turn away from bids for connection.[8]

So while I say connect, connect, connect, it would also be relevant for me to say reconnect, reconnect, reconnect. When we feel disconnected, it's *our* responsibility to reach out, check in, and reconnect. For example, during these times, it's crucial that we identify that we feel disconnected and check in with an "I statement" such as "I'm feeling disconnected. I'd like to reconnect." Figure out a list of bids that work for you and your partner.

* * *

Why is it *our* job to initiate when we notice disconnection? Because somebody needs to! And because *the act of initiating the repair* is more important than *who* initiates the repair. The health of the relationship depends on one person taking responsibility, noticing the disconnect, and attempting to return to the connection. It is selfless because we're putting the needs of the relationship first and before our own needs, including the need to be right. As Sade sings, "Love is stronger than pride." And it takes courage because we face the fear of rejection when we initiate a repair. Prioritizing the relationship by *placing the relationship first* requires both selflessness and courage.

Like Fromm said, love is not a feeling. It is a practice. And as Mr. Spock from *Star Trek* said, "The needs of the many outweigh the needs of the few." In this case, "many" equals the couple, while "few" equals one.

In an ideal world, each member of the couple would take turns to lead the way to repair. Yet, it's likely that one person will be the more frequent leader. If you are the one who usually begins these conversations and wish it to be more equal, "I statements" about your experience may help. Inviting your partner to join in the effort and calling attention to the inequality in a nonblaming way might also be effective. For example, "I feel alone when I start most of the repairs between us. It would mean a lot to me if you could initiate these reconnecting conversations more often."

As close as we may be with our partner, it can feel odd to recognize that we are two *different* people. We need to go outside ourselves and get to know and understand the feelings and needs of our partner, especially when they're different from our own. I like the common expression "Show me you know me." One way to get to know your partner better is by asking directly, "How do you feel loved?" The answer may be surprising. It might not even feel romantic. Because how we feel loved is very individualistic.

Some people have found that recognizing their love language is helpful in this regard. Gary Chapman, the author of the book *The Five Love Languages*, has found that a person tends to have one primary love language, drawn from these five categories:

- Words of affirmation
- Quality time
- Gifts
- Acts of service
- Physical touch

Some studies suggest that we may have multiple love languages, and some people's love languages may fall outside these five, so this model may not apply to all readers.[9] Further, we may not share the same love language as our partners. Still, I have used this model in my practice, and the people who have implemented it have said it was helpful. In whatever case, when we connect with our partners on *their* terms, showing them love and stretching toward them based on those terms, we can experience a closer connection.

I was working with Dafna, a product manager and a mom of two. She'd been happily married for over a decade, but there was some recent marital stress. "I prepare all my husband's meals, make sure the bed is made nicely, and use my product management skills to be on top of the calendar in our home. I do this for him *and* for us, but he doesn't seem to appreciate my efforts. All I hear is that I don't have enough time for him." She continued, "Of course I don't—how could I? I'm doing all these things for him and the family."

Dafna and I discussed the dynamics of the relationship, and it didn't take long to recognize that her love language was probably acts of service and that it appeared that her husband's was quality time. She went home and did the language questionnaire online with her husband and verified this was the case.

This awareness allowed them to have a more intelligent discussion about their individual needs for closeness and the fact that they could accomplish closeness through the lenses of their love languages. Before long, a bridging phenomenon occurred. She needed more acts of service such as him asking how he could help and delivering on that offer. This worked nearly immediately. She reported that his acts of service felt wonderful, like "warm rays of the sun" on her back. It also freed up time for her to give him what he wanted. It turned out that what he wanted was a weekly walk to the local café where they could sit and talk "like college students on a date."

By leaning into each other's love language, each got what they wanted.

This is part of the "Platinum Rule." The Golden Rule tells us to "do unto others as you would have done unto you." The Platinum Rule states, "Do unto others as *they* want done to *them*," or more simply, "Give them what *they* want!" What do *they* need to feel happier and more supported? What do *they* need to feel loved and connected with?

The Platinum Rule can extend to day-to-day exchanges. For example, if your partner comes home stressed from work, they may have specific needs that are hard to anticipate. A quick way of getting to those needs is by asking, "How can I support you at this moment?" Sometimes, they might need a listener. Other times, they need someone who can fix things. It can be helpful to ask, "Do you need me to listen or advise?"

And sometimes, your partner just needs to hear a certain line from you.

You can work together to find what Imago[10] therapist Damian Duplechain described to me as the Spielberg method. This comes from the work of Drs. Harville Hendrix and Helen LaKelly Hunt, whom we met a few pages back, and it is a game changer. Like a good film director, you feed the line to the actor. In this case, you ask your partner to feed you the line that they need to hear. A male in a couple I see chose "You are an amazing dad, and you're sexy too!" and his wife went with "How did I get so lucky to be with you?" It may sound forced, and some erroneously conclude, "If I have to ask for it, then it's not real."

Untrue. We could go several lifetimes never hearing what we long to hear from our partners. And it's not their fault! As close to our partner as we may be, our partner cannot mindread, and they are not *us*. Sometimes they need guidance to be able to say what we want to hear. And what we long to hear might be exactly what our partner feels or thinks; it just may not have occurred to them to say it. I have learned that this was the case from several couples: they simply didn't know what the other longed to hear. But when they learned the Spielberg method, they were grateful to know how easily they could please their partner and what a powerful impact it had on their connection.

Keep It Hot

There's another important element to maintaining connection with a romantic partner: sex.

Come on, you knew this topic was just around the corner!

Sex can be one of the most enjoyable parts of our romantic lives. I don't need to tell you that sexual attraction plays a part in our courtship and our desire to marry someone. Yet as the years go on, it's often something we push aside. We may feel too overwhelmed with the day-to-day tasks of our lives. We may think sex was something we did *before* kids.

According to relationship expert Esther Perel, author of *Mating in Captivity*, one reason that sex often falls by the wayside in relationships has to do with our expectations. When we first start dating someone, it's all about the fun of spontaneous sex. Humans love novelty; we're with a new person, and we're attracted to them, and our main impulse is to get busy exploring that attraction.[11]

But impulsive, spontaneous sex is simply unrealistic for most married couples. On most days, we're engaged in childcare, doing taxes, cleaning up after the dog puked on the rug, and finishing work we couldn't get done at the office.

With all that unsexy stuff going on, if we wait for the impulse, *sex ain't happening.*

Just because sex becomes less spontaneous, though, doesn't mean it becomes less important. Quite the opposite. Sex increases our sense of connection with our partner. It can make us feel really good, and not just in the moment. It changes hormones with a substantial half-life flowing through our bodies, allowing us to feel that connection long afterward.

Another great point from Esther Perel: don't confuse intimacy with eroticism. I often hear themes or variations of, "My spouse and I were intimate on Friday." What does that mean? Did they have a deep conversation? Or did they engage sexually?

By now, you know I care about the accuracy in naming of things, and it seems Esther does too. She mentioned at a conference I attended that two people can be very intimate but not erotic. Another twosome might be erotic but not intimate. In other words, the first may share deep emotional vulnerabilities but not engage sexually; the second may engage in all kinds of sexual behavior but not engage in deep, emotionally vulnerable exchanges. It's important to name these accurately.

Emily Nagoski is an author, professor, and sex educator who shared three secrets of partners with happy sex lives in a *New York Times* article: 1) they are friends, 2) they prioritize sex, and 3) they ignore outside opinions about what sex should look like and do what works for them. She also corrected a common misconception: instead of waiting for desire to lead us to the bedroom, the focus should be on the pleasure we might experience there.[12] Since one of the most common focal points of couples therapy is drive discrepancy (i.e., a difference in sex drive), this is a significant insight.

To improve sexual connection, I recommend yet another seemingly unsexy idea. It's effective, endorsed by Perel and Nagoski, and ultimately, sexy: schedule your sex life. Pick a day and time when you can both be free and make it a priority to show up on time for the date. For the first five minutes, it's a bit of a transition, so it's common to ask oneself, "Will I get into this?" After all, right before the rendezvous, you might have been changing diapers or doing dishes, as parents often are. Or you may have been reading a nastygram email from work.

But if you commit to the date, you may discover you're more into the encounter than you thought.

Ambience- and mood-enhancers are helpful for this context switch: lighting, music, tidying up the bedroom, incense, candles, lingerie, or a myriad of other options are available. If it's helpful to take a bath or shower to wash off the day—together or separately—do that. A key finding from the Kinsey studies is that each of us and our sexuality is unique. Honor yours.

We're never too old for sex or for sex dates, and there's no such thing as having been with a partner too long to enjoy a sexual encounter with them. Sex may look different at different times in our lives. Couples therapist Carol Kramer talked about sex and aging on my podcast. Despite public perception, older people often have deep desires for romantic and sexual connection. Frequency, length of time for the exchange, or the activities themselves may look different as we age. But if sex is important to you, and it is for many of us, then it's important to make time for it in your shared lives.

I've counseled couples who put sex to the side or found they were sexually incompatible over time—often because one partner's needs changed or the circumstances in their lives changed; others realized they were gay or asexual or had unexpected physiological changes. Some were able to find working agreements to this conundrum. For others who were not able to find working agreements or to resolve it, in the end, the relationship often couldn't sustain itself.

Leave Room for the Individual

When I said that Aurianne checked all the important boxes on my profile, it was true. But that doesn't mean everything fits perfectly. As I already mentioned, she doesn't like *The Lord of the Rings* and I don't necessarily want to go to bluegrass festivals, but we still share a lot of our lives through our likes, hobbies, and friends. Yet we also have our *own* likes, hobbies, and friends. And a funny note: Aurianne's love for bluegrass may have rubbed off on me. Last night, we attended a bluegrass concert—a band with the unattractive name Leftover Salmon—and they were awesome! So who knows? I may join her at a bluegrass festival after all.

Yet, while we're undeniably very compatible, we have certain personality traits that don't align. As is the case with many couples, we have different chronotypes, defined as "a person's natural inclination with regard to the times of day when they prefer to sleep or when they are most alert or energetic."[13] Aurianne's a morning person, and I'm a night owl. I love listening to music and chatting, and she can't listen to music and talk at the same time. She's far neater than I am. She's more aware of what she wants and knows how to articulate it. It takes me far longer to figure those things out and to articulate them, which, as you might imagine, means we *both* need to be patient with *me*.

Yet our relationship still works because we know and understand our differences. And we find a way to accommodate those differences. No two people are carbon copies of each other . . . and even though you might wish you had married a carbon copy, it would likely lead to boredom and more of a roommate situation!

For instance, Aurianne is an introvert, and I'm more of an extrovert. There are times I'd like nothing more than to chat for a few hours, but I've had to learn not to take it personally when she wants to have that time for herself instead. Our love languages are different, but we've learned to recognize and accommodate both languages in our relationship.

Of course we want similarities between ourselves and our partners. But even among the most similar people, differences will exist. Used properly, they can strengthen the relationship.

Diversity Plus Respect Wins

Although not a romantic pair, a good example is the brothers Orville and Wilbur Wright. When the Wright brothers were designing the first airplane, they were willing to disagree with each other about the project. They were very clear: conflict was related *to the project*, but it was never related *to the other person*. This commitment to depersonalized conflict, looking at the project as a puzzle, may have led to the magic that caused flight. Poetically, they came to discover that the only way to get the machine off the ground was for each propeller to spin in the opposite direction, one clockwise and one counterclockwise. This was a perfect metaphor for Orville and Wilbur and their connection and appreciation of what each brought to make the project successful.

That's how romantic relationships can work too. We want to work together, with the same aim of getting off the ground. But to really take off and go where we want to go, we must let the other person spin in the opposite direction sometimes.

CONNECTION FORMULA EXERCISE

Do something novel with your partner. When I asked couples therapist and *Hot Monogamy* author Dr. Pat Love (yes, that *is* her real name!) for a relationship tip on my podcast, she was clear: do something novel together. Experiencing something novel with your partner can boost all kinds of connection chemicals and, according to some studies, may even improve your levels of attraction to each other. It can be something like exploring a town you've never visited, going to a concert by an artist you don't know well (possibly at a new venue), or taking a dance class together. The options are limitless. Go for it!

CHAPTER 8

CONNECTING TO FAMILY

I loved my Grandpa Ben. He was the first person to connect with me deeply who wasn't one of my parents. He was entirely unlike anyone I knew. As far as I was concerned, he was someone from a different world—which, in retrospect, was accurate. He had grown up in Bangor, Maine, played semipro basketball, and may or may not have graduated high school. He was one of eight siblings, and his father had abandoned the Russian army and moved across the world to become a junk dealer, pulling a cart with his horse as he hocked items around Bangor.

Starting in my early years, Grandpa Ben made a point of sharing his wisdom with me. He didn't have a lot of formal education, but he had a deep understanding of life. He guided me toward an appreciation for joy in love and work—and he hadn't even read Freud to understand that those were important things. He taught me that if I ever saw anyone out in the world whose day I could make a little better, I should do it.

Of course, not every lesson was profound; some were just hilarious. My family and I still laugh at his parking advice, which he gave me as he was parking at a Fort Lauderdale flea market. He said in his thick New England accent: "Adam, pahk yah cah away from the other cahs so the otha cahs don't hitcha cah." (For those of you not familiar with the sound of a person from Bangor, Maine, he was saying, "Adam, when you park your car, park your car away from all the other cars so the other cars don't hit your car.")

I still think of it and repeat it out loud every time I park in a crowded area.

Perhaps his most lingering contribution to my life was connecting me to my ancestry. He changed our last name from Rolsky to Dorsay because he wanted to do what he could to protect his children from anti-Jewish sentiments and behaviors. But he was also deeply committed to his heritage.

He used to tease me all the time, "Adam, when will you settle down with a nice Jewish girl?" This wisdom is reflected in his generation's *The Wizard of Oz* ("There's no place like home") and for mine, in a TLC song (in this case, I was chasing waterfalls).

I blew off the question for years. What did he know? He was from another, older world. I wanted a complexity in my life that I was sure wouldn't make sense to him, I thought. My grandfather only traveled as far north as Montreal and as far south as Tijuana. He always wished he'd traveled more. In this way, he taught me what *not* to do as well.

Before I settled down, I knew I needed to experience life outside my comfort zone, to grow and be readier for the world. I left Kansas. And I went chasing waterfalls.

Yet I'm thankful he lived to see how right he was in the end. After my wedding, I went to my grandfather and told him, "Sorry for all the crap I gave you. You were right all along." Because of his wisdom, I was better equipped for adult life.

Family Can Lift Us Up

As I write this, my grandfather has been gone more than twenty years, and I still cry—often in my sleep—over having lost him. I still miss him terribly and believe I always will.

We are deeply driven by our familial relationships and dynamics, and we are wired to want to please our parents. This drive does not go away for many of us, even in adulthood. Psychiatrist and Stanford professor Dr. Irvin D. Yalom noted that even years after his mother's death, he was still looking for her approval. He would still ask in his dreams: "Momma, how'd I do?"[1]

Our families shape so much of who we are. At its best, family can be a safe haven, providing a place of honesty, support, and acceptance. Family can provide guidance that carries us through life, as the example of my grandfather illustrates. And it can be a final refuge when all other doors are shut to us. Even when our families fall short of what we need, they influence who we are. Love them or hate them, they are our family. And although the dictionary says the antonym for love is hate, I disagree. I believe Elie Wiesel got it right when he said the antonym for love is *indifference*, a synonym for apathy.

I have never met a person who felt apathetic toward their parents. Conflicted, yes. Apathetic, no.

We humans were built this way. Family dynamics are deep within our human condition and our wiring. We are designed to trust family, rely on family, and desire our family's approval. When it comes to family, it's hard, perhaps impossible, not to care.

When I worked with gang-affiliated youths, why did they join gangs? In many cases, they didn't have a father figure or a strong family connection. Their gang was their surrogate family. It felt better for them to feel a sense of familial belonging to their gang, even if it meant doing things that (they confessed to me in private) felt wrong to them.

In a seemingly different world, I work with a CEO who runs a Fortune 500 company and commands everything in his world. He can get a table at any restaurant or a meeting with just about any person, no matter their status. But he impresses me, at least in part, by how unimpressed he is with himself.

Of course, he's recognized as important in every room he confidently strides into. Except when he walks into a room with his own family. He's deathly afraid of what his wife, his parents, and his kids think about him. This feeling has its roots in something so profound in our lives: we are wired to long for and need family, and family has access to our most vulnerable emotions. We don't always get a sense that who

SUPER PYSCHED

we are as a person is enough from our family of origin. But knowing ourselves, having good boundaries when necessary, and implementing the communication skills described in this book can help us better enjoy our families.

Naming the Dysfunction

The Russian writer Leo Tolstoy once said, "All happy families are alike; each unhappy family is unhappy in its own way."

Forgive me for slightly disagreeing with the master of the nineteenth-century novel, but I think Tolstoy got it slightly wrong:

There are no entirely happy families.

Since no family is perfect, all families have their own version of dysfunction. Some are simply functionally dysfunctional. Would *Modern Family* be watched by anyone, ever, if the family weren't functionally dysfunctional? It was a hit because it was entirely relatable. Their shenanigans made viewers think, "Hey, not so different from my family!"

Functionally dysfunctional families are those in which the parents were *good enough*. They tried to be supportive and reliable. They inevitably missed the strike zone here and there. They yelled at the kids when they shouldn't have or let them get away with too much. They worked too much or missed recitals. They divorced each other. But they always *tried*; the effort was apparent when they attempted to repair the hurts they caused.

Yet some families may have major impediments to performing at their best. These are the dysfunctionally dysfunctional families. And here, Tolstoy is right that such dysfunction comes in an infinite number of shades. The recipe for dysfunctional dysfunction can involve neglect, authoritarianism, overpermissiveness, narcissistic wounding, abuse, or a failure to provide support or acceptance. It might involve verbal abuse, physical abuse, sexual abuse, abusing substances, or toxic, narcissistic focus on one family member over all others.

Sadly, this is just a short list of the possibilities of dysfunctional dysfunction.

Ian, an executive, was leery to see me and had been putting off therapy for years. Why? Because he attended family therapy as a boy and it went poorly. He said he couldn't rid himself of the stink of that experience; he couldn't imagine ever going back to a therapist of any kind.

But he finally decided to give therapy a chance again, and he found me. We quickly established a rapport, and he shared about growing up in a home that felt lifeless. His parents' marriage was hanging on by a thread. The marital tension led to a nightly family dinner-table experience that was excruciating because no one would talk. So Ian took it upon himself to relieve the household by becoming the family comedian and, unwittingly, the common denominator of conversation in the house.

Ian's parents took the family of four to therapy when Ian was eleven and his older brother was thirteen. After a meeting or two, the primary topic of the family began to emerge: *the topic was Ian*. At one point, Ian shouted out, "Why is everyone talking about me?"

The therapist stared very intensely into Ian's eyes and asked the eleven-year-old boy, "Indeed, Ian. Why *is* everyone talking about you?"

The therapist appeared to have gotten it wrong. This fifth-grade boy who was anxiously trying to Roto-Rooter his family home of depression was not the cause of its suffering. But for years, Ian believed *he* was at the source of his family's dysfunction. As we spoke, it appeared that his *parents* were the ones who would have benefited from couples therapy for both their well-being and the well-being of the entire family.

Over time and some good sessions, he became glad that he had come in. He began to recognize the dynamic at home had not been his fault at all.

Ian's case is not atypical. He was gaslit and erroneously became what we refer to as the "identified patient." The family woes were displaced onto Ian. Fortunately, Ian was able to emancipate himself from the weight of these misplaced burdens. On the other hand, some families experience potentially darker realities.

Dr. Reid Meloy, a psychologist who specializes in psychopathy, spoke on my podcast about the dark tetrad of personality features: narcissism, Machiavellianism, psychopathy, and sadism. While most of us don't have disabling levels of those characteristics, some of us lost the family lottery and ended up having to deal with family members who exhibit one or more of these features.

In those cases, we must remind ourselves that their treatment of us is a zero-percent-valid reflection of our worth. It's sad that we can all think of stories of families not just unconsciously making errors but also actively, sometimes purposefully, doing harm to those they should protect.

Debra, a pharmacy sales rep in her forties, was on the brink of divorce when she came to see me. Her children, then ten and eight, "triggered her deeply." She told me they were typical grade-school kids and she was puzzled as to why she felt hatred toward them. When we explored her childhood, the reason she was struggling with her children became more apparent. Her father was an alcoholic, and she described him as a Dr. Jekyll and Mr. Hyde. He was kind when he wasn't drinking, but he became a tyrant when drunk. He hit Debra so many times she said she couldn't even count. The next day, he'd apologize. Her mom was no help. She told her to forgive her father. Debra, being an obedient child, obliged. It took her a while to figure out how old she was when the abuse started. When she looked at her diary, it turned out that it was nine. This information provided us with a path toward healing. It also served as a starting point to release those burdens so she could be present with her own children.

Unfortunately, even knowing about these dysfunctions doesn't necessarily free us from our desire to get affirmation from our family. We can't completely silence the impulse that ties us to family, even dysfunctional ones.

There are no easy fixes to the traumas of childhood, but naming the various phenomena is an important first step to addressing and healing the pain. Therapy with a trauma-informed therapist can help. Joining a support group can also help. And the body is an essential tool here as well. Knowing where we store our trauma in the body itself and learning to recognize and control symptoms of dysregulation can make a big difference in our quests to move through our traumas. Dr. Bessel van der Kolk explains in his book *The Body Keeps the Score* that there is even evidence that the arts, bodywork, dance, and yoga can be helpful to get the trauma to move so we can have more control over this form of pain.

Make Your Own Family

Is your family functionally dysfunctional or dysfunctionally dysfunctional? Only you can truly know. Each family has a line of emotional credit with its members. All families draw on this line of credit. Harsh sarcasm at the dinner table, negative judgment about a life choice, arguments about your career—each of these is a withdrawal on that line of credit. If the bank account is large, this can still leave you with plenty to draw on.

At their best, functionally dysfunctional families stay in the black. Functionally dysfunctional families are good about paying down these loans by having good positive-to-negative interaction ratios—repairing in a timely manner, apologizing, offering support, and giving large helpings of consistent love.

Dysfunctionally dysfunctional families, on the other hand, stay in the red.

Only you know the balance for your family.

If your family is permanently in the red, you've likely been in a lot of pain.

And when that's the case, sometimes the best decision is to limit interaction or, in serious situations, walk away. Familial bonds are strong, but they aren't indestructible. You have the right to regulate interactions or meetings or even sever ties with them and seek more healing family settings to find a sense of healthy belonging.

I don't say this lightly. All actions and inactions have consequences. Cutting out anyone from your life, especially family, will have tremendous ripple effects. But deep consideration—looking under each rock carefully— and coming to a well-investigated, well-thought-out conclusion based on a multidimensional cost-benefit analysis (CBA) can be a lifesaver; it's a tool I use a lot for different decisions. A CBA can be as simple as writing down, on a divided ledger with two halves, "what's good" and "what's bad" about a thing. You can even calibrate each data point with a value based on how important it is to you from 1 to 5. After filling it out, you can add up each side for a quantitative summary.

While it may not be the sole informer of a difficult decision, this simple exercise can at least help you determine how the relationship is working or not working for you and what options to consider. It can give you a snapshot of how things are going, and it can even help you figure out good questions to ask: Are there possible repairs? What expectations can you dial down? Are there any requests you would like to make? Would it help if the frequency of visits was adjusted?

And if walking away from a toxic family relationship is your choice, it doesn't mean you have to walk away from all sense of family. I know people who have created a new family by choosing a community or a group of close friends who get together for birthdays, holidays, and other important events and upon whom they rely when things are tough. They reported the need to find a way to explain to others their decision to walk away from family. One said it quite simply: "It's unfortunate, but there have been unresolvable complications. At this time, I have needed to make the decision to disengage for now."

Develop Deeper Connections

Those who are part of functionally dysfunctional families—biological or otherwise—still have work to do.

Often, we come to look at family as a given. Because the connections are so deep, we assume they are unchangeable. But that isn't necessarily the case.

I have worked with adults and their parents in family sessions. One was a grown woman in her forties who did family sessions with her mother—who was in her eighties. As you might imagine, they inspired me by their commitment to get things right in their relationship before it was too late.

They had a lot of work to do, but they were both invested in improving their connection. Their relationship turned out far better for the work they did. Both said they were hesitant to start and that the process was painful but that the outcome was well worth it.

Not every family requires therapy or has members who are willing to do it; at the same time, in this postindustrial world, families are, in most cases, less connected than ever before. Go back a couple of hundred years, and you'll find that almost every family on the planet was united in almost everything they did. If the family had a farm, everyone was a farmer. Their livelihood was a common denominator, so the entire family's lives revolved around the farm. Parents spent time teaching their children to farm. Everyone worked all day on the farm. In the evening, they discussed the farm and found activities to relax from thinking about the farm.

I'd like to think they played a version of cornhole together.

They may have also gone to church, synagogue, mosque, or temple together—and then back to the farm. The same type of reality was true for a family of cobblers or blacksmiths.

Today, families tend to lack these common denominators of connection. We tend to spend less time together and do fewer things together. We often don't share the same careers as our families, watch the same shows, engage in the same hobbies, or even like the same foods. As cultural traditions disappear, we have fewer touchpoints that draw us together.

Sometimes, pets fill in the gap. They give us one of those touchpoints. This is also a role that sports can play. For many families, playing or viewing sports gives them a positive reason to get together and a common topic to talk about.

While I love a conversation that begins with "How 'bout those Warriors?" that prompt, if it's all we talk about, can only get us so far. Many of us may desire more than that to enjoy the full value of strong familial connection. Luckily, there are ways to strengthen those bonds.

Learn Together

Do you remember how psyched you were the last time you learned how to do something really interesting? Maybe it was a class on painting; maybe it was a personal trainer showing you how to rock your exercise regimen. Whatever it was, it stuck with you. And when you learn those things with another, it can feel like going on a quest together. Questing is something our species has done throughout the millennia, since we were on the savanna. Homer's *Odyssey* is around twenty-seven hundred years old and remains a massive hit, and it even led to the Cohen brothers' Best Picture in 2000 for *O Brother, Where Art Thou?*

We need quests. When we go on a quest with others, we create a bond.

One of the reasons we connect with and make so many friends in school and college is because we've embarked on that quest of learning *together*. We go on road trips. Field trips. Trips to attend conferences to learn or present material. Shared journeys through the vulnerabilities of being young that culminate in late-night conversations.

Most of these things and many others we can do with family—with great outcomes.

Historically, families did this all the time. It was part of being united around a trade. A cobbler taught his sons to make shoes. That's how they spent their hours. They likely taught through the old practice of observation and supervision. I like to imagine they used the medical school method of "watch one, do one, teach one." Cobbling was their educational experience, a bond through a learning quest they shared with family.

We can recreate this experience today. If you have a skill you'd like to pass down, share it with your children. If your parents can do something you admire, ask them to teach it to you. There's a reason that TV shows often depict families bonding over fixing cars or learning to play golf.

During COVID, my son Avin and I learned how to make wine together. Of course, he was too young to enjoy the fruits of his labor, but we both found immense value in following those steps, one after another, and discovering this new interest together.

It gave us a powerful way to spend time together and something to get excited about over the course of several weeks. Without his incredible engineering and science capacities, the wine would have been a massive flop. But it turned out well. The wine tasted all the better for what it represented: the quality time and shared effort we experienced together. I believe my son already has good memories of our time, which will be reexperienced in a few years when we can share a bottle.

Connecting with children is such an important element of parents' lives that the entire next chapter will focus on the different ways to do that.

Ask Better Questions

There's nothing wrong with small talk—in fact, as we'll see in future chapters, it is valuable as a form of conversational duct tape from time to time. But in the absence of bigger talk, it can become habitual and limit how deeply we can connect with those to whom we're closest.

My first tip is this: the rose, bud, and thorn exercise. Ask the others at the table to talk about three things every dinner. The *rose*: something good that happened today. The *bud*: something you learned today. The *thorn*: something that hurt emotionally (or physically) today.

This habit generates better conversations that build and crescendo to areas that would not have been touched without the prompt. It also becomes a ritual, one for which the children and adults involved are prepared. The rose can reduce the negativity bias (by causing us to look at what went well). The bud nurtures the growth mindset (by looking at what we learned and seeing that even adults continue to learn). And the thorn assists emotional intelligence (by naming what hurt and bringing empathy from others to the fore).

While talking about the weather or the big game this weekend is fine, it can feel like mere filler when there are more important things to talk about. Connection can thrive when we dig into those important things.

This is "Big Talk," in the words of podcast guest Kalina Silverman, who's an expert in the art. Instead of spending twenty minutes exchanging content of limited value, we ask questions that mean *something*.

Questions like: What's the most important thing in your life? What do you want to do before you die? Whom do you truly admire? How do you try to live by their example?

If you struggle to come up with Big Talk topics on your own, don't worry—Silverman has developed a deck of Big Talk cards to give you the kindling you need to fire up those big conversations. I have a deck, I *use* the deck, and I love the questions! Please note, you can find a number of similar types of question decks online. You can even write out a list of your own big questions.

But often, it isn't the lack of big questions that keeps us from talking. It's the fact that such questions make us feel so vulnerable that we almost feel ridiculous. For those of us who've indulged, we may associate these questions with being stoned or high or drunk. Only then, when our guard is down, can we ask these so-called silly questions.

Like, what does it all mean, man?

But these questions aren't silly. We simply ask them in that state because our inhibitions are lowered. We also ask them because we *genuinely want to know,* and in that state, we finally stop worrying about what others will think if we ask them. Perhaps they sound funny because we're altered, not at our most eloquent, and we're asking from a place of undefended curiosity and innocence.

This is the same impulse we notice in children when they question everything, incessantly. They want to know why the sky is blue and where we go after we die. That purely curious impulse is still with us. We just have to let it out.

Leaning into this pure state can open the potential for connection. I have a client, Marie, who is very close to her daughter. Marie's daughter has fallen in love with a great young man, and the couple just got engaged.

That meant it was finally time for Marie and her husband, Derek, to meet their future in-laws.

It did not go well.

While Marie and Derek made every effort to get to know the other couple, that effort wasn't reciprocated. They had very little in common, and the other couple showed no interest in bridging the gap. The conversation settled into lukewarm discussions of gardening and the weather, with long periods of silence.

You can imagine how upsetting this was to Marie. She believes in keeping family close, and she is someone who loves and longs for good discussion. How could she do that if every conversation with her new in-laws was destined to go this way?

I suggested that the next time she saw her future in-laws, she bring the Big Talk cards. When she and Derek sat down to dinner with them, Marie opened with a question she'd never have thought to ask before:

"What have you started and never finished? Why didn't you finish it?"

Suddenly, all four of them launched into a conversation about past dreams, ambitious projects, and missed opportunities. They came from very different backgrounds, but they all had a story to fit the question.

Some might say the conversation improved because it was their second meeting and first meetings are awkward. While that may have been partially true, I think it was the cards that made the difference. There are many group dynamics that remain pretty static and predictable, especially over time and amid lots of repetition.

Gentle, fun interventions like Big Talk cards can make things change even in relationships where the dynamics appear static.

When I saw Marie afterward, she was over the moon with her new daughter's soon-to-be in-laws. They were out of the rut, and she enthusiastically said, "Who would have thought we could have such a meaningful conversation?"

Get Family on Video

If you are fortunate enough to have elders in your life, you should focus on asking them big questions. And when you ask those questions, see if you can get their answers on video.

This is what I did with Grandpa Ben. At the time, I was unmarried with no sense of when I'd become a dad. I also knew there was no way my future children would even begin to understand who he was by merely talking about him. So I became an amateur video biographer. I filmed him as he walked through the Publix grocery store, flirting with the blue-haired ladies, trying to get a bargain on fish (it never worked), and carefully checking the items before he put them into his cart with the attention of a chemist doing an experiment. I filmed him while he talked about his life and the legacy he wanted to leave behind. I filmed him with my grandma to capture a real sense of their dynamic and shared family stories. My aim was historical. Grandpa Ben was getting old. I knew I didn't have that much time left with him, and I wanted to make sure his life and the history of our family were preserved for the next generation . . . and that he wouldn't be remembered only for his legendary parking advice.

It's easy to wave such a project off. Deep conversations can initially feel as awkward as asking Big Talk questions. But with practice, it becomes less awkward to ask such questions. And while we don't like to think that our loved ones will predecease us, a video biography creates something of an insurance policy that our loved ones will stay with us in more than just our memories.

The value is immense. Not only does it preserve history, but it also gives us a way to remember our loved ones *as they really were*. Many of us never get our loved ones on video at all. If we do, it's a toast at a wedding or some other special event that didn't really capture their true essence. Grandpa never wore a tux other than at the wedding. Grandma never spoke like that except in her speech opening the new library. It's far better to have a video of them living as they lived, in the settings where we knew them, talking the way they talked about the things that really mattered. There are traits only a video can capture: their essence, their personalities, how they looked, dressed, moved, talked, and sounded. With a video, future generations will have a stronger connection to their past.

These days, I'm so glad I have those videos of Grandpa Ben. I now have a way to access him anytime I think of him and a way to share his life with my own children. I can share moments of his life on video so that he isn't forgotten. Both of my children missed out on knowing Grandpa Ben in person, but thanks to the videos, they can feel connected to him.

Gifts to Give Your Family

I loved my grandfather so much that I put portions of his name in the names of each of my sons. He's still very much a living presence in our lives.

It makes all the difference to me that I was able to tell him how much he mattered while he was with me. So I leave you with some very simple advice: tell those you love how much you love them.

You can do this in any number of ways—from a phone call to a birthday card—but I recommend a particular and well-researched strategy: the gratitude letter. The gratitude letter was designed by one of positive psychology's pioneers, Martin Seligman, whom we last saw in this book being angry with the weeds in his garden.

It's easy to do. Call to mind someone you love who is still alive and has made a measurable difference that improved your life. It needs to be someone from whom you can't benefit financially or professionally. Then put your thoughts into a letter of approximately three hundred words that is heartfelt and clearly describes what that person did to improve your life and how much it meant to you. While gratitude letters can go to any family member you'd like, they can also go to friends, mentors, colleagues, or any other meaningful connection. I especially like sending them to former teachers.

Print it on nice paper or handwrite it. Set up a date for an in-person or live virtual meeting. In the latter case, send the letter to them with the overwhelmingly obvious instruction: *Do Not Open Until We Meet.*

Then read the letter while they have it in their possession.

I like to think of this as yet another insurance policy for us. This time it serves as insurance that we don't have to say those deeply meaningful words solely in a eulogy. We don't want to show up at a funeral with the sense that we could have told the deceased something before we lost the chance.

This is our chance.

These are fairly quick to write—they usually only require thirty minutes or less. But as I've noted, simple is not always easy—and they can be difficult for some people. They can require some real vulnerability. We may feel sappy and exposed when we do this. But in my entire career, I've never heard of a gratitude letter that wasn't worth it. Love and gratitude create real-life currency that is a big part of what we're all looking for and living for. We all want to know we have mattered, made a difference, and were seen.

We want to be loved, and we feel more connected when we know that love is based on something deep and real.

So it behooves us to tell the people who matter in our lives that they matter to us—while we have the chance.

Research shows that the positive aftereffects, the powerful feelings from writing and receiving such a letter, can last for weeks.[2]

Have I sold you on this idea? I hope so!

CONNECTION FORMULA EXERCISE

Choose someone in your immediate, extended, or created family, and write a gratitude letter to them. Be specific—think of what they have done for you to make your life better, and thank them for it. Write about three hundred words; they will likely fit on a single sheet of paper. Print it on a nice sheet of paper or handwrite it in a way that's aesthetically pleasing. Set up a date to read it to them, in person or virtually. If you'll be meeting virtually, send it to them in advance and ask them not to open it until the date. Then read it to them live over video. Notice how it feels before, during, and after. Do you feel more connected?

CHAPTER 9

CONNECTING TO CHILDREN

Sam was a software engineer in his late forties who had two children. He wanted to be a good father, yet he was also anxious to increase his job security and income. At forty, he had decided to go back to school on nights and weekends to get a master's degree in engineering to "stay ahead of the curve," as he put it. But between work and school, he missed out on his kids' golden years. He was present when he could be, but school and work took him away from precious and irretrievable time with his children.

By the time he had obtained his master's, it was too late. His kids didn't want anything to do with him.

He was hearing from his other guy friends about the cool things they were doing with their kids—going on bike rides, tailgating at baseball games, or engaging in some other cool shared hobby. Sam's kids, though, did not have those kinds of inclinations. They spent a lot of time on their phones, deep into PewDiePie and other YouTube influencers. Sam thought the videos his kids watched were "beyond mind-numbing." He didn't know how to spend time with them if all they did was stare at their phones.

There appeared to be no prospect of a common denominator.

Sam came to my office distraught about how he'd missed out on a unique window of time in his children's lives. Hearing him, I empathized and said I thought there were still potential opportunities to connect with his kids.

He was incredulous. But with a new perspective and the wisdom of "trying something different," Sam began to feel somewhat optimistic. We worked diligently to think of small ways to start deepening his connection with his children.

One thing we agreed would be a good way in was to enter his children's worlds. He sat next to his children, watched PewDiePie, Mr. Beast, and other influencers, and tried to see the videos through his children's eyes. To his surprise, he came to like many of the videos. He also got to know what his children were into and formulate a common vocabulary with them through the videos.

But he wanted more.

Like many parents, each night, when Sam would ask his kids his daily question over dinner, "How was your day?" he'd get the requisite limp response of "fine" without much eye contact or follow-up. Sam was discouraged. To counter this, we began with the "rose, bud, thorn" exercise at the dinner table, described in chapter 8. Initially, he didn't ask his kids to participate—the parents just modeled it through talking.

It was a small change at first, but seeing their parents do the exercise with levity, ease, and pleasure, his kids started to notice and take interest. The conversational prompt started to turn around Sam's relationship with his kids. They began to participate in the exercise, and over time, Sam entered his children's world. Little by little, he learned more about who they were, who their friends were, and how they really felt. Sam, who described himself as a "typical engineer," realized that he'd never really spoken with his kids about emotion. This small but effective exercise opened a whole new world to him and a new way to connect with his kids.

Sam said, "I did the math. My kids will be here for just a few more years, and then I'll only see them occasionally. I'm sad about the time I missed, but I'm grateful we used this time to establish a deeper connection."

The last chapter was about connecting with family. This chapter is about connecting with our children, but it is not intended to be a scholarly or thorough evaluation of child development, let alone parenting advice. Like in the previous chapters, my intention here is to suggest ways to enhance our presence and connection—in this case with our children.

Much of what is discussed will focus on connecting with children when they are teenagers or younger, still living at home, but many of these things will also work for adult children. While connecting with adult children can have its complications, it's been my experience that no matter the age of our children, *they are still our children*. So whether our child is eight and going to gymnastics or forty and the parent of our grandchildren, connecting with our children starts with where Sam started: entering *their* world and demonstrating to them we can see their world as they see it.

Go on a Quest

Once Sam entered his kids' worlds through the videos and the "rose, bud, thorn" exercise, he decided to up the ante even higher with the buddy trip. He decided to have a one-on-one experience with each of his children, overnight, one child at a time. Having this type of shared, curated experience with your child can strengthen and deepen a connection like nothing else.

I recommend to many of the people I work with to go on a "quest" with their kids. This quest can be a literal buddy trip—going camping for a night or two together or to a hotel, even if it's nearby. Doing these with some regularity can be immensely enjoyable for both of you and can yield huge benefits. The fact is this: shared novel experiences generate various feel-good chemicals that create and sustain connection. All you need to do is a little thinking and planning.

Now that my older son is in college and my younger son will be out of the house in a few years, I lament not doing these kinds of trips more frequently with my older son. So I'm making it a point to increase the frequency of these quests with my younger son, and I'll be stoked to do them moving forward with my college boy if he's willing!

Driving for long distances, sitting side by side with nothing but the road ahead of you and behind you, can create space for important, relationship-enhancing conversations. This type of buddy trip may be especially conducive to conversation for boys. Throughout the millennia, males have engaged in activities like hunting and farming side by side. While many boys are amenable to prolonged eye contact, many are not. The same can be true for many girls or nonbinary children. So if you have a child who doesn't love sustained eye contact and who may find it intimidating or uncomfortable, an hours-long car trip with both of you looking forward might help to slowly reduce that tension.[1]

The curated experience doesn't have to be something as elaborate as a road trip. You can do a local "quest" over many days or weeks. For example, zero in on your child's favorite food: pancakes, hamburgers, ramen—whatever it is. Then make it your shared quest, as parent and child, to find the best place for that food in your entire town, city, or geographic area. Come up with a rubric for how you'll rate the food experience (taste, look, scent, freshness, quality of service, etc.), and then, after trying out all the locations, you can conjointly name the "best" place for whatever your child loves.

This idea could also be brought to life in your own kitchen. There are a gazillion recipes online. Why not find the best recipe for the food your child loves?

Obviously, the shared activity doesn't need to revolve around food. It could be any loved activity you do together. You could do a month of hiking, biking, crafting, model building, exploring board games, or literally any other activity with your child that *they* deem awesome. Another fun one: the two of you can choose a book to read out loud together in a cool spot. You can even find ways of ranking the activities, games, or books, if that's fun for you. As with the food examples, the rubric you draw up would be based on whatever categories you *both* think are important.

Another great resource is Atlas Obscura.[2] It's a free website that has all kinds of local, often super-weird and fascinating, attractions. It's a way you can become a tourist without even traveling. Just go to the Atlas

Obscura website, find something odd, interesting, or cool, and off you go! You'll be amazed and surprised to see just how many odd, curious, and unknown attractions are within a tiny distance of your home.

The great things about the quest are not just the shared experiences but also all the components that lead to it and the connections that come after it. Connection possibilities are boundless in the quest's creation stages, which include, at the very least, planning the quest, finding all the restaurants or hikes or whatever it is you'll do, and coming up with the rubric and criteria for rating the experiences.

Then you have the experience itself. In the moment, you are more present with your child. The act of rating makes you pay more attention to what's happening. You aren't thinking just about the food but also about the ambiance of the restaurant or the quality of the service. On a hike, you are paying attention to the sights, sounds, smells, and other cool characteristics of the forest. This activity helps to make you and your child more mindful of their surroundings and experiences, increasing sensory and even interpersonal awareness. It helps them connect with you, but because nature can do this like nothing else, it can also help them connect with nature, which has shown to be good for our mental health (more on this in chapter 15) and with themselves.

A good rule for you and your child is to put the phones and other distractions away. As Japanese psychology expert Gregg Kretch reminded me on my podcast, tea ceremony participants only comment on what's in the room. While it may be good to allow for other, deeper, conversations about external thoughts, a tea ceremony-like outlook might be good to aspire to. Staying focused on what's going on between the two of you will definitely enrich the experience.

Then, when the experience is over, you get your postgame analysis. You talk about the experience, use your rubric, and think about what you want to do differently next time. You may end up with a scientist on your hands. And for sure, some potential positive side effects from this include mindfulness, gratitude, bonding, memories, and new parent-child traditions that can provide ongoing connections throughout both of your lives.

Finally, by following through with this planned task, you establish yourself as a reliable, trustworthy, and loving person. By doing what you say you will do, you improve the quality of your connection.

You may face some resistance at first. Make it fun. Find a way to insert levity and optimism into the forthcoming event and be open to changing plans if necessary. Saying something like, "Introduce me to your favorite songs on the drive" may provide the WD-40 to rid the squeaks. In all likelihood, you'll have a blast and your child won't want the quest to end, making the initial resistance a mere memory. You'll know you're on the right path when after doing it a few times, it becomes essential to your relationship.

In the end, it's not about the quest itself. It's about your relationship as parent and child and the life-giving connection the two of you create.

Self-Compassion and Parenting

"Parenting is hard" was the simple phrase uttered at the beginning of our interview by podcast guest psychologist Dr. Susan Pollak, who authored *Self-Compassion for Parents*. She also said Freud got it right when he referred to parenting as "the impossible profession." This is all the more reason for us parents to apply the self-compassion techniques described in earlier chapters.

When we're compassionate with ourselves, we parent better. We are kinder to ourselves and kinder to our children. I remember a time when I was short with my son over something that embarrasses me to this day. I yelled at him for squinting his eyes when I was trying to give him instructions. I yelled because I thought he was mocking me.

He was not. He was probably trying to pay attention, or, who knows? He may have had dust in his eyes.

I felt ashamed by my poor response, which was based on my misinterpretation. I made a futile attempt to forget. It seemed like my only recourse since I had not received the memo yet on self-compassion.

I apologized to him years later for having yelled at him, but he'd forgotten about it by then. I hadn't. In fact, it still bothers me from time to time.

When I was short with my son, I was hard on both my son and myself. If I had possessed the ability to engage in self-compassion in any of the three forms (which I described earlier and will revisit now), I would have been better able to apologize on the spot rather than doing so years later. For example, if I had considered the perspective of *common humanity* and thought, "Every parent struggles, and I'm no different," I might have been able to apologize. Or if I'd engaged *mindfulness*, seeing the situation for what it was, not bigger or smaller, and thought, "You didn't read your son correctly, Adam," I might have been able to apologize. Or if I'd been able to tap into *self-kindness* and heard the voice of a friend saying, "Dude, we all screw up!" I might have been able to apologize.

To paraphrase a thought from Brené Brown, shame makes us feel unlovable and causes us to go into our shell and hide. That is exactly what I did.

Self-compassion allows us to be easier on ourselves, better with our children, and model being kind to ourselves. It facilitates our connection to ourselves and to our children. It can take time to learn to do it well, but the pursuit is worth it for our own sake and for our children's.

Teach Your Children Well

Dr. Damon Korb is a behavioral and developmental pediatrician, a parenting expert, and the author of *Raising an Organized Child*. He was a guest on my podcast and talked about raising and connecting with children at various stages of development.

One of his thesis statements is that *if a child can safely complete a task themselves, they should do that task themselves*. If they can fold their laundry and put it away, then parents should train their children to do just that.

You would be surprised by the age at which a child can do these kinds of things after being taught. Some children as young as three or four can put away their clothes. Some kindergarteners can make their own lunch, with little or no support. It turns out many children have the ability to take on these kinds of tasks, but most parents end up doing them instead.

Why? Because in the moment, it seems easier. Teaching a four-year-old to fold and put away laundry is a slow, painful process. They'll get it wrong and wrinkle the clothes. When they make their own peanut butter sandwich, more peanut butter may end up on the counter than on the bread. Most parents don't want to take the time to sit with their kids and teach them because of this.

I get it—it feels so inefficient, and the amount of patience it takes can be immense.

And sometimes we don't want to teach our children—perhaps consciously or unconsciously—because *we* want to feel needed. Damon mentioned on my podcast that he angered many Australian parents when he suggested children make their own lunches. In between laughs, he noted he nearly caused an international incident.

Aussies, I feel you and love you (and imagine Damon does too). And here's my take: if there's a hard line around one or two areas where you want to feel needed, protect those. Yet you can do so while trying your best to find other ways to teach your children life skills based on their current abilities.

I say this because by not teaching them how to do these things themselves, you and they miss a powerful opportunity for a lot of good stuff, including teaching agency. Agency is the feeling of being in control of actions and their consequences. Having agency has been shown to be predictive of many good outcomes in a child's life and overall mental health.[3]

Because I love the grill, I've taught my teenage son how to grill and how to smoke meat. Given that fire can be dangerous, there was a lot of supervision. He loves it. It took some activation energy to get us there, but with a tweak here or there, he's making great stuff and feels a sense of agency.

Teaching children in this way is also a powerful opportunity for connection.

Sure, on the front end, this kind of teaching is a time suck. But think about it: if it takes us ten days to teach a kid to make lunch and we are making about nine hundred lunches over five years (just guessing), that's some nice savings on the back end. If my math is correct, you could save about fifty-six hours over the next five years, or essentially 2.5 full days, by investing one hundred minutes of teaching time.

Coordination through improved communication and trust-building is a superior form of connection. It makes the two of you more of a team and may yield benefits in other ways down the road. By coordinating with your child in this way, you are increasing your connection with them.

Another potential benefit: By demonstrating clear communication and patience, you may be influencing your child's future as a leader or teacher. Having experienced your clear communication and patience, they may in turn become the same kind of patient, clear communication leaders for others that you were for them.

* * *

On the other hand, teaching our children can involve the arts. Create a list of albums you love to listen to and introduce them to your kids. This music is a part of your legacy of connection with them, and the lasting connection through that soundtrack will be indelible. You and they will hear certain songs from certain road trips, projects, or other connected times in your lives, and it will bring each of you back to that moment. Introducing my sons to Led Zeppelin while we were doing a big building project was memorable to all of us. It even reshaped how I hear the music. And my sons are both Zeppelin fans as a result.

Or, create a list of movies and/or shows to watch and introduce to your children. That can be its own kind of quest. While watching movies may not be a flow-based activity, lasting, enjoyable, and sometimes edifying connections are created here even if they don't require much exertion. Revisiting Edward and his scissorhands was a moving experience for all of us. And revisiting that family of Bradys or *Pee-wee's Playhouse* and seeing my young children falling off the couch laughing hysterically was super bonding. We had a shared vocabulary afterward.

And if you watch movies, listen to music, or take in some shared art, don't forget the debrief! That's potentially the richest part. Engage and talk about how the art landed with you. Make this a source of great conversational connection and geek out with your children. Learn from them. It's art. You may have taken a college course on appreciation of one of these art forms, and you may be able to share some cool insights. Your child can likely do the same, and you may be blown away as you see or hear about the art through their eyes. Both of my sons have repeatedly done this for me, and like me, you may never hear the music, see the movie, or experience the art quite the same way again.

Far from the Tree

Even though our children come from us, they are not us. A great book by Cornell professor Dr. Andrew Solomon titled *Far from the Tree* addresses this concept.[4] As much as we might like to have a "Mini-Me" as in *Austin Powers*, Solomon reminds us that our children are unique individuals by arguing that, "there is no such thing as reproduction." He also states, "We must love them for themselves, and not for the best of ourselves, which is a lot harder to do. Loving our own children is an exercise for the imagination." All of this was certainly true for Raquel, a sociology professor at a local university. Her daughter, Ashleigh, was, as she put it, "the spitting image of me in every way." She showed brilliance in academics from a young age and all the way from childhood to college said she wanted to be a professor "just like Mommy."

One day, Raquel came to my office and told me she was overwhelmingly sad. She said that Ashleigh had abruptly left her doctoral program to start an organic farm in Oregon. Her grandparents had left Ashleigh a sizeable chunk of money in their will, and Ashleigh had decided to "follow her bliss."

For Raquel, Ashleigh's decision to change course was heartbreaking; she even said she felt betrayed. Raquel and I explored the losses associated with Ashleigh's decision: a loss of continuity, legacy, as well as the connection she had felt with her daughter throughout their lives together. Raquel said that if her family had had a coat of arms, it would have included service, education, tenacity, hard work, and family loyalty. As Raquel saw it, all those components of the family coat of arms had been turned upside down.

After many months, when the opportunity presented itself, I asked Raquel if she saw even the tiniest of virtues in Ashleigh's pursuit. Raquel acknowledged that Ashleigh was brave, or as she put it, "intrepid." After a year, she even said, "Ashleigh was dealt a good hand, and she decided to do something very different from what I or anyone in her family had ever done." And seeing Ashleigh work so hard to assemble a team, learn horticulture, and do something of service had allowed Raquel to see that Ashleigh was, in fact, following the family's coat of arms. But Ashleigh was doing it her way. Raquel understood this and was able to give her full support.

Connecting through the Years

As our kids age, our opportunities for connection constantly shift. I remember when my firstborn was a baby and our friend Susan said, "Enjoy each stage. You might be annoyed at times, but you'll long to return to those stages once they're gone. It goes by quickly."

I thought of Susan often as each of my sons grew. Indeed, our opportunities for connection shift based on the developmental stage of our kids and what they are interested in. Our children's primary job is to become increasingly more autonomous as they age, thereby needing us less or in different ways, and this causes our opportunities for connection to change over time. So it's of utmost importance to focus on the ways we can connect with our children during each stage of their lives.

Pokémon GO walks may turn into long bike rides. Going fishing may morph into archeological digs. Remote-control airplanes may fall by the wayside in favor of robotics. Kids are constantly changing, and we parents can pay attention and gently look for new openings to connect with our children and their evolving interests.

Each year of life, starting with infancy through kindergarten, then through the tween and teen stages, and all the way to adulthood, our children will mature and need us less. The stages of individuation and separation are healthy, real, and sometimes heartbreaking. So when I counsel parents of small children in my office, I imagine myself as Dickens's Ghost of Christmas Future, saying, "Lean into your creativity to figure out how to stay connected with your child's needs, and be willing to change with them."

While the strategies I discussed above fit for most ages, here are a few age-specific strategies that can help:

Young Kids

During the first three to five years of their lives, deep and present connection with our children is at its most essential. They need us during these years in ways that require our uninterrupted focus. One great tip: A way we can learn to be focused and present with our children is to notice things about them. Zero in on their clothes, the toys they play with, and their observable behaviors. Watch them like you're a sportscaster at a game. See them and comment on what they're doing, speaking objectively on what you see your child is doing, in the present tense: "I see you picking up your toy truck. You're now moving it all the way across the carpet. You're crashing it into a car!" Doing this keeps you connected with them in present time and allows them to feel you experiencing them. This fortifies your connection with them.

And it keeps your attention where it belongs: on your child.

Dr. Becky Kennedy, a child psychologist, talks about how having "play, no phone" time (or PNP time) for as little as ten minutes a day can dramatically increase your connection with young kids.[5] This is when—you guessed it—you play with your kids with no phone or other distractions. There's always so much going on in young kids' lives, and usually, all they want to do is sit and play, specifically with you. Giving them that undistracted time will do wonders for your connection.

Tweens/Teenagers

Most kids start to actively break their connection with us when they reach the tween years. They want to be more independent and start to figure out their own identity. We parents need to give them this space to find out who they are.

But we can remain interested in their lives and connect with them when we can. As with the PewDiePie example, if they're into soccer and we're not, we can become interested in the sport by getting curious and asking them questions about it. Then we can connect with them on a level beyond just chauffeuring them to and from practices and games. If they like *Roblox* or *Fortnite*, we can get into it ourselves, even if it means we are spending some free time practicing. We can ask them about their friends and try to get to know them.

This age is when the "rose, bud, thorn" exercise from the start of the chapter can help find those connection points. Tweens and teenagers often seem to want nothing to do with us, but finding those moments to open up a brief conversation can help us build and maintain a foundation for a deeper relationship with them.

Adult Children

The process of our children growing up and leaving the house can be one of the most painful yet joyful experiences of our lives. I cried long and hard the day I dropped my oldest off at college.

Yet I am so happy about the young man he's become. Like me, most of us feel a strong connection to *both* of these truths if we've been there.

The way we connect with an adult child depends on who they are and our relationship with them. If they are no longer living in our house, there are fewer natural opportunities for conversation and connection. We have to be intentional about them, which is why texting, calling, visiting, and making ourselves available vis-à-vis their preferred medium, as well as increasing the frequency of communication, can help.

If your adult child lives at home, adult expectations and boundaries can be crucial to staying in the positive zone. This living situation could comprise an entire book, but suffice it to say that clear communication is crucial. That sounds pretty business-y, sure, but another piece of important business is the business of play! Stay playfully engaged with your adult child. Find ways to create sweetness and levity through age-appropriate themes and variations on what has been shared in this chapter.

Much of the connection we have with adult children relies on the connection we had with them when they were kids. But there's some good news: it's never too late to deepen what we have.

Authoritative Parenting

There are four parenting styles described by developmental psychologist Diana Baumrind: authoritative, authoritarian, permissive, and neglectful. As parents, of course, we need to be in charge. But we also need to stay loving. Many parents have trouble incorporating these two seemingly opposing directives.

The worst outcomes occur when parents are *neglectful*. Neglect occurs when a parent doesn't provide basic essentials such as adequate clothing, shelter, medical care, or supervision. This can lead to disastrous outcomes relating to the child's health, safety, and well-being. Essentially, the child is left with the belief that they don't matter at all, and they tend to fare the most poorly of the four types.

Some want to be their children's "buddies" and get drunk with their non-drinking-age kids. The research on this is clear: it's not advisable and can lend itself to bad outcomes. In fact, this type of overly *permissive* parenting without boundaries can lead to antisocial behaviors for the child later in life.[6]

Some parents can be too *authoritarian* and miss out on the loving aspect of the relationship. They can be too cold and distant and focus more on the behaviors of the child rather than how the child is feeling and what they need. This interferes badly with connection. These parents *correct* more than they *connect*. They say, "Do what I say, not what I do." This can lead to subservience in the child and can reduce the child's sense of agency in the world. It can also lead to rebellious acting out.

If we find ourselves primarily in any of the three aforementioned parenting styles, what we want instead is to become an *authoritative* parent: a friendly coach. I've heard many people use the term "authoritative" when they meant to say "authoritarian," which we just defined as a person who dictates. In stark contrast, *authoritative* parents are clearly in charge, setting expectations, and being appropriately demanding while being warm and loving. Think Ted Lasso or Mary Poppins. We are in our child's corner, cheering for them, but also the coach and in charge, making sure the plays go well. Our role as a parent is a given and not questioned. We are friendly, but during these formative years, we're definitely *not* their cool Cabo drinking buddy.

Sam became that *authoritative* parent. He also learned that it was never too late to find a connection with his child. No matter how old, no matter how long we've felt disconnected from them, we can always start right now and build a stronger relationship with our child. Maybe we've missed out on some early years. While we can't get those back, we can start anew with patience, perseverance, and the plans we've covered in this chapter.

CONNECTION FORMULA EXERCISE

Go on a quest with your child. Figure out what they love—whether that's a type of food, a genre of music, or even finding rocks—and go out into the world, seeking to find the best of that thing. Go through all the steps: cocreate the rubric, set your course, go through the discovery, and debrief afterward. Once you go on a first quest, it may be the start of a series of quests that go on throughout your entire lives together.

CHAPTER 10

CONNECTING
TO FRIENDS

I first met Aaron when I was eighteen. Witnesses to that first meeting said it looked like long-lost brothers finally reuniting. We started talking music—the Violent Femmes, The Smiths, the Surf Punks—and immediately became inseparable. Once we started talking, we pretty much never stopped.

There were differences too. He played soccer and piano. I was more into football and guitar. But each of us had something that fed the other.

We ended up going to college together. Every night, we were the last people in the dining hall because there was so much to talk about.

Aaron was highly intelligent, and his interests appeared to have no limits. After closing out the dining hall, we still weren't done talking, so we'd walk to the pool hall and play pool for hours. We didn't care who won. We just liked playing and talking and goofing around. We were inseparable throughout college, and we cheered each other on. And as you'll hear, that friendship continued to make a major difference later in my life. I would be screwed without him.

The Truest Relationship

Eric Barker, who wrote *Plays Well with Others,* described friendship on my podcast as the ultimate democratic relationship. The thing about friends, he said, is that they are expendable. They aren't family. You can opt in or out of a friendship at any time. The only thing keeping a friendship together is mutual positive regard.

People have maintained such relationships since the beginning of time. Crack open any ancient story, and you're almost certain to find it filled with friends. We're designed to have friends just as we're designed to have a romantic partner. We have wired prosocial tendencies. Pay attention the next time you meet with a friend, and you'll notice your tone slightly changes to match theirs. Your posture shifts to align with theirs. If they scratch their head, odds are you'll do the same shortly afterward.

This is called mirroring, a sign of connection that we share with other primates. It's a nonverbal signal that we like this person, we trust this person, and we want to sync up and connect with this person. We have what's called a "mirror neuron system," which helps us imitate others and increases our empathy.[1]

Throughout the millennia, humans have needed humans. We used to live in villages filled with people who played various friendship roles in our lives.

Friendship is democratic, but it is also necessary. We have evolved to need friends.

In the movie *Castaway,* when the Tom Hanks character is so desperate for a friend he starts talking to a volleyball, no one thinks it is ridiculous. Everyone understands his need. In fact, we understand it so deeply that many of us cry when Hanks loses Wilson during his escape from the desert island. If we thought about crying over an inanimate ball, we might feel silly. But we were crying because he lost his last chance for social connection, recognizing how profound that need is, and we felt his desolation without it.

Support through friendship is so powerful that it can add years to our lives. A study found that friendship in adulthood likely counteracts adversity experienced early in life and gives us longer lives.[2]

Friends also help us by *spotting* things we don't recognize in our own life because we're too close to them. As Marshall McLuhan said, "One thing about which fish know exactly nothing is water." Our friends spot what we're missing—the good and the bad. Friends are the ones to set us straight and call us on our BS. They also tell us that we're funnier and more attractive and more charming than we give ourselves credit for.

And they may also be honest about our faults and give us feedback we don't want but badly need.

Nothing summarizes all a friend can do like what my friend Aaron has done for me. Every night, as we ate together, a common theme in our conversation was that we'd both become psychologists and go into practice together one day.

Things didn't go exactly as planned. Aaron became a psychologist shortly after college. I did not. Years later, during the period in which I was wrestling with the idea of going back to school, I confided in him that I wasn't sure I could do it.

We were at a Honolulu sushi bar when he started talking about his work. He loved his work, and I did not love mine. I broke down, nearly crying into my sake over the fact that I never became a psychologist.

"I should have done it," I said mournfully.

"You still can," he replied.

I wasn't in the mood for a pep talk. We'd been down this road, and even though I was the one to bring it up, I sharply demanded that we drop the subject. It was too painful for me to explore, especially since I was certain there was no meaningful way to alter my career.

"I really don't want to talk about this again!" I said emphatically.

But Aaron cared more about my life than my boundaries. He wanted me to be super psyched—no matter how painful that would be.

"You can still do it," he said with a bit of levity and a lot of passion.

When we reviewed this conversation recently, he told me I looked like I might jump across the table and clock him. To be clear, I've never done anything like that in my life, but apparently, I looked unusually pissed.

In spite of that fact, he wouldn't let it go. He reminded me that Aurianne would support me in this pursuit. He reminded me he would support me. Everyone wanted me to pursue my dream.

It took hearing him and knowing I had that support to finally take that crucial step on the path I continue to walk to this day.

The Difficulty of Modern Friendship

One of my favorite podcasts is *Conan O'Brien Needs a Friend*. I think Conan consistently breaks the speed limit for generating high-volume and high-quality humor.

But the genesis of that podcast, as you can perhaps guess from the title, was a question Conan once had: Did he have any *real* friends? If the hilarious, brilliant, and likable Conan O'Brien has wondered about that, then it seems safe to assume that we have too.

The truth is, it appears to be harder to make and keep friends than in years prior. These days, we move so often that it's hard to maintain relationships. According to the US Census, the average American will move more than eleven times in their lifetime.[3] We often move first in childhood, breaking those early relationships. Then many of us leave home to start college or go elsewhere for our first job.

Then we may move for the next job. And the next job.

Even if we stay in one place, it's no guarantee we can secure long-term friendships. Our friends may be the ones to move. And besides, we work so much that it can seem hard to find the time for friendship. Many of us have no boundaries in our work, and we're anxious about saying no, relegating ourselves to being on call nearly 24-7. We try to compensate by making friends at work, which can be great, but there are risks with transience there too; they often leave, or we leave, or one of us gets promoted or changes teams . . . and we fall out of touch.

Freddy, an executive I work with, first came to me because he was lonely. He'd had friends all his life, but he woke up at forty and realized they'd all disappeared somewhere. No stranger himself to disappearing,

Freddy was born in Virginia, went to college in Texas, studied abroad in France, went to grad school in Boston, and now works in Silicon Valley. In each place, he made friends, but he couldn't maintain those relationships over such distances, especially since he sometimes went years without getting back to one place or another.

Without friendship, we are profoundly lonely, and loneliness is costly to our health. It's likely connected to the spike in depression and anxiety we've seen over the last couple of decades. That depression and anxiety spike has occurred at the same time the number of friends people have has plummeted. In 1990 a full third of all people had ten or more friends. Only 16 percent had two or fewer friends. Today, those numbers have basically flipped.[4]

A lack of friendship also forces us to rely too much on family—creating an unnatural burden on those closest to us. My wife is one of the best spouses on the planet. But she doesn't want to watch the Golden State Warriors with me; she simply doesn't like watching sports. If I had no friends, though, I'd be forced to either watch alone or—and I would not do this—impose on her something she doesn't like to do.

Esther Perel, the aforementioned author of *Mating in Captivity*, has said that when we lived in villages, we had different people close by who'd do different things with us. She notes that things are very different today: we now rely on our spouse to provide everything from the village. But if we lean on our spouse as our sole and primary relationship, it puts immense stress on that relationship.

The process of overrelying on our spouses is a lot like starving: in the same way the body starts to consume muscle that it badly needs just to stay alive in this scenario, a marriage is threatened by toxic stress on the couple due to one or more partners being starved for friendship.

Finding Friends

To create those new friendships we desire, the first thing we have to do is create space for them. One of the biggest problems of modern life is that we're exceedingly busy. We work long hours, and when we aren't working, we've got to-dos coming out of our ears, and during the moments of downtime, we're strapped to our screens out of habit.

We live in a new world that lionizes busyness, information, and efficiency above all else.

But go watch any show or movie that involves friends, and you'll notice that most of the time, the characters aren't busy. They aren't on phones. Even workplace comedies rarely involve much work.

This is intentional because friendship often requires time to hang out and sync up. I've sometimes referred to this dynamic as the "hang and vibe" friendship, as opposed to the activity friendship. This is the friendship that exists just because we like each other, a process that author Will Schwalbe describes as alchemy, the process of turning lead into gold. Will is the author of *We Should Not Be Friends*, a memoir chronicling an unlikely forty-year friendship between the author, a gay man, and Chris Maxey, a straight and high-ranking Navy SEAL officer. He explains that over time, this alchemy leads to a profound comfort. Friends can come as they are, be who they are, and know they're loved.

That requires time, space, and being off our phones and connected with our friends. Just being. There may be a goal like showing up and helping a friend with a task. But generally, it's the willingness to shed work and other identities for a while and just be present with one another. It's two or more people talking about life; sharing fears, longings, whatever is on their mind; and knowing there's someone acting as a supportive witness.

When we're young, friendship often requires nothing more than geographic proximity. We're seven, and a kid between six and ten lives across the street, so we're friends.

As adults, particularly with new friends made in adulthood, we often do the activity friendship model. This is when we have a shared interest that bonds us to each other. That could look like a local campaign, serving on a board together, an amateur sports team, or a book club. The point is that it's a place where people with the same interests gather with the time and inclination to create connection.

Often, once you have those components in place, it's easier to create the "hang and vibe" friendships than you might think.

Embrace Difference

A shared connection is important, but that doesn't mean we should only seek friendship with the like-minded. One of the greatest gifts of friendship is that it can help us think differently. A hallmark of psychological well-being is the ability to be mentally nimble—the term used is "cognitive flexibility." For sure, having friends who are a bit different from us increases our cognitive flexibility. Friends from different backgrounds can pop the bubbles we find ourselves in, challenging our cultural, political, and personal beliefs.

Think back to the friendship described by Will Schwalbe in *We Should Not Be Friends*. He and Chris Maxy added spectacular richness and support to one another's lives. It was their values of kindness and other virtues that allowed them to transcend their differences. And their differences may have increased their bond as well.

The science is in on this. The diversity model is better—whether we're talking about neurodiversity, culture, age, religion, disability, or pretty much any other form of difference. Different perspectives, different opinions, and different approaches make us stronger.

One of my dearest friends, Scott, has a very different background than mine. I'm the Jewish son of a physician from California. He grew up in a Protestant family on a farm in a remote area of Kansas. The closest fast-food restaurant was hours from his home. We did not grow up with the same perspective on life. Yet we share core values and are super well matched, and we have a lively, supportive connection. Without question, my life is better with Scott in it. Our friendship has opened up so much room for new ideas, new directions for work, and new inspiration for both of us.

Reaching out beyond our comfort zone is always a challenge. There is a natural instinct to stick with our own "tribe," however we define that. And as we age, we tend to narrow our perspectives and interests. Left to our own devices, we contract over time, occluding our focus and limiting what interests we're willing to entertain, which can mean becoming more rigid with age. As a child, we'll take on entirely new hobbies to hang out with the kid across the street. As an adult, if we're a superfan of classical music, we may not put as much effort into a potential friend whose primary interest is professional wrestling.

But if we want to make friends, stretching is the way to go. And if we're willing to stretch, we can find connections with almost anyone.

To that point, I had the honor of interviewing actor and professional musician Daryl Davis. I first read about Daryl in Adam Grant's outstanding book *Think Again*. I couldn't believe what I had read, and I had to hear his story firsthand. Daryl has played with some of the greats: Chuck Berry, Muddy Waters, and B. B. King, and he even had an acting role in HBO's megahit *The Wire*. Yet his greatest accomplishment might be the friends he's made. He's an African American man, and he's made numerous friends with members of the KKK.

You read that correctly.

But it gets better. Because of his ability to connect with others, he's been personally responsible for motivating over two hundred members of the KKK and other hate groups to leave their organizations. Through honest, open dialogue, Daryl got to know these men's values and helped them critically consider these values relative to their role in their respective groups. He enabled them to recognize being in a hate group went against their values.

So they left.

Daryl told me he has dozens of KKK robes in his basement from those former members who renounced their beliefs. Each robe is a testament to his dedication to connection. Daryl's courageous acts create massive positive ripples that likely affect thousands of people in current and future generations.

When you open yourself to the challenge of difference, you may be surprised at the strength and value of the connection that develops. Supreme Court justices Ruth Bader Ginsburg and Antonin Scalia were friends despite having almost no legal opinions in common. Similarly, a beloved friend of mine is from the South and quite conservative. We get along fantastically, and I am positive he's opened my mind and helped me understand more about the world than I possibly could have without him.

With a little effort, these friendships can lead us to profound new experiences.

Each Friend in Their Place

Friends are a big deal, and when we find them, we should seek to discover their superpower and play to that strength.

As mentioned, in the village of yesteryear, we would have had many connections and a real community. Some of those connections would have been our drinking buddies. Some would have helped us find food or fix things. Some would have been our mentors and offered us guidance. Some would have been there to discuss family problems. And so on.

We need those same dynamics in place with our friends today. Just as Aquaman can swim really well but can't fly, and Spider-Man can do awesome things with his web-making but isn't such a great swimmer, one friend might be the first person we call to help us move but the last person we call to talk about relationships. One friend might care about emotions but not sports. One friend might understand family stress; another, work stress. And one friend may just be the friend we call when we want to geek out over *The Lord of the Rings*, a person who, in my case, saves my wife from unnecessary boredom.

All of these friends have value. We sometimes dismiss the idea of varying levels of intimacy in friendship. And while we may be looking for best friends, not acquaintances, there's value in all shades of friendship.

Drive-Away Test

Whomever you choose as a friend, you'll be giving them your most precious nonrenewable resource: your time. Remember, you can lose your money and get it back. You can lose your health and get it back. But you can't lose your time and get it back.

A good use of time is being in reciprocal relationships with a healthy give and take. You can ask yourself: Does the friendship feed me or bleed me? Obviously, you'll want to feel fed by your friendship—you want your cup filled—and you'll want this for your friend too. Even in the best friendship, we may feel bled or depleted at times, but it's better that those experiences be in the minority. A great way to discern whether you are being "fed or bled" is to do what I call the "drive-away test." Imagine you've been hanging out with a friend, whether in person, on the phone, or even online. How do you feel driving away or leaving the hangout? Do you feel taller, happier, renewed, or do you feel deflated, exhausted, or perhaps even used?

These are important data points to consider. And sometimes, friendships come to an end after such considerations.

Recognizing a friendship is over can be deeply painful. One of my clients, Craig, had a close friend named David. Craig described David as a great guy who had a rough childhood that led to anger issues in adulthood. Craig had seen evidence of David's anger, but it was always turned toward other people, and Craig believed that his friend would never act out that way toward him. He believed this because in his eyes, *their* relationship was different. They were so close, best friends. Until the day that David exploded at him, hard. Craig described it as shocking. Even though he knew David had the capacity to behave this way, Craig didn't know how to make sense of how his friend could do it to him.

And then it happened again. And again.

Eventually, Craig realized that this friendship was more harmful than good for him. He told me a breach of trust had occurred, and he couldn't get past it. After a lot of thought, Craig made the difficult decision to part ways with David. The brotherly love between them remained, but in Craig's words, "The friendship had a good life. And it took us far . . . as far as it could go."

Are your friends improving you? Are they lifting you up and seeing the best in you, like Ben Affleck's character in *Good Will Hunting*, who demands that his best friend (Matt Damon's Will) make the most of his life? Or are they dragging you down, holding you back, and filling your life with negative feelings?

Oprah Winfrey once said, "Everyone wants to ride with you in the limo, but what you want is someone who will take the bus with you when the limo breaks down." Are your friends ready to take the bus with you? Or are they there for the limo rides?

Sometimes, the answers to these questions are not what we had hoped.

The Blessing in Former Friends

Ending a friendship does not mean the friendship was a waste. In fact, when a friendship ends, much of the good stuff can be saved for both parties. Craig and David had many great experiences together. Those memories didn't disappear after they said goodbye. Craig made it clear to me that his life had been permanently upgraded by knowing David.

I asked Craig if he and David had a final conversation. "Yes, but it was brief." What did it include? "We both literally told each other a few things we'd gained from our friendship. And we parted by saying thank you and wishing each other well."

Naturally, many of the people who see me struggle with this. They express grief at the loss of a friendship. An attachment has been formed, and when a cherished friendship ends, it can feel almost like a death. That grief is understandable, and it must be felt. In addition to the natural grief we feel, we can dial into how we are better people for the priceless gifts received from this fellow traveler through their friendship. And we can reflect on how we made their lives better too.

Part of being human is our capacity to bond. And when the bonds break, even for all the right reasons, the disconnection hurts. For a time, we traveled the same road together. We took care of each other and learned from each other. And now, that journey is over. We are sad, and we can also be grateful. This doesn't make the hurt stop hurting, but it allows us to see the blessing beyond that hurt.

And sometimes, friendships come and go without a breakup, instead reaching a natural time-based end. Not long ago, Aurianne and I went on safari in Africa, where we met Kate. She was traveling on her own, and we immediately clicked. For those three weeks, she felt like a friend for life. We gave each other good medicine, sharing stories and providing genuine support for one another.

We may never see her again.

But that doesn't change the fact that we will always appreciate Kate and cherish those weeks together. The sweet moment of our friendship is realistically over, and we're grateful for having experienced it.

I Just Called to Say I Love You

There is no friend like an old friend. I recently asked my older son, Avin, what connection was most important to him. He told me it was his friends. He knew his family was stable and supportive, but he's at the age—early college—when friends are crucial because they really help form the person we become.

Avin has known one of his best friends since kindergarten. Another joined the group in second grade. I have no doubt these three will be at each other's weddings and will take care of one another throughout their lives. If we are lucky like that—to have such close and supportive friends— it behooves us to do whatever we can to keep those connections alive.

To maintain connection with friends, the most significant thing we can do is spend time with them. If we find someone who we value as a friend, we should reach out—even if we must do most of the reaching out ourselves. In friendship, as in life, we can only control our controllables. And if this relationship is important, then it's important to keep it up.

As in your romantic relationship, the key with friendship is to connect. I know that sounds obvious, but there's often a chasm between what we know and what we do. So in addition to reaching out on the fly, you may want to use calendar reminders to reach out at the appropriate intervals in case daily life gets in the way.

Ideally, get together for an in-person hang session. If you can't do that, a Zoom call is a great alternative. Yeah, I know many of us are tired of Zoom, but if it's a friend on the other end, it tends to be energizing. If you can't do that, go down the communication food chain with a phone call, an email, a text, and so on. Some connection is nearly always better than none, but for most people, the more personal the interaction, the better.

Of course, how much you need to reach out is different for every friendship. On my podcast, psychotherapist Britt Frank—author of *The Science of Stuck*—explained there are two types of friendships: hummingbirds and scorpions. Hummingbirds need to eat every day. For them to feel fed, they need to be in touch with or see their friends every day. But, in Britt's words, "Scorpions can eat a ton in one shot and then not need to for a while." For them, a friend connection may only be necessary once a month.

Whether it's daily, weekly, monthly, or yearly, I imagine you've seen that all it takes is the shortest amount of time to reestablish connection. An eight-minute call can get the dopamine flowing and remind both of you just how connected you are in spite of the time that elapsed.

The point is to find ways to keep that connection going. It may seem an inconvenience some days, but as you get off that call, you'll remember that investing in friends is worth it.

CONNECTION FORMULA EXERCISE

Reach out to an old friend just to tell them you were thinking of them and wanted to hear how they are doing. It doesn't have to be any more than that—just put yourself out there and see what happens. Feel free to repeat with someone else. Who knows? Maybe you'll restart one of the greatest friendships of your life.

CHAPTER 11

CONNECTING
TO ANIMALS

I used to hate cats. I mean *hate*! I didn't even like pictures of them. Then I met a little guy named Yoda.

Yoda came to me indirectly. I was in my twenties, dating and living with a woman who loved cats. While she was working on her degree, she wanted feline company and asked me if I would be OK with her adopting one.

I was not.

But she kept at it until finally, I reluctantly agreed, with clear conditions.

"Listen," I told her, "here's the deal. Get the cat, but the cat is *your* cat, not my cat. I will not clean up after the cat. I will not pet the cat. The cat doesn't come into the bedroom. And I get to live as though the cat isn't even there."

I know. I sound like a monumental jerk here. But imagine something you hate, and then imagine bringing it into your home! This was a *major* accommodation.

And knowing me as she did, she knew my concession was huge, so she agreed.

Still, she wanted me to be a part of the adoption process. I went with her to pick out a cat. My then-girlfriend had a very particular type of cat in mind. She wanted a short-haired female. The adoption volunteer had one, but as soon as it came out of its kennel, the first thing it did was bite me.

"You see what I mean?" I said in exasperation. "This is why I hate cats."

That cat obviously wasn't coming home. The volunteer suggested another.

"I have another cat. Quite possibly the best cat I've ever met. There's just one problem . . . this cat isn't short-haired. Or female."

She brought this comically massive Maine Coon fluff ball out for us to see. The cat jumped out of her arms and into my lap, headbutting my nose in greeting. I was transformed in an instant. Seconds before, I hated cats. Now every cell in my body wanted to take care of this beautiful little creature. I wanted to hold that cat forever.

That was Yoda. He slept in my arms that night. From then on, we were deeply bonded. When my girlfriend and I broke up, she generously recognized Yoda and I were a single unit, and she let me retain kitty custody with her blessings.

But that didn't mean things were easy. Yoda came with some major problems. Within months of adopting him, I found out he had FIV, feline immune deficiency virus—basically cat HIV. He also had asthma. In medical terms, he had simultaneous hypoimmune and hyperimmune disorders. Because of the FIV, I needed to fortify his immune system, but if I fortified it too much, it would inflame his asthma. Still, if I didn't give him the drugs to strengthen his immune system, then it would create potentially deadly complications with his FIV.

I was told he had at most a year to live. But my love for my cat made me into a veterinary health care warrior: I wasn't just going to accept that diagnosis. At the time, I was single and had no children; Yoda was my one expense, and I spared no expense.

He meant the world to me, and he gave me so much more than I ever gave him. Every second I spent with him was healing. He always slept on my chest. He would greet me at the door. His love was infectious. He won over literally every cat hater who met him. And I wasn't going to give up on him.

I used traditional, allopathic Western medicine, but I also went to a Chinese medicine vet and a pet nutritionist. I tried anything and everything within reason to give Yoda a few more months of high-quality life with me.

My efforts paid off. The one-year estimate became five great years. Then, in year five, I received more bad news. Yoda was diagnosed with lymphoma. Once again, I tried everything. The only potential dealbreaker would be Yoda's level of distress. I had nonverbally promised him that if he was in real pain, I wouldn't keep him alive at *his* expense. But until then, we'd try everything.

This time, the focus was on palliative radiation treatments. Those treatments bought us another high-quality fifteen months together.

Finally, on Martin Luther King Jr. Day 2002, Yoda suddenly declined in health rapidly. He was withdrawn. I called the mobile vet over, and she told me it was time.

Even today, all these years later, I can't think about that day without tearing up.

Animal Village

My relationship with Yoda was extremely special to me, but if you've ever had a pet, you probably know what I'm talking about. We humans like to think of ourselves as separate and above the rest of the animal kingdom. But the truth is, by our nature, we are meant to be surrounded by animals.

Since that time long ago in the village, animals have been a part of our daily lives. There might have been dogs, cows, chickens, sheep, and pigs on every farm, and cats in every household. Every town had horses trotting down the roads. We were deeply connected to those animals as well as the people in our lives.

Returning to this connection was one of the central reasons my friend Philip, from the previous chapter, packed up his life a few years ago, bought a farm, and moved out to the country to dedicate his time to sustainability. Before the move, he found himself completely cut off from animals. "We didn't have pets or time for pets," he told me.

He opted not to continue living that way. Now he's one of the happiest people I know.

A former pulpit rabbi, Philip added, "My tradition says I have an obligation to take care of animals before all else. Now I feel more connected to life around me in a way I never did."

There's natural therapy in walking a dog or petting a horse. This isn't speculation: animal therapy has been demonstrated to decrease anxiety and loneliness while also reducing pain, fear, and worry. Animals offer support and improve social interactions.[1]

The animals around us are marvels, and as a bonus, they're often just as eager to connect as we are!

Little Teachers

I never really had pets as a child. When I was around four, we had a dog for a brief stint, but he wasn't a good fit for the family. My mom found him a home with a single man who drove off with our dog. Our home was petless for over a decade afterward, until an adorable dog, a cairn terrier who looked exactly like Toto from the *Wizard of Oz*, surprised us by wandering into our yard.

Or, more accurately, he looked like a poorly maintained Toto. He was unkempt, and there was no trace of a human counterpart or any ID tag. Although he appeared to be neglected and surrendered, we diligently tried to find his human. After many weeks, no one had surfaced, and he became our family dog. But I was seventeen at the time and would soon head to college, so I had little time to bond with Pepper.

As I've explained, Yoda was my first real, intimate connection with an animal. Along with love and friendship, his greatest impact on me was his ability to teach me lessons I needed to learn. Like his namesake, he had a way of imparting wisdom that changed my life.

It's true, he never taught me to lift rocks with the Force or to wield a lightsaber, but his lessons were just as valuable. As a guy with ADHD, much of what I learned from him related to my improved executive functioning as I cared for him during his sickness. He needed care, and I was the only one in his life who could consistently provide it. His disease was not the teacher I wanted, but it was the teacher I got.

Through this care, he taught me how to become more resourceful and how to discipline my mind enough to follow through on his diverse treatments. With no less than three vets with different specialties advising me, there were plenty of treatment regimens, which was very hard for someone with ADHD to keep track of. Yet such was my love for this fluffy feline that I *never once* missed a dose.

My ADHD was still present, but I found I could navigate around it when my cat's care was on the line. That's a lesson that stuck. And it gave me the training I needed to become a father. I learned to be the spokesperson for a voiceless loved one when working with medical authorities. I also learned to care for his needs first.

Another lesson he taught me was the value of *quiet*. At the time, I was a very unbalanced extrovert. I was so extroverted that I believed I couldn't be alone or be truly quiet. But Yoda showed me how to find what I refer to as "my inner purr." He showed me the value of being alone and what self-soothing looked like. Because of him, today I'm an ambivert—the extrovert I was but with a profound appreciation of solitude.

But Yoda's greatest gift, his greatest lesson, was the one that animals so often teach their human companions. He showed me I was intrinsically lovable. Neuroscientist Dr. Gregory Berns has shared on my podcast and in his book, *How Dogs Love Us*, that many dogs love the way humans do.[2] He got the idea to test this hypothesis from his own experience. His dog, Callie, seemed to truly love him. So Berns trained and ultimately placed Callie in a functional MRI machine. He found that when she saw her beloved human dad, the same regions lit up in her brain that light up in humans when we feel love.

Cat psychologist Dr. Kristyn Vitale, star of the Netflix special *Inside the Mind of a Cat*, shared on my podcast that she believes we will one day find the same is true for cats. As "man's best friend," dogs have received the lion's share of research on animals, but Vitale is confident that with more research, we'll find cats also love us. And while I will never get to test this under the rigors of science, deep down, I am convinced that Yoda loved me.

Need more evidence that pets can change our lives? Carol Novello is the author of a book called *Mutual Rescue*, and she shared valuable information about the pet-human bond on my podcast. She described that we not only rescue pets but our pets, in turn, also rescue us. She shared the science of how pets are good for us as well as what they can teach us. One of her stories included an overweight man who was able to finally obtain the habits he so desperately needed to become healthier . . . by adopting an overweight dog. With his canine companion, he exercised and had a buddy with whom to become healthier according to his own standards and wishes.

For those who are willing to listen and learn, animals can be incredible teachers. Their lessons are everywhere. Cats can show us what absolute relaxation looks like. Dogs know how to greet everyone openly and enthusiastically and how to live in the present moment. Birds display keen abilities to sing and communicate. Even snakes and lizards can show us the value of a good day spent lying in the sun or the discipline of motionlessness.

There's a reason yoga poses and martial arts styles are named after animals. Humans have been learning from their animals since the beginning of time. Perhaps it's time we started learning from them once again.

Beth Anstandig, an author and therapist, wrote a book called *The Human Herd*. She described in our interview how badly we need to look to animals, learn what we forgot as a species over time, and improve our futures by looking at our past. She shared scientific data that horses know—and never forget—how to care for themselves and others in their herd. She has created an entire curriculum on leadership, called Natural Leadership, based on the intelligence of horses and other animals, and the program appears very successful.[3]

We Generally Outlive Our Pets

If you're a dog person, I'm sure you'll agree with a quote attributed to author Agnes Sligh Turnbull: "Dogs' lives are too short. Their only fault, really."

And barring the super long-living animals, like the cockatoo that can live for more than seventy years, the quote could be applied to most human-animal experiences. Part of my way of dealing with the sadness of pet loss is to properly memorialize my amazing animals. I aim to honor the relationships I had with them as well as their indelible effects on me.

For several years, I volunteered at Humane Society Silicon Valley as their pet-loss counselor. In addition to witnessing some of the hardest cries I've ever experienced—yes, those fuzz balls can make us cry harder than just about anything—I learned some good ways of maintaining the connection even after the pet is physically gone.

To lock in and preserve the connection with your pet, I recommend writing a good eulogy and sharing it with those whom you love and trust. It's all the better if they knew the pet. Write out the pet's story and the qualities of the pet you loved, and if you can, write what your pet *taught* you. You've heard that Yoda taught me a lot, and I can say the same for all my furry guys. I imagine that if you dig deep, you'll find that your pet taught you too . . . and these are things that keep the bond alive long after they've departed.

I even went one step further with my pets. After my dog Motzi, a collie who looked just like Lassie, died, I wrote out all of the names of the people he connected me with in my neighborhood. The list was long and contained names of people who matter to me. Studies have shown that people are more likely to engage people walking a dog than those walking alone. My walking relationship with Motzi corroborated that study.

Pets Are "Meant to Be"

Be the Person Your Dog Thinks You Are is the title of a book by C. J. Frick. I imagine most pet people don't have to ask if the title makes sense. The title is a quote in and of itself, and I believe we can substitute the word "dog" for "pet"! Our pets love us unconditionally and appear to be our biggest fans. They seem to see us in the best light and may provide a mirror for us to see ourselves in ways we can aspire to.

With this kind of love, they may even evoke our best selves. Just their presence and their unique abilities to connect with us can improve our health. Studies show that pets can reduce our depression and anxiety, help us heal faster from illness, and improve our lives. Our animals may make us happier, friendlier, and capable of exhibiting more levity.

But ultimately, one of their most precious qualities is that we love them and they love us. That synergistic, reciprocal back-and-forth that we humans need so badly to feel safe in the world constantly emanates from our interactions with our pets. They are our friends and companions. They're our family. Once we have that purest of connections, it just feels like it was meant to be.

Virtually all pets come with a cool, fun, or even spiritual story when they enter our lives, further increasing our connection to them. *How I Met Your Mother* was a hit show; I'd propose a show called *How I Met My Pet*. All three of my most beloved cats, including Yoda, have great origin stories. So does Raffi, our current family dog. For the longest time, I was resistant to getting another dog after Motzi. By this time, we had kids, and life with cats is far lower-maintenance.

So I put up a qualifier. If we were going to get a dog, I told Aurianne, it *had* to be a doodle. Essentially, a Muppet-like dog was my dream dog, and I would want that dog to be trained, to be certified, and to work at my office as a therapy dog.

While out on a walk, I bumped into a beautiful doodle. I called Aurianne over to check him out. Once she saw him, she told me, "If you wanted *that* doodle, I would say yes," so I called the breeder, who said she had the perfect dog for a therapist.

And that's how Raffi came to join the family. Clearly, he was meant to be.

CONNECTION FORMULA EXERCISE

If you don't have a pet but love animals, consider getting one. It's a big step, but if you are looking for instant connection, conscientiously deciding to adopt a pet can be one of the quickest ways to get it. (By conscientious, I mean assessing everything you can to ascertain if having a pet is right for you, reducing the prospect of postadoption remorse.) Yes, it takes a lot of activation energy. But once you get over that hump and get into a groove, you've got a dedicated animal friend and, possibly, a teacher. If you don't want to get a pet of your own, consider spending time with one, being a sitter for a friend who has one, or just hanging out with a furry critter and seeing what it's like.

PART IV
CONNECTING TO THE WORLD

CHAPTER 12

CONNECTING
TO WORK

If you're like most people, you will spend about one-third of your life working.[1] That comes out to around ninety thousand hours for the average person living an average lifespan. In our overworked culture, it's likely that for many of us, it'll be even more.

For those of us lucky enough to love what we do, that's a blessing. Rain or shine, I'm always grateful to be a therapist and work with people I can help. But not everybody has that luxury. While the majority of us are satisfied with our work, according to Deloitte research, only about 13 percent of us actually feel passionate about it.[2] We tolerate it, but we aren't super psyched about it.

Most of us think of work as something we *must* do instead of something we *get* to do. That can create a lot of wear and tear over time. It's tough to put in ninety thousand hours when we don't really want to be at work. When we don't feel there's any meaning in what we do, the hours go slowly, resentment may grow, and our health often suffers.

I learned this hard lesson earlier in life, during my time as a bank teller.

I took the job during my first effort at graduate school. It offered me the best income I could get and the flexible schedule I needed while I focused on my studies. The job itself made sense, but initially, I hated it. I felt undervalued. Customers treated me like a meat-based, barely human ATM. They often wouldn't even look at me. They sometimes carried out the transaction as if I weren't even there. I felt unseen, and I resented it.

For about eight months, it felt like time froze as soon as I walked in for a shift. When the workday finally ended, I'd come home exhausted to a degree that far exceeded my level of physical exertion.

I might have remained that way for the next two years if I hadn't happened to read *Man's Search for Meaning*, by Dr. Viktor Frankl. Frankl was an incredible man. A Jewish psychiatrist, he'd survived Auschwitz. As he pondered why he had survived when so many others had died, he developed an incredible insight: "What man actually needs is not a tensionless state but rather the striving and struggling for some goal worthy of him."[3]

Essentially, Frankl had found meaning in his life even in those horrific circumstances. What's more, finding this meaning was a *choice*: "Everything can be taken from a man but one thing: the last of the human freedoms—to choose one's attitude in any given set of circumstances, to choose one's own way."[4]

This meaning helped him survive; I turned Frankl's wisdom to my own situation. My life was infinitely better compared to his. If Frankl could find meaning in one of the worst experiences in human history, I could easily find meaning in a reality he would have envied.

Inspired, I started thinking about how to give meaning to my experience as a bank teller and how it could positively shape my life moving forward. *What could I learn in this experience that would help me in my own life?* Perhaps even when I become a psychologist?

That's when it dawned on me. As a psychologist, I would see all kinds of different people. To have any impact on them, I'd need to be able to make a genuine human connection with each of them. Was there a way I could learn to do that with my customers?

I analyzed my shift in my head and realized I served about 120 people each day. I gave myself a task: Could I take myself from being a meat-based human ATM to creating a shared experience with the diverse group of people whom I served? Could I get them to smile or laugh during our transaction? At least 119 of those 120 people? (I gave myself an allowance of one belly flop per day.)

Suddenly, my work went from a bore to a challenge. To quote podcast guest and mingling maven, Susan RoAne, I went from a bank teller to a bank *listener*. I had to sharpen my skills and stay on my toes. As I changed that mindset, the hours began to fly by. What had once drained my cup started to fill it, and my customers reacted positively. I became super psyched to do my job because I had found purpose.

The Road to Vocation

Mythologist Michael Meade said on my podcast that we're not just Homo sapiens; we are Homo symbolicus, meaning we're creatures who seek meaning. With that in mind, we want our work—those ninety thousand hours—to *mean* something. We want it to offer us a place where we can learn, grow, and find a sense of purpose. I often ask people who see me, "What are the vocational muscles you want to flex as you work? And what are the muscles you want to grow at work?" Through these questions, they're able to ponder what's important to them well beyond work itself. Their answers tend to speak to their longings, their values, and the things that really matter to them.

Han was a no-nonsense, nose-to-the-grindstone guy who came from Korea, earned his MS in the States, and became a senior director at a local company. He was struggling at work and had run out of gas. We looked at what was happening, and when I asked him about the vocational muscles that might be meaningful, his brow furrowed. He even scoffed. He'd never considered such a notion, and he resisted the question. The language made sense, but conceptually, that was not how he was raised; while he was growing up in Korea, the focus was on getting the best-paid job.

I thought Han was done with the question, and I considered it DOA after that session. But to my delight, and out of the blue, a month later he said, "I've been thinking about that vocational muscle thing you asked me about."

"I'm all ears," I said, rather surprised.

"I'm incredibly good with the science of my work, and that's why I've always been gunning for CTO. And I'm still gunning for CTO."

He looked at me and winked, a prompt for me to ask more, and I was happy to play the game. "Got it—so what's the twist?"

"Simple," he said. "I'm going to get my promotion by connecting with my colleagues and being less of a 'work-only' guy." He told me about his time in the military. He said he loved the camaraderie and feeling like part of a unit. But when he started work, his parents told him that work was very different from the army and getting along with people didn't matter . . . he'd be promoted only for his individual merits. He took that to heart, and he became known by his colleagues as exceedingly competent but cold and disconnected.

He wanted to get to CTO by calling upon the military version of himself. Perhaps he would be a kinder and gentler version of the military version of himself. In any case, he became the version of Han that put his team first—leading the way. His work relationships improved dramatically. And after two years, he was CTO.

* * *

Meaning in work generally consists of two elements: flow and fulfillment. Flow, discussed in previous chapters, is a state of focus in which our skills are sufficiently challenged. I often like to think of flow as the overlap of meaning and challenge. When something is meaningful and challenging, time goes by quickly. In a state of flow, we feel so connected and immersed, we can work on a project for two hours thinking we've been doing it for only thirty minutes.

Finding flow in work is a strong predictor of happiness. Research has shown that flow gives us a sense of accomplishment.[5] Yet sadly, this is the opposite of how many of us feel at work.

In some ways, the problem is that many of us have a *job* when what we need is a *vocation*. The word vocation comes from the Latin *vocatus*, or "calling." A calling is more than a position. It's *what we're meant to do.*

There are many roads to vocation. Here are three ways we can generally find more purpose and more flow in the activity that takes up most of our waking hours.

Reframing Work's Purpose

The first thing we can do is change our perspective on work in general.

Adam Grant, mentioned earlier, has encouraged people to change how they speak about careers. We often ask children what they want to *be* when they grow up. But according to Grant, we should instead ask them what they want to *do* when they grow up.

This is because the static job comprised of the things they want to do may not even exist yet. When I was in college, the title "web designer" was not in existence and therefore not something a person could *be*. However, the verbs associated with web design, like *doing* graphic design, were.

Drawing from Grant's lessons, focus on the dynamic *doing* part of the job, not the static *identity* part.[6] What verbs would you use to describe what you like to *do* at work? This is relevant to adults, not only to children.

Sadly, work and our jobs are so deeply ingrained in our identities, we have trouble separating the *being* from the *doing* as they relate to work.

Dr. Janna Koretz's concept of enmeshment, mentioned earlier, can come on strong with our jobs. When we're enmeshed with work, we do not and cannot separate ourselves from our professional titles. I spoke with her on my podcast about this idea. After the episode, I heard from various elected officials, clergy, and professionals whose job titles seeped into their identities; they told me, "That episode was all about me."

So what can we do?

If we move away from the idea of "I *am* a doctor, astronaut, janitor" to "I *work* as a doctor, astronaut, janitor," we create the space for the rest of our life to take its rightful place in our thinking.

I take great joy and pride in being a psychologist, but it is not my entire existence. I am also a father, friend, husband, son, neighbor, podcaster, and much more. Like you, I contain multitudes.

Although I said earlier that I *am* a psychologist, it would be more accurate to say I *work* as a psychologist. (Had I said that earlier, without this explanation, however, it might have sounded a bit strange.)

I found the following piece of advice from a great article in *Psychology Today* helpful: do the opposite of the demands of your job during your off time.[7] If you work in an über-cerebral job, make sure you do something body-based over the weekend, whether it's hiking, yoga, using a sauna, dancing, getting a massage . . . just get into that body of yours. If you work in a sedentary job, make sure you do something super physical: gardening, woodwork, construction. If your work involves a lot of physical labor, try things that stimulate the mind or spirit: read a book, watch a documentary, listen to a podcast, or go to a museum.

When we tap into more parts of ourselves throughout the week, we shrink work into its proper role. And with a greater sense of identity beyond work, we can also shrink our work problems into a more appropriate size. Without this perspective, a setback at work could ruin your child's birthday party or a night out with old friends. Having a greater sense of yourself beyond work, not enmeshed with the title or job, can create more space for more connection.

Finding Purposeful Work

Tennis great Andre Agassi wrote in his brilliant memoir, *Open*, that he never wanted to be a tennis player. In fact, he hated the sport. It was his father who pushed him into it.

Far too many of us are like Agassi in our own careers. It's as though we're told we should be playing baseball, but deep down, we long to be competitive swimmers, quietly underwater for the entire workout. We're just out of place, doing the wrong thing adequately when we could be doing the right thing expertly.

This is how I felt in my career as a sales rep. I was good at it. I made the president's list more years than not. But I knew I wasn't doing what I deeply wanted to be doing. At the job, I was using a tiny percent of the vocational muscle I longed to flex at work.

For those of you who feel overwhelmed by this topic, I recommend returning to your VIA Inventory results from chapter 4. The VIA can give you a sense of what you value most, including in work. Doing this can help you repurpose your current job, like I did at the bank, or it can help guide you toward a career you're better suited for.

Each strength can be found in numerous jobs. For those who prioritize creativity, there are ways to find fulfillment in careers like journalism, marketing, and design. A great critical thinker might find meaningful things to do in law or as an engineer. If you place a high value on wisdom, you might find teaching, mentorship, religious studies, or philosophy have some cool paths. People who value courage might work as firefighters or test their mettle as public speakers.

Often, gaining a sense of direction in work is enough to find that career that really *calls* to you. Then it's up to you to take the steps to get there. And it may take time. As my mother-in-law would remind me, "The time will pass anyway. Why not get the degree so you can get the job you want?" Online, in-person, and hybrid go-at-your-own-pace classes are available.

Most courses do not require a hard-core rush. And I was reminded in a podcast interview with Dr. Benjamin Bolger, a perpetual student, that we can all accomplish more than we imagine through planning and time management. Ben has completed seventeen degrees, from the AA to the PhD—mostly coveted master's degrees—from schools like Stanford, Harvard, Brown, and Columbia.

We need to lean into why we're doing it. If there's a big enough *why*, we can often find the *how* to solve a problem.

Another option is considering part-time work to supplement your full-time gig. One of my engineer clients has signed up to be a volunteer firefighter. Another is going to EMT classes while keeping his job in finance. Meanwhile, others have gone for complete overhauls and taken the chance on major changes: lawyer to restauranteur, sales rep to musician, real estate broker to party planner.

Each of them is doing something that FEEDs them with the flow, educate, energize, depth acronym laid out in chapter 2.

Finding Purpose in Your Current Work

I know some of you are not in a position to go out and strive for that dream job right now. There can be a multitude of reasons why now is not ideal. It took me more than a decade to find my opportunity, and for some, that opportunity never comes.

But that doesn't mean you have to give up and accept that you'll always have a job you hate. The same tools that help you find a dream job full of flow and purpose can help make the job you already have meaningful.

Using the VIA, you can seek out the various elements of the job that give you meaning. It's not just my story of my time as a bank teller that illustrates this. Dr. Martin Seligman, mentioned earlier, tells a story of a single mother working as a server. She worked long shifts and received poor tips. She didn't get along with the staff at all.[8]

Once she took the VIA, though, she discovered something about herself: it turned out she really cared about interpersonal intelligence. And when she thought about it, she was in the perfect position to flex that muscle.

This one realization transformed her job for her. Suddenly, she found she could rock every shift. Her colleagues loved her. Her tips vastly increased. The time on her shifts flew by. She found purpose and flow in a position she previously found unbearable.

There's a story often told about Christopher Wren, the architect of Saint Paul's Cathedral in London. One day in 1671, he was strolling along, checking the progress on site, and he came across three bricklayers.

He asked the first what he was doing, and the response was "I'm building a wall."

He asked the second the same question. That bricklayer responded, "I'm working hard to feed my family."

And the third answered, "I am a cathedral builder. I am doing my part to build the Kingdom."

For the second and third builders, work had deeper meaning. It was the same job, but they found the value that spoke to them. Back then, people didn't really choose careers, but they could still find purpose in what they did.[9]

Dr. Amy Wrzesniewski is an organizational psychologist and professor at Yale School of Management. She found that a particular group within a hospital janitorial staff had higher levels of satisfaction with their jobs than many of the physicians there. They had engaged in a work style she refers to as *job crafting*, "quietly creating the work that they wanted to do out of the work that they had been assigned—work they found meaningful and worthwhile." The cleaning staff expanded their duties beyond the heavy, dirty work they needed to do. They also self-deputized and became ambassadors of human relations at the hospital. They got to know the patients and genuinely felt the fact that they, the cleaning staff, were a crucial part of the healing experience of patients.[10]

They developed relationships with their patients. And some of those relationships continued even after the hospital stay.

Job-crafting is real. To some extent, it's what I did as a bank teller. To some extent, it's what the single-mom food server did.

Challenge yourself to see how you can get your job done and do a little extra that floats your boat.

Is there an element within your work that speaks to you and possibly contains a path you can expand? Does some skill potentially relate to what you hope comes next in your life or some other aspect of your life that is important to you? Is there something that gives the work meaning and provides you with a challenge?

There is no doubt in my mind that being a bank teller with meaning was the training ground for everything I've done since. My career as a psychologist, my corporate work, my role as a husband and father, my work in my community—in every case, I use or used the same skills I started to develop the day I decided to find meaning in my bank teller work.

So here's the question I asked Michelle (as always, a pseudonym), a software engineer at Google: Could your job serve as a place of learning where you develop skills that help you in your career and life outside of work while you deliver big for them? Could you begin to see Google.com as Google.edu as if they were providing you with a well-paid internship?

Michelle identified people skills as something she needed to improve. Google became the beneficiary of her deliberate practice to improve in this area. And she got a promotion.

See if there's a way to get beyond just going to work for a paycheck, and, instead, find ways to use work to learn cool things at your job while doing your job well. Doing so will allow you to become stronger throughout your life. This may not be the opportunity you want, but it's the opportunity you've got. So how can you rock the opportunity you've got—and find some purpose and flow while doing so?

Find a Mentor

Whether you are taking that step toward your dream job or trying to make the most of the job you've got, one person can almost always make the path easier and clearer: a mentor.

You've already met some of my mentors in this book, but one mentor relationship in particular was the big driver in my career: my relationship with Martin Doerner. He was my boss at Kumon, where I was a regional manager, recruiting, training, and supporting franchisees of after-school learning education centers.

Again, this was not my ideal position. While it was better than being a bank teller, it was still not my *vocation*. But Martin had a way of challenging me and giving me the work lessons that would serve me for the rest of my life.

The man was one of the smartest and most talented people I'd ever met. He was a walking encyclopedia who could find solutions to seemingly impossible problems. He was also an intimidating maverick, a straight shooter who said it like he saw it. Martin refused to play office politics.

I believe he could have been the company's CEO if he'd just played "the game," but that definitely was not his way.

He didn't play games. He cared about what was real. He was demanding, capable, and passionate about the work and making those around him better. He was just the guy I needed to improve my skills as a regional manager.

My initial interaction with him came after he first witnessed my presentation on everything a prospective franchisee needed to know. I was told by others it was something I did well, so I was feeling confident about my umpteenth performance, but this time he was in the audience. He'd never seen me present, and I expected him to be full of praise. When I got back to my desk, I saw a note from Martin. He'd left me twenty bullet points on how the presentation could have been better . . . of which at least nineteen were absolutely correct.

For some, this would have been extremely deflating, but it was just the kind of kick in the butt I needed. This man had gone out of his way to show me how I could improve, and I was going to show him I was worthy of being his protégé.

Not everyone wants a mentor who's so demanding, but I did.

A mentor is like a therapist, in that each has to create *safety and challenge* for those they connect with. In therapy, the mixture of safety and challenge is cocreated by the therapist and patient. The same can be true for a mentor and mentee. Too much challenge and not enough safety can overwhelm the mentee and inhibit growth. Too much safety and not enough challenge, and a mentor is perpetuating stagnation. It's a balance that's unique to each relationship.

I've always appreciated the spirit of a quote attributed to Dallas Cowboys Coach Tom Landry: "The job of a football coach is to make men do what they don't want to do in order to achieve what they've always wanted to be."

If you find someone like Martin, with that mix of safety and challenge that works for you, they may be able to provide you with the guidance you need to get where you want to go.

After I spoke with Andy Lopata about his upcoming book on

mentorship, which he's coauthored with Dr. Ruth Gotian, the takeaway was this: if you want to be excellent at what you do, find a mentor. The mentor doesn't need to be older than you. As in the situation of Olympic coaches and athletes, they don't even need to be better at your game. The mentor just needs to be able to help you bring up your game.

Avoid the False Path to Work Connection

One thing these mentors may be able to help you with is keeping you on the right path to success—however you define it. There are many temptations in pursuing a career that can lead us down dark and unfulfilling roads.

Plenty of my clients come to me filled with regret because they went to business school to make millions or they work in tech because they thought it would improve their status. But without purpose, now they hate their jobs as much as I hated working at the bank.

Undeniably, money, power, and fame can offer some nice side benefits. We imagine they will be a panacea, but none fixes what's broken in us or gives us the sense of value that was previously missing. They may have moments of highs—like a candy bar—but they don't have the slow burn of real connection. And often, they're a major letdown.

Many of the rich and famous people I have met have told me the same thing: fame and money alone are extremely anticlimactic. And fame itself can bring additional problems as they relate to connection.

While I've not met him, I've heard Brad Pitt and so many like him can't go anywhere in the world without being bothered. Undoubtedly, he must struggle to know who actually likes him and who just wants something from him. Navigating authentic connections can get a lot harder when you have something others want.

In the famous words of actress Rita Hayworth, "Men go to bed with Gilda but wake up with me."[11] Gilda was her most famous role, a sexy fantasy that others projected onto her. Fame made it harder for Hayworth to connect romantically. It became a barrier, blocking connection with others.

We all have interests and values that exist beyond work. In the same way we can't hope to get all our connection through our spouse, we shouldn't aim to get all our flow and fulfillment through work.

This is a lesson many learned during the pandemic. Forced to work from home, with more time on their hands than they'd had in years, people suddenly discovered the *intrinsically* good stuff. That's the stuff we like just because we like it, in and of itself. Unlike the *extrinsic* stuff—the stuff we do for rewards—the intrinsic reflects who we are. People found that they really liked gardening or baking bread or learning card tricks. People picked up new skills and tried new activities—at first to stave off boredom but eventually because they found such connections added joy to their lives at a time when they seriously needed it.

That's what hobbies and volunteering can do for us. They allow us to express ourselves and connect in ways that don't have to relate to how we make money. We do things we like . . . just because we like them. We do things we care about just because we care . . . and they're external reflections of our internal worlds.

These activities help us live our full *ikigai*. This is a Japanese term that means "your reason for being or your purpose in life."

Ikigai involves four circles (see the diagram on the next page) all coming together as if in a massive Venn diagram. In one circle is what we're good at; in another is what we love; in a third, what the world needs; and finally, what we can be paid for.

These four circles in turn overlap, creating the space for our passions, mission, vocation, and profession.

Any time we can achieve some element of *ikigai*, we tend to feel more purposeful and happy. A hobby likely will not offer you all these components. We probably aren't going to receive any financial compensation for it. And it may or may not be something we're already good at.

But these outside activities will almost always hit a number of points on the *ikigai* quadrants all the same. And that means we are netting more positive connections in our lives through them.

In an ideal situation, your work will include what you're good at, what you love, what the world needs, and what you can be paid for. If there is one code to crack in one's professional life, it is finding the connections captured in *ikigai*.

If You Can, Take *Thoughtful* Risks

To get where I wanted to go, I had to get uncomfortable. After I dropped out of graduate school in my twenties, the easiest thing to do would have been to stay at my corporate job. But to reach my vocation, first I had to do the work to tame my ADHD. Then, in my late thirties, I chose to return to graduate school, which meant working a full-time job while pursuing my doctorate and raising a family.

And once I had the dream job, to move forward in that career, I chose to take further big risks. One of them involved a major, household-name tech company in this area. I was offered the chance to develop a resiliency program to help teams suffering from vicarious trauma as they dealt with counterterrorism and child safety issues.

My instinct at first was to refuse to even apply. Who was I to take on that kind of role? Wouldn't a professor from a major university be better? Once again, it fell to my wife, Aurianne, to speak sense to me.

"What are you talking about?" she asked me when I tried to talk myself out of it. "You're the perfect person for the job both professionally and personally."

So I applied and prepared an entire presentation for my audition. Yet when I walked into the room for the big interview, I read the people in the room and realized my prepared presentation would flop. I heard a nagging voice inside me telling me to take a chance and go in another direction.

Ditching my plans, I skipped the PowerPoint I'd brought and launched into a new idea that I formed as I spoke. I felt a bit like George Costanza from *Seinfeld* hearing his own pitch the first time he gave it. I called my program a "two-way TED Talk."

At the end of my presentation, I was told that I was just who they were looking for and the job was mine.

Later, I learned that the person who interviewed before me presented a very similar program to the one I'd originally created for the interview. I'm so glad I listened to my inner voice and pivoted.

That can be the kind of risk required to get where we want to go. I know that some of us are not in a place to take such risks. We may have financial obligations and family responsibilities. Or we may have to finish degrees or undertake more training.

But if we see an opportunity and feel guided by a clear, intelligent inner voice, we should listen to it carefully. We can listen with both our thinking mind and our feeling mind. And then, for extra credit, we can listen with our body's intuition. If we have smart, trustworthy people in our lives, it behooves us to talk it out with them. And if we come to the realization that the opportunity is good for us and the benefits outweigh the risks, we can take an intelligent risk. While there are no guarantees we'll get it, not trying is a guarantee we won't. If we leverage this form of intelligence, it might be the moment that changes everything.

CONNECTION FORMULA EXERCISE

Revisit your VIA results from chapter 4. How can you use what you learned from this exercise and connect more deeply with your work? Can you turn your dot-com job into a dot-edu experience? Jot down some ideas that come to mind.

If you'd like to repurpose your job, like the food server in this chapter, can you use your VIA results to assist you in using a strength and finding a way to connect it with flow?

CHAPTER 13

CONNECTING TO COMMUNITY

I served for many years on the board of the school my sons attended. As with so much in my life, my instinct when I was offered the position was to turn it down. At this point, you probably know who convinced me to do otherwise. Once again, it was my wife, Aurianne.

And again, I'm so glad I listened to her. These days, I look at my volunteer work on that board as one of the most rewarding things I have ever done. But it didn't start out that way. The first year, the board struggled under the weight of enormous difficulties.

The morale of the parents was at an all-time low. Attendance was the lowest ever, and attrition was at its highest rate ever. I found myself on a board of brilliant people—health, legal, financial, engineering, and education professionals at the top of their industries—but solutions never seemed to surface.

To bring the school back to its former glory, we had to somehow find a new head of school within three months so they could be installed before the next school year. The person we chose couldn't just be *good*; they had to be exceptional enough to rescue a sinking ship.

Making matters even worse, we had very little money to convince the new head to join us.

But with the impending deadline, the team got to work. We created a system to find talent, interview with tough vetting questions, and court our best candidates.

Amazingly, after a few weeks of intense work, we found the right person for the job. He was incredible.

Within two years, we had the highest rate of attendance in the school's history. The parents and the students were committed. The school was spectacularly revived.

It was an immensely rewarding accomplishment made even more valuable by the fact I got the chance to work alongside a group of people I respected and truly enjoyed being around. After that summer, we were bonded for life.

Creating Community

One of the most important benefits hobbies and volunteering can offer us is a chance to build community. The need for community is deeply wired into our psyches, and it's only recently that, to borrow from the title of a book by legendary political scientist Robert D. Putnam, we've started to bowl alone.

The incidence of depression is at an all-time high. Coincidentally, people report having fewer friends than ever before. On the other hand, people in strongly connected communities often have lower incidences of depression.[1] Statistics show that people in those communities often sleep better. And being in a strongly connected community can add years to your life.

One of the world's five "blue zones"—places where people live longer than average—is Okinawa. The people of Okinawa have a term for their social circles, which start in childhood. They are *moai*, which means "to meet for a common purpose."

Over the summer, while I was in Tokyo, I met a cab driver named Tadashi from Okinawa. He told me his *moai* were central to his happiness and overall well-being.

Of course, pursuing *moai* is not the only reason people are living longer there, but it almost certainly helps. Community offers us a sense of belonging and purpose, and having this sense of belonging lets each person in the community know they are part of something and cared for. That creates stability, conforms with our needs for attachment, and allows our nervous systems to relax more consistently. It reduces cortisol and stress-hormone production and conveys to us that we are safe.

"You and I" together are more powerful than either of us is alone. Being human, we are wired to want to feel that we are part of something. A sense of belonging, participating, or engaging on behalf of a group can fulfill that need. Throughout the millennia, that's been the primary purpose of tribes. Long ago, this belonging aided our survival. Today being a tribal member is largely optional, but the innate drive to be *part of something with purpose* remains. That's what *moai* provide us, and we don't need to live in Okinawa to create our own versions of them.

In today's world, creating community can require some effort. We have to seek out those who share a common purpose. There are many options available to us, and often, the easiest common purpose through which to connect is a shared hobby or volunteer activity.

Finding Hobbies

One thing that often slips away from adults is engaging in an activity simply for the sake of the pleasure, joy, and fun it provides. As kids, we played kickball not to learn a particular skill but because kickball is fun.

Humans aren't unique in enjoying play. Dogs love to play chase or catch. Dolphins play, and so do horses. Yet while adults still long for play, we often neglect making time for such activities.

Hobbies help us rediscover the joy of play for play's sake. I've been heartened to see, in recent years, more people joining adult kickball leagues and the rise of pickleball. Far from being silly activities, these are expressions of our joyful humanity. As a fellow human and a psychologist cheering on humanity, I'm super psyched when I see people in their element, doing their thing!

I have tried to seek out similar activities in my own life. One of those was improv. When I joined my improv group many years back, the teacher told us, "This will be the most fun you can have with your clothes *on*."

She was right. Our clothes were always on, and it was easily the most fun thing I had done. Sue Walden, my teacher, set the group up to keep all the serious parts of life out. There were strict rules against sharing our careers. We were meant to engage people, not the roles we played outside the group. This wasn't a place to network; it was a place to have fun and let our freak flags fly, We were meant to be our true selves, and no self-limiting identities, like those from work, interfered.

Hobbies can connect us to a sense of wonder we experienced in childhood as we learn something new or express some once-hidden part of ourselves. When we're experiencing this while connecting to a community of others experiencing it, it can feel even more rewarding. Who knew you could be part of a barbecue team? Who would have thought you could learn to start running marathons with groups in your forties or even far later, as so many of my friends have?

Pursuing hobbies may also yield unexpected benefits. Practicing improv boosted my listening and engagement skills as a therapist. Martial arts may help you to both blow off steam and focus more the next day. But those are just bonuses. The objective is the joy and, potentially, the community you build as you share in these life-affirming activities.

While the aforementioned are generally considered safe and can boost your overall well-being, there are certain community- and group-based activities that are likely best avoided or limited.

A person who saw me, Nate, had to come to terms with this. Nate's a classic adrenaline-seeker, and he was part of adrenaline-seeking communities. He went from being in a motorcycle racing community to being part of a paragliding community. Up until recently, he loved nothing more than being with his communities that did BASE jumping and wore wing suits.

Well, he does love one thing more: his wife and kids. Now that they're in his life, and he's committed to being alive *with* them, he has chosen to nix those extreme and potentially life-ending activities for now.

So we've found hobbies and activities to get him *nearly* that rush without the risk. We've come up with exciting activities he can do with his family—enjoying the collective rush of going snorkeling with sea turtles, for example, or doing a week of hiking and camping on the Grand Canyon floor or whitewater rafting with them. While he has said it's not the same high he experienced with his communities through these extreme sports, the high he gets to experience with his loved ones easily offsets the deficiency. He has also said it's more aligned with his values as a family man and that his aim is "to stay alive while feeling alive."

And this is often the case with dangerous hobbies like BASE jumping, which, by the way, seems to have the highest death rate among extreme sports. Unless we absolutely must partake in such hobbies, there's almost always another related activity that can give us some of the thrill with less of the risk.

Lastly, on the topic of group activities, have you ever considered a charity run or bike ride? There are few better ways to combine your personal fitness needs with creating community and meeting friends. I have done multiple charity rides—shout-out to the California AIDS Ride—and have found the training rides themselves motivating and bonding. I have friendships that are alive today and memories that will last a lifetime from participating.

The Shortest Route to Happiness

Hobbies are great, but if we want a pure hit of joy, volunteering can be magic. Performing acts of service has been found to be one of the best ways to improve our mental health. It's a powerful shot in the arm that can reduce stress and alleviate depression and anxiety, conditions that can cause us to get stuck in our heads and can perpetuate a negative, inward focus. Performing acts of service, on the other hand, allows us to get outside of ourselves. It can also give us a sense of meaning and purpose when we feel we have little or none.[2]

All of this is to say, volunteering can improve our mental health. Put simply, anxiety fills our mind with worries about the future, while depression can plague us with ruminations about the past. Feeling useful by doing good can quiet the mind and keep us connected to our possibilities in the present.

Recently, I heard Arnold Schwarzenegger in a documentary talk about how his father's wisdom changed his life. His father simply said, "Be useful."[3]

Turns out, Arnold's dad knew what he was talking about. Feeling useful is essential to reducing loneliness and improving our health. Being with people or being cared for by people isn't enough for us. A study of the elderly found that those who didn't feel useful were more likely to experience disability and die sooner than those who remained useful.[4]

Volunteering even once a month can be helpful to your mood.[5] Some studies suggest there's also value in trying different types of volunteering. Spread your time around various activities to find those that really speak to you.[6]

That last point is key. When you volunteer, do it because it is meaningful to *you*. For some, there's nothing more important than feeding the unhoused, while others find more value in cleaning up trash in the park. Perhaps you really love animals and want to spend time helping at the local no-kill shelter. Or you might prefer attending to calls at the suicide prevention hotline.

Whatever is best for you is likely the best path forward. If there's a vocational muscle, then certainly there's a good case for a volunteering muscle that wants to be developed. There's no right type of volunteering. Like in the "drive-away" test after seeing a friend, ask yourself after you volunteer: Do you feel better for having done it? Are you more fulfilled going than you were coming? Are you looking forward to coming back?

My guess is that once you find the type of volunteering that speaks to you, you won't ever want to stop doing it. It can feel that good.

Volunteering, engaging in hobbies, and generally connecting with community can take up a lot of time. I can't begin to count the number of hours I spent trying to find a new head of school for my sons' school. Some of the time spent on the board was, yes, frustrating. And at times, it even became kind of a whack-a-mole joke at home: "Honey, another meeting for the head of school search just came up!" While it can feel exhausting, this type of exhaustion will likely be the meaningful type and is far less likely to be the empty type.

CONNECTION FORMULA EXERCISE

What's one hobby you've wanted to start or a volunteer opportunity you've considered? Try it—don't think about it; just do it. Sign up for that class or that shift at the local nonprofit. Sign up for that organized charity bike ride or run. Maybe you'll just go once. But you also may find a new passion. Saying yes can lead you to all kinds of life-affirming directions.

CHAPTER 14

CONNECTING TO ART AND INSPIRATION

Back in the spring of 2008, I was visiting my friend Jed, who lived in Hoboken. Jed is known by my family as the "coolest guy ever," and he lives up to his title.

That spring evening, we were listening to his vinyl collection (of course it was vinyl!) when an album came on that blew me away.

"Who is this?" I asked.

"Les Paul."

I couldn't believe it. It was the guitar legend whose music I knew only superficially but whose Gibson guitar model I had seen in the hands of countless legends.

I asked hopefully, "Is he still playing?"

"Yeah, he still plays in Manhattan on Mondays."

I jumped out of my chair and said to Jed, "Dude, I am looking outside your window at Manhattan . . . and today *is* Monday."

We rushed out to see him perform, and we arrived right on time for his set at the Iridium Jazz Club. I didn't know it at the time, but Les Paul had only about a year left to live. He was about ninety-three when I saw him, but you wouldn't have gotten that impression seeing him on stage. What

I saw was a man tearing it up, playing some of the most beautiful guitar I've ever heard, living and expressing pure joy. I've rarely seen anyone so alive. Jamming. Harmlessly and shamelessly flirting with women. Using every bit of his mojo and artistic energy.

Scratch Your Creative Itch

Friedrich Nietzsche described art as the highest form of human expression. I love the idea that art can be the byproduct of our imagination, creativity, individuality, and life force. You can find caves in Indonesia that bear the art of the dwellers who resided there . . . at least 45,500 years ago![1] The dwellers are long gone, but the art remains, giving us a graphic window into the psyches of our ancestors. When I consider the profound need of modern-day people to express themselves artistically and then think about those cave drawings, a 45,000-year bridge emerges speaking to the universality of art and its expression.

For that reason, I've separated a discussion of art from the hobby chapter to give it special focus. The arts, after all, for most of us, are a hobby. We attend concerts or play guitar for the joy of it. But there's something special about the arts. They have the potential to unlock flow and creativity in our lives that can be uniquely fulfilling and regenerative.

Experiencing art and expressing ourselves through it allow us to seek out and create what delights us. Our love of art is uniquely personal and individual. A music teacher I knew believed strongly that the violin was the greatest expression of human experience. I happen to know people who feel most alive playing the kazoo. So whether we love blowing glass or engaging in the culinary arts, our preference will be unique to each of us. Art is about finding what moves us, often deeply, and fills our cup.

There is virtually no limit to what we can consider art. When we see Steph Curry drilling threes from near half-court and come to understand what he's doing, we know it's not just athletics; it's art. What counts as art can be as unique as art itself. For some, opera is cacophonous noise, and for devotees, it's a pinnacle of achievement. To some, flowers are just pretty adornments to life, but if we're into *ikebana*, Japanese flower arrangement, they may be a peak form of expression. Seek whatever form of art speaks to you, and then attempt to speak through it.

You Have Something to Say

Some of my best podcast episodes involved guests who told me before-hand, "Why are you interviewing me? I have nothing to say."

My son's former fifth-grade teacher, Mr. Sleep—yes, that's his real name—whom I brought on the podcast, told me that. He was certain he wasn't interesting enough to be interviewed. But, surprise, his episode spoke to people in a big way! It has more downloads than my popular episode with Steve Kerr, one of the most fascinating of humans, who is also one of the winningest players and coaches in NBA history.

Somehow, so does the one with my father, as well as the one with pediatric oncology nurse Marc Bader, both of whom also erroneously told me before the interviews, "I have nothing to say."

Turns out, all three of these guys had a lot to say!

I include these mischaracterizations of self because I think many of us erroneously believe we lack the creativity to express something of worth. This belief may also keep us from starting an art project or any other creative act. We may wrongly believe we are deficient in some way, whether it be education or a cultivated palate, and thus unable to truly appreciate art. We all have an internal saboteur, an internal critic, and the job of that internal part is to make sure we don't make ourselves look like idiots or experience humiliation. A part of us could also be afraid that we'll become a stupid meme, that everyone will laugh at us—or if we're actually hoping to be funny, that no one will laugh . . . or that they won't laugh in the way we'd hoped.

This internal saboteur keeps us safe, but it also keeps us from testing our limits and expressing ourselves. On one level, we can be grateful for this inner critic, whose intention might be to protect us. But we don't want it to dictate what we do or don't do and allow it to decrease the quality of our lives. As long as we're not being reckless (and we probably aren't), to borrow from psychologist Susan Jeffers's great book title, we need to "feel the fear and do it anyway."

If we don't, we may come to regret it. An important study involved asking people on their deathbeds about their biggest regrets. The study revealed that these individuals had few regrets over their failures. Their regrets were about meaningful things they *didn't do* . . . what was left undone in their lives. The regrets were about the potential love relationships they didn't take a chance on, the travel they put off, and yes, the art that they never created.[2]

* * *

We don't have to be brilliant to create art, and we don't have to create brilliant art for it to have value. The intrinsic act of creating it for ourselves and expressing ourselves through our chosen art form gives value to our lives. Already, in my own life, I have regrets about roads not taken due to my own self-limiting belief that I had to create something unusually great to create at all.

And I imagine there might have been times that you've felt that way too.

I also imagine most of us can remember doing art projects when we were children. We probably enjoyed it not because we were aiming to become Picasso but because the act itself was pleasurable. We tended to lose ourselves in the creative process. I love the TED Talk by Sir Ken Robinson in which he describes a young girl drawing in class. Her teacher asks her, "What are you drawing?" The girl answers, "I'm drawing God." The teacher then says, "But nobody knows what God looks like." The girl responds, "They will in a minute."

We all still have a version of that child within us. Imagine the joy she must have been experiencing as she drew her masterpiece. This is an innately human characteristic: a desire to express ourselves. Yet so often, that desire is blocked by social comparison or that annoying inner critic. For example, we might opt out of singing with the thought "I'll never be able to sing like Andrea Bocelli" or with our inner critic warning us, "Don't even try—you're gonna look stupid!"

Let's reclaim our birthright—let's make art!

Even great artists realize this and sometimes step outside of their area of brilliance to express themselves in new ways. Yo-Yo Ma is perhaps the most celebrated cello player of all time, but that didn't stop him from trying his hand as an actor in *Glass Onion*. Actors like Kevin Bacon and Scarlett Johansson have released albums of their music. They may not be as talented at music as they are in their primary careers, but their musicianship is an important component of their self-expression. Engaging in these creative activities will likely stave off regrets later in life for them.

But we don't even have to release anything to the world for this to be worthwhile. Legendary novelist Kurt Vonnegut once responded to a group of high school students who asked for advice. He told them to go home and write a short poem, then, without showing the poem to anyone, tear it up and throw it away in separate trash cans so it would be impossible to reconstruct later.

The reason? According to Vonnegut, "You will find that you have already been gloriously rewarded for your poem. You have experienced becoming, learned a lot more about what's inside you, and you have made your soul grow."[3]

It's never too late to experience that becoming. The saying "You can't teach an old dog new tricks" has now been proven false. Modern neuroscience shows we continue to create new neural connections no matter how old we are.

It's never too late to learn to play music or to paint or to find the activity that gives you inspiration. Leonard Cohen put out his first album at thirty-three. The artist Edward Hopper gained recognition only in his forties. The author Annie Proulx didn't start publishing her novels until she was fifty-seven. And my father is relearning piano in his eighties.

Whatever your age, art is not off-limits. Perhaps we can reclaim the child we once were, when we enjoyed art for its own sake.

Experiment for Yourself

You may already know what kind of art you want to experience. Perhaps you have always wanted to learn an instrument—or you already know how to play one and just need to get back into it. Maybe you've wanted to dance, paint, write, create a garden, or cook. Perhaps you've wanted to explore more varieties of art forms. Getting into art includes any pursuit that involves the creative process as either one who creates it or as one who takes it in. Or both. Regardless, there's real value in trying new things or renewing your relationship with something abandoned. You may find that you love the abandoned activity more than you imagined or that the new activity somehow reinforces the old one. Many people find that engaging in two artistic activities can strengthen both in unexpected and synergistic ways.

The arts are not mutually exclusive. They're a sandbox full of related toys we're invited to play with whenever we want.

I recommend that in our artistic explorations, we allow ourselves to be guided by fun, curiosity, or a desire for growth, a bit like the FEED model in chapter 2. When we see an artist create—whether it's a musician on stage or a chef in the kitchen—what we usually notice is how much they enjoy what they're doing.

However, a lot of great art has come from suffering, sadness, and heartache. Engaging in art and creativity is one of the finest coping strategies we have. Without question, when we are in life's darker spaces, art may be what gets us through. Yet, I remember learning about great authors, musicians, and other artists who were depressed, drank copious amounts of alcohol, and smoked similar amounts of tobacco. Sadly, many died young. I had been under the impression that these were the prerequisites to being a great writer or artist. But pain and suffering are not the only drivers of great art.

I'd like to address a notion popularized by Friedrich Nietzsche: "What does not kill me makes me stronger." It was more recently paraphrased in pop lyrics by the powerful voice of Kelly Clarkson in the song "Stronger": "What doesn't kill you makes you stronger." These words are potentially true but also potentially false. What doesn't kill us *might* make us stronger, but it could also make us *a lot* weaker. It depends on our coping and response to the thing that didn't kill us. Do we cope with life-depleting habits, like disconnecting from our values or dissociating with substances? Or do we cope with life-enhancing habits (like art) that make us stronger?

But back to art. One time, when Aurianne and I were in Venice, we stepped into a cathedral where a string quartet was playing Vivaldi's *The Four Seasons*. This was our last vacation before becoming parents. Aurianne was seven months pregnant. I'm a bit embarrassed to say, I didn't want to do the "Vivaldi thing." I'd heard Vivaldi for years and believed I had maxed out on him.

Stepping in, I found out things were even less enticing than I had imagined. The only seats left were in the front row. We were five feet away from the cellist, which meant it would be difficult to sneak out early without offending someone.

But once the music started, I was transfixed immediately and knew my life was changing for the better. I may have heard *The Four Seasons* a hundred times, but watching that cellist, I felt like it was the first time I'd ever really *heard* it. He was so enraptured by the music that he was putting me and, I imagine, the entire crowd into a blissful and hypnotic trance.

I spoke to the cellist after the performance. I asked him how long he'd been in this quartet. Six years, he told me. He said he'd been playing the same piece of music six times a week for six years. That was over 1,800 times! I asked, "How have you not become tired of it? How can you appear so engaged and in love with the music that you make it look and sound like you are playing it for the first time?"

He looked me in the eye and said, "When music is this great, it always feels like it's the first time."

That redefined my sense of the depth of love a person could feel for art. That's the kind of feeling any of us can find in art—the sort of connection that's available when we go searching for it, create it, and try to find our beloved in the form of art.

* * *

Here's a life-changing concept that Jeremy Utley, a professor at Stanford's school of design (d.school), shared on my podcast: *quantity generates quality*. In other words, more ideas generate better ideas. Sometimes a great idea is a bad idea with a small tweak. So keep on creating. Allow yourself to fail, and remember what Dorie Clark says: "Failure is just data."[4]

Lastly, great ideas don't happen in a vacuum. I used to sit at my desk with a cup of coffee just hoping to be inspired by my mind alone, without any prompts or other stimulation. It didn't work for me. I only understood why after I spoke with Jeremy, who told me that great ideas arise from what we've been exposed to. This is kind of a theme and variation on the writer's axiom "Go with what you know."

So it behooves us to expose ourselves to the many things that interest us and venture outside our comfort zones. From these experiences, we can take two seemingly disparate ideas and connect them, potentially creating something mind-blowing.

You know, like connecting a mobile phone to an MP3 player to a web browser. Now that's a great idea—I think I'll call it an iPhone!

Really Listen

Whatever art you choose to embrace, take the time to enjoy it. A lot of us only listen to music as background sounds without really immersing ourselves in it. Or we put a movie on and pull our phones out. We take in art at a museum at a brisk pace or use it as a chance to chat with our friends about unrelated topics while missing the hard work of geniuses.

None of these things is bad, but it serves us to remember what our elders told us in school: "You get out what you put in." If we want to get the most from art, we benefit when we give it our full attention. Instead of doing three things at once, give yourself to the art; give the art a chance to really get in, and let it take you places.

If you're a foodie, in addition to taking pictures of your food, use a mindful approach and focus on the colors, textures, and flavors of what you're eating. Read a book in silence. Or put the headphones on, close your eyes, and give your focus entirely to the music.

Steve Jobs used to listen to Bob Dylan with headphones in bed, letting the music be his tour guide. It's impossible to imagine that activity didn't influence where his mind drifted—toward incredible destinations.[5]

That's the power of art—when we let it speak to us and through us.

CONNECTION FORMULA EXERCISE

Pick a song, any song. It could be your favorite song or one that you just thought of out of nowhere. Put it on, close your eyes, and listen to it the whole way through. Don't do anything else but really *listen* to it. Pay attention to how your body feels and what reactions you are experiencing as the music flows through you. Try to bring *that* level of awareness to any form of art you experience—good food, paintings in a museum, or the flowers right outside your home. You'll get out what you put in.

CHAPTER 15

CONNECTING TO NATURE

In 2020, Aurianne and I were set to go on our first vacation as a couple since having kids. You can imagine how excited we were to get away and have a novel bonding experience together.

I bought our tickets at the beginning of March. We were going to Rwanda—to be with a brand-new culture and take in some incredible nature. As I'm sure you remember, two weeks later, the whole world shut down. Our tickets were canceled. Not only were we missing Rwanda—we weren't leaving the house.

As the world opened up in 2021, we were all the more determined to get away. This time, we booked a trip to Costa Rica and started at the Osa Peninsula. This is the most biodiverse location on the planet. We were staying in an eco-hotel reachable only by SUV and boat.

I knew it would be amazing. But my experience there still blew me away.

The sounds of birds, insects, and monkeys surrounded me. The constant buzzing of electrical devices and car engines that constituted my everyday life was suddenly absent, replaced by the breeze I heard and felt through the trees. My whole body felt simultaneously enlivened and at peace. This was just where I longed to be.

Aurianne noticed that my transformation was more than just mental.

My appearance actually changed. My face softened and looked more relaxed. My posture improved. The cadence of my speech slowed and became more intentional.

There was only one potential downside. Sleep has always been elusive for me. Would all the sounds from the insects, birds, monkeys, rain, and wind keep me up?

It turned out to be quite the opposite. On that first night, as I listened to the buzzing of nocturnal creatures and other sounds, I fell into one of the deepest and most regenerative sleeps of my life. And that experience repeated every night of the trip.

Natural Animal

My ability to sleep was likely somewhat enhanced just by being on vacation. But since I've had plenty of rough nights while in hotels, it dawned on me that being in nature was in itself good for me.

The reality is that we are creatures of nature, and being around nature can make us feel happier. Connecting to the sounds, beauty, and other stimuli of the natural world can give us a sense of peace and awe and make us feel more alive. Nature has the power to offer us profound connection in the four ways this book outlines: connection to ourselves, the ones we're with, the world, and something greater than ourselves.

Running around in the sun, hiking through the trees, sitting in a boat while the waves lap up against the sides—that's what our ancestors did all day every day. Even though most of us don't do this now, it's what we're designed to do all day. And when we do it, we feel good.

Nature provides us with at least two largely side-effect-free antidepressants: it provides sunlight, and it provides the setting for our biophilia need, which is defined as a drive to connect with nature. Sunlight can have a powerful effect on our mental health. Some studies even suggest it can be as powerful as antidepressant medications.[1] Research on biophilia has shown that it improves our well-being. In fact, even biophilic interior design has been demonstrated to be an effective treatment for many issues such as depression, migraines, and chronic pain.[2]

When you think about it, this isn't really surprising. Our brains as they were 35,000 to 100,000 years ago were not designed to exist in the artificial spaces we've created. We spend most of our time in artificial boxes filled with artificial noises. Whether it's the office with the subtle drone of air-conditioning, the house with the refrigerator's hum and the hiss of electrical devices, or the car with the grumble of its engine, there are always artificial sounds all around us. And while we might not consciously think about these sounds, our brains take them in and process them. That adds stress to our lives.

To relieve this stress, there's no substitute for getting out and connecting with nature. Step into the real sun, listen to real birds, smell real flowers, and surround yourself with real trees. Artificial high-intensity light can be incredibly helpful for those with seasonal affective disorder, but an hour outside in the bright sunlight can feel all the more nourishing. And we all know how artificial strawberry candy cannot compare to biting into a fresh, ripe, *real* strawberry. Our bodies and brains know the difference, and they tend to crave the real thing.

The more we can connect to nature, the more access we have to an internal experience of contentment and calm.

Julian Treasure is a musician, author, and a man with some of the most popular TED Talks ever. He is an expert when it comes to listening. He spoke on my podcast about his concern that with the deforestation of various habitats, bird populations are on the decline. As a result, birdsong is also on the decline. This is troubling because throughout the ages, birdsong has communicated to us that things are safe in our environment. This is because birds only sing when they feel safe; in contrast, when birds are quiet, the lack of sound signals to us that a threat may be present. With deforestation and less birdsong, even when things are safe, our brains may be more on alert. To counter this, Julian encourages us to make it a point to listen to birdsong—again, preferably of the natural variety, though he also suggests that even a recording of birdsong can have healthful effects.[3]

Take a Forest Bath

Recall the story of my friend Philip in Chapter 11, who left city life behind and bought a farm. Visiting his farm is one of my favorite things to do. The smells, sights, and sounds of the animals, as well as the crops, trees, and mountains, all feel like a vision of Tuscany.

Philip has reaped the benefits. Every day, he's up at 5:00 a.m., ready to work the entire morning on his farm. He's one of the happiest people I know.

I recently asked him about his choice. "We have found so many ways to make our time more efficient. But we've narrowed our experience," he told me. Efficiency and sufficiency are at odds. Modern life, without much access to the natural world, has come to feel "very sterile and limiting."

He listened to his impulses; he made sense of his longings. Over time, he found that he was yearning for a different way of life, and he was fortunate enough to listen to his inner voice and find a way to follow it by creating something big.

There are things we can do to reconnect to the natural world and rejuvenate, even if we don't buy a farm. We can start by seeking out nature around our home and engaging with it. If you have a yard, spend some time out there gardening or sitting under a tree. If you live near a park, go for a walk. Get a well-rated camping hammock and find a perfect spot between two trees, like my son does—you'll have a repeatable private-resort experience for a few bucks. Consider leaving the headphones and screens behind, or use them intermittently. Take the dog on a walk that gets you closer to more trees and farther away from major roads. You can play birdsong on your phone and buy some plants to fill your home. And if you have space, get a grill! At the grill, you can spend afternoons out around the trees and in the grass while cooking a great dinner. And for the vegetarians and vegans, there's a lot of great stuff for you to grill to honor your inner caveperson.

Even the occasional foray into the natural world is likely to reduce anxiety and depression.

But if possible, we should seek out those opportunities to get off the grid. There are likely city, county, state, and national parks, along with other beautiful places, close to your home. When you go, you'll see that most are seriously underutilized. Get out there and get into nature.

★ ★ ★

The Japanese have developed a mindful practice called *shinrin-yoku*, which translates to "forest bathing." These are long walks in nature in which a person seeks to be calm and quiet while allowing the atmosphere of nature to seep into them.

This is a powerful antidote for the stressors of modern life, and, relatedly, there's a reason outdoor behavioral healthcare (OBH) for at-risk youth has found remarkable success. OBH treatment includes backcountry travel and wilderness-living experiences, adventure experiences that foster eustress—which is the beneficial kind of stress—and using nature as a crucial part of the therapy.

It seems that pulling children and teens away from the pressures of modern life, disconnecting them from technology, and teaching them nature skills brings them back to a more natural, positive state. These therapies increase autonomy, respect for others, and communication skills—all because they're founded on engaging with nature.[4]

Most of us know instinctively that nature offers a primal way to refill our cups. For most of us, the big barrier to entry is this: *activation energy.* It takes preparation and effort, which means it requires time and a bit of delayed gratification, to get out there and do it. It also means planning and packing. I know, not fun! Yet I'm sure we can all think of high-value activities that start with planning and packing.

And then there's the travel time: if we live in the city, it might take us an hour or more to get away from modern civilization.

Those barriers have caused me, on many occasions, to pass on natural experiences and just chill with a streaming show or some other easier option. But I know that when I put in the effort, it's always worth it. It will probably be the same for you. Like so many connections, nature requires a little effort if we want to benefit from it. But once we put the effort in, the value is nearly immediate.

CONNECTION FORMULA EXERCISE

Take a forest bath. Go for a walk in nature and attempt to quiet your mind by noticing the different shades of green, as well as the new buds emerging. Notice anything else that catches your eye, your ear, your nose, or your skin. You don't need to find a pristine forest. You can walk around your neighborhood and rediscover the nature around you. Notice the differences each season brings. Notice a tree or plant you've never taken the time to appreciate. Or like my middle school biology teacher taught me, hang out in your backyard, close your eyes, and listen intently. Listen to all the natural sounds you can identify. We are primed to connect with nature—just give that primal inside-self a chance to come out and see what happens.

CHAPTER 16

CONNECTING TO ANCESTRY AND TRADITION

Joel ben Izzy, a well-regarded storyteller and author, shared on my podcast that he regularly asks unusual questions to deepen conversations. For example, instead of asking, "What's new?" he asks, *"What's old?"*

Our connection to the past can root us in deeper meaning that we miss if we only take in what's new. In his book *Black Swan*, Nassim Taleb writes that we are attracted to what is old because it has something to offer us. If something has been around a long time, there's a greater likelihood there are truths we can learn from it. It's like an old tree that has managed to sway through storms and outlast droughts and fires. If something ancient reaches us, it is because people have recognized its value and have chosen to pass it down for centuries.

The old also gives us the chance to bring the past into the present. Consider this: Paul McCartney once met with the philosopher Bertrand Russell. Russell was raised by his grandfather John Russell. And John Russell met Napoleon. That means someone alive today is only three degrees removed from the man who nearly conquered Europe more than two hundred years ago.[1, 2]

The past is closer than we think, or as William Faulkner put it, "The past is never dead. It's not even past." And all that is old reminds us of this.[3]

This connection was once built into society. In that ancient village, we would have listened to the stories of our ancestors through our elders. Some of us would have even sat around fires at night, learning these stories with drums and the captivating voices of the elders. Those stories would have given us a sense of place in our society and in the world. Our history guides our present, and without question, sometimes to look forward, we need to look backward and know our history. This might allow us to avoid making huge errors; as George Santayana said, "Those who cannot remember the past are condemned to repeat it."

Or it might allow us to discover a gem that might be lost if it isn't kept alive.

We can still find ancient connections in many forms. For some, they can be accessed through architecture. One of the charms we find in visiting Europe is the oldness around us. We walk into pubs and inns that have been running and active for five hundred years. There's so little that is that old in the United States. When I took my sons to Tadich Grill in San Francisco, the oldest continuously running restaurant in California and the third-oldest in the whole country, it felt ancient to us, but it's only been there since 1849. That's a tiny historical blink in Europe.

Here, those looking to commune with the ancient may find it in sacred Native American grounds, a museum, or in nature. Our mountains and the sequoia forests possess the ancient in the form of trees that mark their age in millennia.

Otherwise, in this "new world"—and indeed, in the old one as well—we have to find the connection in tradition.

A Loss of Tradition

These days, and to our detriment, we have veered away from listening to those older than us. Kids tend to listen to influencers on TikTok. Their parents tend to listen to podcasts. Their grandparents tend to watch cable news. And the influencers for each generation tend to be very different people.

Something is lost if we only connect to people from our own generation. In doing so, we lack perspective and direction. We are meant to "dance with our ancestors" and with our entire tribe and carry forward the traditions handed down. It's how we're designed to live. I often think about how deeply Maya Angelou understood this when she said, "If you don't know where you've come from, you don't know where you're going."[4]

Unfortunately, many of us are losing touch with our anchors to the past. The past is our inheritance. Without it, we can feel lost. Tradition gives us the deep-seated meaning we humans need, a sense of identity, a feeling of connection to our community even if it isn't in our immediate view, as well as so many tools for life. It can offer us ways to cope with suffering, ways to connect directly with our community, rites of passage to mark the important moments in life, and a system to navigate life and grief.

I knew how to connect to my father-in-law because he came from old-world Brooklyn. I didn't come from there personally, but I knew about that world through my grandparents, who had shared their own stories with me. I understood the ethos, and it mattered to my father-in-law that I could talk with him about egg creams, stickball, and the Brooklyn Dodgers.

In India, people know just what to do after a loved one dies. They have a tradition. The body is burned, and the ashes flow into the river—the same river that offers life to the whole community.

When Aurianne and I were getting married and her father was dying, we could lean into the Jewish wisdom from our ancestors that "nothing stops a wedding." A wedding always takes precedence. This tradition gave us a direction that we could choose to accept or not—but it helped us lean into our truth from a deep knowing of who we are.

These days, we have too few directions. And while we may think of constraints as stifling, they're often quite helpful and can even be freeing. The absence of rites of passage and rituals to express grief or joy can leave us rudderless when we most need direction and initiation. Humans long to be and need to be initiated; we need a wisdom-based system to assist us in the hard moments and a set of ways to comport ourselves in circumstances where it's hard to improvise.

Essentially, we need a playbook for life, and for most of us, such a playbook has been misplaced.

Discover Ancestry

As a young boy, I realized there was a power to old things. My grandfather had an attic full of old pictures, clocks, lamps, recording devices, and mechanical stuff that seemed to come from a different world. It was all so removed from my life. It felt like there was something almost magical there, like every item had a story to tell. I was curious to know those stories. What was this weird old painting of my grandfather? Who painted it? Where was he? Why had the artist painted him?

That interest in our past has stayed with me. Even in my years trying to define myself outside my tradition—in my early twenties—I went and found solace in the ancient ideas of Japan. And eventually, I came back to the old ways that were mine.

My world is so much richer for knowing Japan. And my life is so much richer still for coming back to my roots after seeing a profoundly different and wise system.

For some, accessing this richness is as simple as taking what you have been given and continuing to share stories, follow rituals, make them your own, and dig into old wisdom.

For many, though, it's more complicated. Most people don't have this direct, clear line to their ancestry anymore. But there are ways to access tradition and bring it into your life.

Excavate Your History

Years ago, I lost a man I held in the highest regard: a Holocaust survivor from my community named Alex Bauer. I'd always felt close to Alex. Since I was a little boy, I had this strong connection with him. He had been through an unimaginable version of hell in Auschwitz, but it was hard to believe it. He was so full of light. A greeting from Alex could light up one's week, and everyone I knew felt the same about him. He was at my bar mitzvah and my wedding. Near the end of his life, we'd lead religious services for older people together.

At a recent funeral, I met a Hungarian man who happened to be Alex's nephew, though he hadn't known him well. Once he introduced himself, he immediately asked me, "Please tell me everything you can about him."

There was this hunger in him to know the man who had passed, to connect to a precious part of *himself* that was now physically gone.

I admire that. If you have older relatives alive now, I suggest asking them directly for these stories, like I did with my Grandpa Ben in chapter 8. You may find that family and cultural traditions are not as distant as they seem to you. It may be that many traditions died out only in the last three or four generations and that it is within your power to revive them.

There may be old family recipes you could pick up or old family holiday activities you could reincorporate.

If you lack such family members, there are other methods of excavation. Some take up the hobby of tracing your family tree as far back as possible. Consider doing a DNA test to find out your ancestry or geek out to an ancestry website, like my younger son is doing now. You may discover links to ancient cultures and traditions you had no idea were right inside of you.

Such links are an invitation to reconnect to the past in a way that nurtures your present and your future.

Adapt Traditions

Of course, some traditions may strike you as outdated or not to your taste. Some may feel like a burden more than a blessing. In that case, you may want to continue them with your own revisions in a way that suits you and your family.

This is the right of every generation. Again, it's a testament to the fact that when good and healthful traditions survive, they're all the more powerful. It means that so many generations have decided the value of that tradition was worth preserving.

For instance, our family still lights candles and says prayers many Friday evenings, just as I'd dreamt we would. Our family still recites the traditional prayer over bread and wine. But there's also a traditional prayer to say to our children, and its nonpersonalized tone didn't speak to me. So I created a new one. I've been reciting it on Fridays since my oldest son was two.

I believe that's our right as inheritors of our past . . . and if we enact this type of tradition in a way that really connects with our family, it may have a better chance of surviving with future generations.

Adopt Traditions

If you don't have such traditions in your own past, don't worry. There's nothing to keep you from drawing on the traditions of others. In my backyard, I have statues of Buddha. In my office are statues of Ganesh, the remover of obstacles, as I think of him as the patron saint of all things related to psychotherapy. These objects speak to me. I don't view them as deities but as symbols of ancient wisdom that aren't at odds with my Jewish identity. Instead, they offer me great value in my life, so I have incorporated them.

You can do the same.

You don't have to be Jewish to say the Shema or Christian to say the Lord's Prayer. Aurianne spent six months learning about Vedic traditions in northern India. She's still Jewish, but she's been informed by those traditions. I've been deeply informed by my experience in Japan and Japanese traditions. I've heard of Mormons who did their mission in another country remaining firmly grounded in their LDS beliefs while enriching their lives by bringing back language, cultural wisdom, and some great recipes from their host countries.

You can make these things your own just as people have all over the world. As Japanese culture author Robert Whiting said on my podcast, when the Japanese imported baseball from America, their approach to various aspects of the game was distinctly Japanese. Korean taco trucks are awesome. Hawaiian music with a reggae beat is pure island bliss and appropriately called Jawaiian.

Adding traditions doesn't have to take away from who you are; it can expand who you are.

Make New Traditions

I often think about Muhammad Ali. There are so many angles from which to consider this great man. But the one I'm going with now is that he, like so many African Americans, was deprived of knowing his lineage. And like Malcolm X, Richard Pryor, and others, he went to Africa in search of his past, looking for traditions, feeling what was real in his heart. An African American colleague of mine did the same. She's lived in Madagascar for years . . . and from what I can tell from her posts on social media, it appears to have been a sort of homecoming for her, allowing her to connect with her ancestors.

A Korean-born colleague of mine, Dr. Joshua Heitzmann, talked about being adopted by a Caucasian family in rural California. He described the myriad challenges and losses relating to tradition and identity post-adoption. One of the recommendations he has for fellow Korean adoptees to feel empowered is to consider learning the Korean language as one of the many ways to reclaim some of what was lost through adoption. The adoptees cannot control their pasts, but learning about their culture in this way is one of the methods to have some control over their futures.

We can even find new traditions in how our families celebrate birthdays. We can choose which holidays are important and how they are marked. We can develop rites of passage and rituals of initiation. For example, we can choose an age that signifies when our children enter adulthood and create a ritual around that threshold. Or we can ritualize a meaningful anniversary of any kind for a family member. The sky is the limit.

Creating traditions with our family can be easy. We can create a special menu for Independence Day, or mark Fridays as pizza night or Saturdays as family-movie night.

And we can look into traditions around meaningful life events that have been practiced throughout history. If we like them, we can modify them to fit our needs.

Dig for it. You may find treasures. If the past isn't there for you to draw from, you can create it.

CONNECTION FORMULA EXERCISE

Meet with an elder in your family or community. Ask about one of their traditions or something they remember doing regularly as a child. Try to find a way to bring that into your life—either through adopting it fully or adapting it to fit your own context.

PART V

CONNECTING TO SOMETHING GREATER

CHAPTER 17

CONNECTING TO SPIRITUALITY

Some people experience the world as chaotic and nihilistic. I generally perceive the world a bit differently. Meeting Aurianne as a child, losing track of her twice only to fall in love with her and start a family with her twenty-five years later has felt miraculous. Further, the winding path of my career and the beautiful journey I am watching my sons take in their own lives makes me think that there's something going on beyond my perception.

This is not a preposterous notion. Objectively, there are things transpiring right in front of me beyond my perception. Bees can see ultraviolet light. Homing pigeons use olfactory detection to find their way, and bats use echolocation to find prey. Without question, there are phenomena we cannot perceive with our human brains . . . but they are happening, nonetheless.

I don't aim to define what that *something* is, because it is beyond what the limits of my brain can understand. However, contemplating this mystery gives me comfort and provide me with meaning. And for me, that's enough.

While religion and spirituality can provide structure and comfort to many people, a powerful reminder of the human spirit can be found in the following story. It's about those who don't believe in God or something greater than themselves, the importance of atheism, and is attributable to Rabbi Levi Yitzhak of Berditchev, who lived over two hundred years ago. One version of this story about the Hasidic rabbi is found in Martin Buber's *Tales of the Hasidim*:

> A rabbi was asked by one of his students "Why did God create atheists?" After a long pause, the rabbi finally responded with a soft but sincere voice. "God created atheists," he said, "to teach us the most important lesson of them all—the lesson of true compassion. You see, when an atheist performs an act of charity, visits someone who is sick, helps someone in need, and cares for the world, he is not doing so because of some religious teaching. He does not believe that God commanded him to perform this act. In fact, he does not believe in God at all, so his actions are based on his sense of morality. Look at the kindness he bestows on others simply because he feels it to be right. When someone reaches out to you for help, you should never say 'I'll pray that God will help you.' Instead, for that moment, you should become an atheist— imagine there is no God who could help, and say 'I will help you'."

Find Value in *Something*

This book takes no position on God and religion. While I am obviously Jewish, I have no interest in convincing you of any theological point. But I do think there's value for many of us in finding *something* greater than ourselves to believe in.

Since we humans are meaning-seeking creatures, finding meaning has been shown to provide comfort and reduce stress at various stages of life, including in our dealings with death and loss, and to offer us comfort when we're in pain.

Perhaps the best word to describe this *something* is "spirituality." Wikipedia's definition of spirituality resonates with me: *an individual's search for ultimate or sacred meaning and purpose in life*. Maya Spencer, in a paper written for the Royal College of Psychiatrists, phrased it this way: "spirituality involves the recognition of a feeling or sense or belief that there is something greater than myself, something more to being human than sensory experience, and that the greater whole of which we are part is cosmic or divine in nature."[1]

As I see it, an awareness of anything greater than myself can help me connect with a sense of the spiritual. When I connect with another person, the connection of "we" can feel more powerful than each of us is alone. Creativity that takes us to new places can be experienced as spiritual. Being present for a beautiful sunset, joyfully playing with our kids, experiencing deep love, finishing a meaningful day of work or volunteering—all of these can help us connect to a feeling of something greater than ourselves.

Some people see components of God or gods in these expressions. And some don't.

If we are open to incorporating spirituality into our lives, it can bring our lives coherence and meaning and offer us consolation when we're hurting.

Practices in this area can also improve our health. Spirituality and prayer have been shown to have salutary effects. Research suggests that prayer (and its cousin, meditation) reduces stress and anxiety.[2] Prayer is regulating, whether it's theological or not. It involves going into a meditative state, speaking something out, and putting it into the hands of some *other*. Lisa Miller, a psychologist and author, has noted in her book *The Awakened Brain* that people who identify as spiritual—regardless of their beliefs—show fewer signs of depression and anxiety than people who do not.[3]

Gratitude

There is a Jewish prayer we are meant to recite upon waking. In it, we thank God for giving us another day of life. It's a reminder of the blessing we all experience each day we are alive.

It's easy to lose track of that blessing. Life is complicated and sometimes painful. Many of us wake up thinking only about our obligations for the day. Without attention, we may forget the blessing and take the fact we are *living* for granted.

In his book *Somewhere a Master*, Elie Wiesel recounts the story of a rabbi who woke up every morning not believing in God. Throughout the day, he would seek evidence of God's existence. He hoped that by the time he went to sleep, he could believe again. It was a daily ritual.[4]

There's real value in seeking out and acknowledging the blessings of our life. Simply by looking, we can find many things to be grateful for.

Not long ago, gratitude was seen as an almost New-Agey idea that we couldn't quantify, like something we occasionally experienced in a prayer or in a birthday card. Until recently, there hasn't been much research focused on the impact gratitude has had on our health. That's no longer true. Positive psychology has now linked gratitude with greater happiness throughout our lives, and functional MRIs show important cerebral improvements for gratitude practitioners.

And no wonder—gratitude propels us to recognize the great things in our lives that we might otherwise take for granted. Our brains are designed to conserve energy and to keep us alive. Once we have obtained our desired goal, relationship, or whatever that *target thing* is, our brains are designed to stop thinking about it. We stop paying attention to these great realities. Instead, we fall into automated rhythms that cause us to habituate to the new reality. Doing so is an efficient use of brainpower. But it keeps us from experiencing gratitude.

There's a classic joke told by many theologians that depicts our capacity to habituate in this way: A grandmother and her grandson are walking on a beach when an unexpected wave crashes on them, taking the grandson with it. The grandmother, overwhelmed with grief, cries to the heavens, "God, please bring him back to me. Without my grandson, life has no meaning!" Moments later, a wave comes in carrying the grandson to safety, good as new. Upon scooping him up, she cries to the heavens, "He had a hat!"

We hear that joke and laugh. We may even think, "I'd never do that!" Yet we humans, with brains wired for survival and conserving energy, are prone to ask for the missing hat.

When I started dating Aurianne, I thought about her all the time. I was courting her. Was she into me? Would I ask her to marry me? Would she say yes? But years later, it could have been easy to lose sight of how much she means to me. Like a thermostat, habituation leads us to the *new normal* and says to us, "What used to be awesome is now ordinary."

Gratitude helps me see that she's just as miraculous today as she was when we first started dating. One of the wisest ways to counter this aspect of our brains is to use this mantra: what we appreciate *appreciates*.

Relatedly, Buddhist monk Thich Nhat Hanh—named the "father of mindfulness" for his role in bringing Buddhism to the West—stated in *The Miracle of Mindfulness*, "People usually consider walking on water or in thin air a miracle. But I think the real miracle is not to walk either on water or in thin air, but to walk on earth. Every day we are engaged in a miracle which we don't even recognize."[5]

Often, we only realize what we have in each moment when it is taken from us. We ignore the miracle of our health until we become sick. We forget the incredible value of having fresh, hot water in the shower until the hot water heater breaks or there's a drought.

But there are many millions of people in the world today who lack health and what we consider basic comforts. Two billion have no access to clean water, and 46 percent of people lack access to basic sanitation.[6] If you are reading this book, you are likely among the fortunate who have grown accustomed to these modern comforts.

But we don't have to take them for granted. We can wake up and embrace the blessings of our lives. We can switch out of autopilot in our relationships and find the aspects in them that we're grateful for. We can offer gratitude to those people, for our health, even to the stoplights that we might curse on the way to the office but that work remarkably well to keep us safe.

So it bears repeating, what we appreciate *appreciates*. The more we show something gratitude, the more it thrives and the more it has to offer us in our lives. When we appreciate life more, a great thing can happen: our problems can feel smaller, and our cups may feel fuller.

Savoring Experiences and Presence

As far as we know, we'll only get to experience life this one time. Why not enjoy it to the fullest? One way to do so is to be more present with and to savor the moments of our lives. An important contribution to the literature of positive psychology has been the idea of savoring, which is defined as "the use of thoughts and actions to increase the intensity, duration, and appreciation of positive experiences and emotions."[7]

Benjamin Hoff wrote a book called *The Tao of Pooh* in which he reimagined Winnie-the-Pooh as a Taoist master. It is both a pragmatic and deeply spiritual book. It also taught me a lot about enjoying life to the fullest by using Pooh's relationship with his beloved honey as a powerful metaphor.[8] As I have come to see it, Winnie-the-Pooh offers instruction based upon how he enjoys his favorite snack. He enjoys the experience of his honey not just once but three times: he savors the experience of anticipating the honey, he savors the act of eating the honey, and he savors the sweet memory of having eaten the honey.

Savoring is a big deal. Positive psychology includes the word "savoring" as a term that involves intentional thoughts and behaviors to focus on a positive feeling to increase the intensity and duration of that experience. Sadly, many of us aren't really there when great stuff like Pooh's honey is flowing. Reflecting this is a cartoon from the *New Yorker* by Mick Stevens in which a man and his wife are on a beach vacation and the man says, "I can't stop thinking about all those available parking spaces back on West Eighty-Fifth Street."

Living like this disconnects us from the beauty and the time-limited nature of vacation. Sadly, many of us engage in practices that cut us off from the present moment.

I imagine that, like me, you've gone to nice restaurants and seen a family of four on their devices while eating their meals. Are they savoring their experience? Doubtful.

But not Pooh. He is not distracted from any of these moments. He is not pushing the anticipation away from consciousness as he looks forward to his honey. When he's eating honey, he's entirely present and not on his phone or applying some of his brainpower to other things, diminishing his enjoyment of the honey. And afterward, he appears to bask entirely in the positive memory of the honey.

Many of us could learn from Winnie-the-Pooh. When we're looking forward to something, we may be so eager for the reward that the wait can feel more painful than pleasurable. Or we may push it out of our minds so that we're not distracted by the potential discomfort of waiting. Yet, when we do that, we miss out on the "looking forward" portion, which can release higher levels of dopamine than the reward itself.

Often, when we get the desired thing or experience, we're distracted and thinking about something else.

And when it's all over, we may even forget about it.

A sense of connection to something greater than ourselves can help tame these impulses. Many religions include rituals of remembrance and mindfulness-inducing prayers before important events. Muslims, Christians, and Jews have formal prayers before meals. For well over one thousand years, Japanese people have said before eating, "Itadakimasu." It means "I humbly receive" and is an act of submitting and showing gratitude by recognizing *all* the forces that allowed the meal to occur.

All of these acts aim to keep us mindful and present with what's happening. Mindfulness has a multitude of healthful benefits: reduced anxiety, better decision-making, improved sleep and cardiovascular health, and other benefits are cited consistently in the literature.

Jesus, in the book of Matthew, advises us on how to be present: "Therefore do not worry about tomorrow, for tomorrow will worry about itself. Each day has enough trouble of its own."[9]

Rumi, the Sufi (Muslim mystic) writes, "This is Now. Now is all there is. Don't wait for Then; strike the spark, light the fire."

Consider, too, this beautiful Zen Buddhist quote: "Do not dwell in the past, do not dream of the future, concentrate the mind on the present moment."

Trace any religious or philosophical tradition, and you will find seemingly unending stories full of wisdom about being present and advice on how to pursue being present. One of my favorites is an old story about a Mother Superior at a convent who took delight in her meal of partridge, gushing over how delicious it was. One of the other nuns was surprised the Mother Superior would bring such enjoyment to her food.

"Mother Superior," she said, "shouldn't you reserve that verve and energy for our Lord Jesus Christ?"

Without missing a beat, the Mother Superior responded, "When I'm with Christ, I give him all I have. When my time is with the partridge, I give *it* all I have."

Awe

In a line often attributed to Albert Einstein, he gives us a decision to make: "We can go through life either as if everything is a miracle or nothing is a miracle."

Which is it? That's for each of us to decide. As for Einstein, he ended his quote with this: "Our best selves emerge when we see everything as a miracle."

This is the power of awe. Awe is like gratitude on steroids. It's been described as *radical amazement* by Abraham Joshua Heschel. It includes seeing extraordinary natural things like Niagara Falls or human-made things like the Pyramids in Egypt. It can also include the feeling we experience when we see something that we initially perceive as ordinary but then see it for its true, spectacular nature. These can include things like witnessing a beautiful sunset, observing a child discovering something for the first time, or experiencing a moment of human kindness. To quote my colleague and podcast guest Dr. Jonah Paquette who wrote a book on the subject, awe makes us say, "Wow!"[10]

Consider a normal fire in a normal fireplace. Generally, we may pass it by or perhaps sit down to warm ourselves on a cold evening beside it. But every once in a while, we might *really* look at it and truly take in its beauty. Isn't fire amazing? It keeps us warm. It roasts our marshmallows. But that comforting chemical process in our hearth is the same process that burns down forests. It is a spectacular force of nature that has within it powerful capacities that are potentially healing, pragmatic, and destructive all at once.

The words "awesome" and "awful" come from the same etymological root. Awe is defined as a feeling of reverential respect mixed with fear or wonder. It's that feeling of walking up to the edge of the Grand Canyon and seeing just how vast it is and how far down it really goes. We see how big it is, and it simultaneously shows us just how small we are.

Or, a giant storm may call to mind the lyrics of Sting: "On and on the rain will say how fragile we are."

An awestruck state of mind causes us to be more kind, more serving of others, and less self-absorbed. Amid the solar eclipse in Oregon in 2017, strangers hugged each other. Jonah shared that there was a physiological basis for this behavior: brain imaging reveals that when we experience awe, we exhibit the same presentation as someone on psilocybin, the psychoactive element in magic mushrooms. We are less self-conscious and more focused on our connection to others.

That's pretty awe-some!

One of the best ways to integrate awe into your daily life only takes seconds and can be done with ordinary things from our lives that we might otherwise overlook. Like the fire example above, it turns out that we don't have to go to some place awe-inspiring like the Taj Mahal to experience awe (although, by all means, go if you can!).

Physician and author, Dr. Michael Amster, endorsed a method on my podcast which he cleverly created (with his coauthor Jake Eagle), and we can do it by following the acronym AWE. He has researched the AWE method extensively and has had good outcomes relating to various aspects of our physical and mental health.

The "A" stands for *attention*. Michael shared that he was awestruck while, of all things, making pancakes. He zeroed in on the process of starting with liquid batter. As the batter comes in contact with heat, it slowly morphed into a solid right before his very eyes. He could observe this by merely slowing down and being aware. As you can see, this is not difficult; we can do this too.

The "W" stands for *wait*. Sticking with the pancake example, we take a moment after observing the phenomenon of liquid pancake batter becoming a solid right before our very eyes.

The "E" stands for *exhale and expand*. Deeply exhaling not only activates the parasympathetic nervous system, which is necessary for our rest and digest relaxation response, but it also allows us to take a moment and let the awe moment expand, feeling into what we've just experienced.

Engaging in this practice just three times a day, which only takes about a minute each time, can yield a very high return on investment of time.

Consideration for Others

In order to survive, we humans have developed some selfish impulses. Given the wrong motivations, we can find ways to justify almost anything. For that reason, connecting to something greater than ourselves can assist us in being oriented to being better people.

The philosopher Martin Buber gave us another binary choice: we can choose to relate to others by "I and It" or "I and Thou."[11] In other words, we can choose to see others as objects we can manipulate (seeing other people as "It") or as fellow humans deserving reverence and honor (seeing them as "Thou"). By raising the value of these interactions, we find new ways to authentically appreciate and connect with the people in our lives.

Seeing others through the lens of greater reverence can reinforce that *what we appreciate—or rather, who we appreciate—appreciates.*

Finding Meaning

We've established our basic human hunger for meaning. Living in this era of technological advancement brings many blessings, but it can also include a deep vein of cynicism.

Finding our unique connection with the spiritual can restore that meaning we need. Whether we look to the spirituality of Western or Eastern religions or traditions, or other wisdom-based ethical frameworks, finding ways to leverage their wisdom may help us address life's big questions. These frameworks are old, contain years of thought, and may support us as we engage in the timeless act of "standing on the shoulders of giants."

There's a story in the Bible that I often think about and has informed my own spirituality; it may be helpful to you too. Please feel free to consider using it or adjusting it in any way for your own quest. It involves Jacob, the second son of Isaac, who is returning home after being in exile. On the bank of a river, an angel wrestles with him all night—they are alone. It ends at sunrise in a stalemate. As the sun rises, the angel wrenches Jacob's leg, causing a permanent limp, and gives Jacob a new name: Israel, meaning "one who strives."

This is a poignant story. I think it has spoken to so many over the centuries precisely because it depicts what I think we are all meant to do in our lives: strive and wrestle with the tough questions.

CONNECTION FORMULA EXERCISE

Combine the power of mindfulness and gratitude by spending some time reflecting on and giving thanks for the good things in your life. This can be done in silence or by sharing with another. You can call it prayer if it suits you, or just make this kind of reflection a part of your gratitude practice. Remember, what you appreciate appreciates.

CONCLUSION
FILLING YOUR CUP

"What is it you plan to do with your one wild and precious life?" wrote poet Mary Oliver.

It's my hope that this book has helped you deepen your connections to yourself, to others, to the world, and, if you're inclined, to the spiritual.

But that doesn't mean I just want you to be happy.

The goal has been to help you find your formula for what makes *you* feel connected. Because if we are feeling connected to ourselves, others, and the world, it's a sign that we are alive and vitally engaged in something uniquely meaningful to us.

Identifying what is meaningful to you creates data that help you know *what your cup is* and *how to fill it*. Filling that cup will not make you happy all the time, but you'll care more about what you are doing because what you're doing is meaningful to you, based upon who you actually are. Living a life that is consistent with filling your cup with what matters to you will make you more psyched and energized even if what you are doing objectively sucks.

Let's think about some things that objectively suck:

- Being stuck repeatedly with needles.
- Being forced to stay awake through the night.
- Feeling an intense amount of pain all throughout your body.

While those three scenarios are all objectively aversive, people willingly go through those experiences each day. We get our bodies tattooed with needles because the art is so meaningful for us. When the tattoo continues to contain meaning, we look at our bodies, and we remember more about *why* we got that tattoo and less about the experience of pain.

New parents go through many sleepless nights with their kids, but they do so because their children depend on them. The parent may also look back fondly on those memories as chances to bond with their young child, who's now grown, and find themselves missing that precious stage of the relationship.

And of course, childbirth is one of the most intense experiences of pain someone can feel, but women regularly choose to go through it. Some even do so without pain medication to feel more connected to the experience and to their baby.

Why do we do these things? Because they fill our cup. Because they are meaningful.

When we do things that are fun but aren't meaningful, we might enjoy the experience, but the half-life of the pleasure may be short. A weekend in Vegas might be fun, but hedonism alone doesn't sustain us. If we can combine the hedonism with something meaningful—a great friend with whom to enjoy the experience or seeing an artist live who is deeply important to us, for example—we're more likely to benefit and remember it fondly over the years. While many of us think we'd rather have more bachelor weekends that are entirely full of hedonism and nothing else, those memories may not sustain us in our old age.

By comparison, there's the story of my mother and her best friend from childhood. My mom's friend's husband was in the process of dying. My mom and her friend were on opposite coasts, and they spent the entire night on the phone together. My mom was happy to sacrifice her sleep for her friend, even though she had a plane to catch early the next morning.

She went to the airport after their all-night phone conversation and discovered something that shocked her: she wasn't tired at all. At that point, my mom was a woman in her eighties operating on no sleep, and she reported feeling energized. How could that be?

Going to the airport with no sleep may suck, but doing it because she had a deep, meaningful connection with her oldest friend made it so much easier. Meaningful connection makes just about everything easier.

* * *

When you know how to fill your cup, there is more of you to go around. As you implement some of what you have learned from this book and increase your ratio of meaningful activity and meaningful connection, the wear and tear on your system will likely be dramatically reduced.

There's an ancient Chinese proverb that goes: "The best time to plant a tree was twenty years ago. The second-best time to plant a tree is now." You may have missed out on many connection opportunities throughout your life. But there is no time like the present to start leaning into the four types of connection.

When we feel connection and feel connected, we are affirmed and we have found what is meaningful to us.

Go out and fill your cup. You now know some ways to do so; keep learning what works.

Let's get super psyched together.

ACKNOWLEDGMENTS

Thank you to my parents, Dorothy and Richard Dorsay, who gave me life and who supplied wind at my back as I wrote this book. I'm grateful beyond words for your love and all you have done to help me get to this place.

To my sister, Jenny, who has been cheering me on the entire way and whose laugh is like manna from heaven.

To my incredible friends—David Gaertner, Bob Haroche, Scott Shute, Philip Ohriner, Bonnie Bernell, Aaron Kaplan, Susanne Weir, Jed Goldstein, David Sabes, and David Straus—who have been there for me, who have championed me, and who have consistently challenged me to dig deeper, take chances, and go for what I have wanted.

To my mentors, Allen Greenberger and Martin Doerner. I am tearful as I write your names. I wish you both were here, and I'm simultaneously so grateful to have learned from you. Your teachings ring out in all the words in this book.

To Grandpa Ben. You always believed in me from your heart, even when there appeared to be no data to support you in doing so. I love you, Grandpa, and I miss you every day. To my late father-in-law, Alvin Jacobs, for entrusting me with his beloved daughter and for telling me I'd find fulfillment in my career even when I couldn't imagine it. To my mother-in-law, Tamar, who gave me the best gift I've ever received.

This book could not have been written—or certainly not as well—without the help of some superb connections to incredible people in my life. First and foremost, my wife, Aurianne, sat with me for countless hours as I rewrote and edited my first draft. Aurianne—your generous heart and brilliant mind helped midwife the book into its current form. I am so grateful to you for being my copilot in this process. My sons, Avin and Bren, helped me as well. Avin, in particular, you helped make the cover beautiful. Bren, you often helped me with how to express a thing when I was blocked. It is mind-blowing to see you both aid me in solving high-level intellectual and artistic problems.

Thank you to the always funny and equally brilliant A. J. Jacobs for writing the foreword to the book. A. J.—you're a hero-turned-friend and someone whose company is so much fun that our interactions have a half-life that lasts for days.

I am also profoundly grateful to the friends and colleagues who weighed in with their expertise to edit and offer insights I would have otherwise missed (named alphabetically):

Julia Alloggiamento, Joel Ben Izzy, Bonnie Bernell, Betty Carmack, Kathryn DeZur, Cindy Ebenfeld, Craig Factor, Leonard Felder, Britt Frank, Alan Friedman, Melissa Goldberg, Bob Haroche, Renee Haroche, Harville Hendrix, Rachel Herz, Ken Jacobs, Janna Koretz, Laurie Leung, Nancy Levin, Jennifer Dorsay Love, Mesha Joy Machamer, Slade Machamer, David Marcus, Meredith McBranch, Lissa Minkin, Lisa Nissenbaum, Carol Novello, Sven Ohah, Philip Ohriner, Eric Olsen, Susan Pollak, Matthew Prull, Elinor Rivera, Jill Rosenberg, Sara Saatchi, Jerrold Shapiro, Scott Shute, Irena Smith, Aaron Suhr, Natasha Walstra, Patricia Williams, and Nathan Zadkovsky.

Thanks to my incredible team at Amplify, including Naren Aryal, Brandon Coward, and Eric Schurenberg.

And I would like to thank all the guests on the *SuperPsyched* podcast. You have made me and my audience smarter and have contributed mightily to this book. And without my brilliant, world-class talented producer, Paul Bahr, the podcast would be an amateur enterprise. You make it professional. I am beyond grateful for your partnership.

I would also like to thank my dear friends, not yet thanked above, some of whom have also been workmates, who have shaped me over the years. You have helped me become who I am today. In no particular order, you are: Arnnon Geshuri, Xander Love, Sir Norman Melancon, Janet Weber, Nanette Rowe, Gary Leight, Gary Embler, Lilia Sheynman, Jessica Byrd-Olmstead, Richard Mahan, Erik Tenbrink, Brent Green, Elizabeth Buchanan, Sharon Mason-Parker, Hayden Craig, Tejasi Bilgi, Suniti Barua, Jorge Wong, Steve Harris, Zack Sleep, Addy Krantzler, Irvan Krantzler, Shannon Hickey, Tom Hinds, Stuart Krigel, Marc Bader, Eric Tannenwald, Larry Fox, Jeff Rosen, Brian Fox, Matt Braker, Alan Kessler, May Shih, Julia Petchey, Charles Wiz, Leslie Brezak, Masako Tanaka, Otto-san Tanaka, Kazutaka Nagashima, Kiyoko Nelson, Diana Clayton, señor Robert Davis, Susie Herrick, Arnie Nierenberg, Abe Bromberg, Dan Goldensohn, Cynthia Hernandez, Errol Shubot, Michael White and the DO team, Bronwyn Saglimbeni, Arno Michaelis, Dydine Umunyana, Marcela Rivera, Zvi Weiss, Krista Regedanz, Loic Jassy, Yosi Amram, Marlena Lyons, Kandilee Peters, Andrea Sprague, George Parker, Meryle Sussman, Elizabeth Winkleman, Donna Hill Howes, Paul Rousseau, Robert Lieb, David Auld, Ron Haynes, Tom Hlevanka, Bill Zemanek, Dan Khorge, Gerald Kinoshita, Joshua Berkenwald, Dana Romalis, Daniel Pressman, Richard Cohan, Jaqueline Richards, Sean Hanagan, Yukiko Hatanaka, Jay Livingston, Victor Sanchez, Lois Vidt, Arnetta Garcin, Yael Chatav Schonbrun, Alex Baur, Larry Bargetto, David Pugh, Vedant Agrawal, and the people who come to me for professional services. While confidentiality keeps me from naming you personally, I can unequivocally say that as I have aimed to help you, you have contributed to my life and caused me to grow. I am grateful to you for the honor of your trust.

NOTES

PART I: SUPER PSYCHED

Chapter 1: Connection Is Everything

1   National Academies of Sciences, Engineering, and Medicine, *Social Isolation and Loneliness in Older Adults: Opportunities for the Health Care System* (Washington, DC: The National Academies Press, 2020), https://doi.org/10.17226/25663.

2   Social Science Research Council, "Youth Disconnection," accessed October 24, 2023, https://www.ssrc.org/programs/measure-of-america/youth-disconnection/.

3   "Stress in America 2023: A Nation Recovering from Collective Trauma," American Psychological Association, November 2023, https://www.apa.org/news/press/releases/stress/2023/collective-trauma-recovery.

4   Adam Grant, "There's a Name for the Blah You're Feeling: It's Called Languishing," *New York Times*, April 19, 2021, https://www.nytimes.com/2021/04/19/well/mind/covid-mental-health-languishing.html.

5   Terry P. Humphreys, Laura M. Wood, and James D. A. Parker, "Alexithymia and satisfaction in intimate relationships," *Personality and Individual Differences* 46, no. 1 (2009): 43–47, ISSN 0191-8869, https://doi.org/10.1016/j.paid.2008.09.002.

6   Graeme J. Taylor, R. Michael Bagby, and James D. A. Parker, "Relations between Alexithymia, Personality, and Affects," in *Disorders of Affect Regulation: Alexithymia in Medical and Psychiatric Illness* (Cambridge: Cambridge University Press, 1997), 67–92, doi:10.1017/CBO9780511526831.007.

7   Stijn Vanheule et al., "Alexithymia and interpersonal problems," *Journal of Clinical Psychology* 63 (2007): 109–117, https://doi.org/10.1002/jclp.20324.

8   Graeme J. Taylor, R. Michael Bagby, and James D. A. Parker, "Relations between Alexithymia, Personality, and Affects," in *Disorders of Affect Regulation: Alexithymia in Mediscal and Psychiatric Illness* (Cambridge: Cambridge University Press, 1997), 67–92, doi:10.1017/CBO9780511526831.007.

9   Viktor Frankl, *Man's Search for Meaning: An Introduction to Logotherapy* (Boston: Beacon Press, 1962).

10 Daniel Gilbert, *Stumbling on Happiness* (New York: A. A. Knopf, 2006).

11 Cassie Mogilner, "The Pursuit of Happiness: Time, Money, and Social Connection," *Psychological Science* 21, no. 9 (2010): 1348–1354, https://doi.org/10.1177/0956797610380696.

12 Kristine Klussman et al., "Examining the effect of mindfulness on well-being: self-connection as a mediator," *Journal of Pacific Rim Psychology* (2020): 14, https://doi.org/10.1017/prp.2019.29.

13 Elisa Makadi and Diana Koszycki, "Exploring Connections Between Self-Compassion, Mindfulness, and Social Anxiety," *Mindfulness* 11 (2020): 480–492, https://doi.org/10.1007/s12671-019-01270-z.

14 Dunigan Folk and Elizabeth Dunn, "How Can People Become Happier? A Systematic Review of Preregistered Experiments," *Annual Review of Psychology* 75, no. 1 (2024): 467–493.

Chapter 2: Why We're So Disconnected

1   Michell L. McNicol and Einar B. Thorsteinsson, "Internet Addiction, Psychological Distress, and Coping Responses Among Adolescents and Adults," *Cyber Psychology, Behavior, and Social Networking* 20, no. 5 (2017): 296–304, http://doi.org/10.1089/cyber.2016.0669.

2   Leonard Reinecke et al., "Digital Stress over the Life Span: The Effects of Communication Load and Internet Multitasking on Perceived Stress and Psychological Health Impairments in a German Probability Sample," *Media Psychology* 20 no. 1 (2017): 90–115, DOI: 10.1080/15213269.2015.1121832.

3   Eberhard Fuchs and Gabriele Flügge, "Adult Neuroplasticity: More than 40 Years of Research," *Neural Plasticity* (2014), https://doi.org/10.1155/2014/541870.

4   Janna Koretz, "What Happens When Your Career Becomes Your Whole
       Identity," *Harvard Business Review*, December 26, 2019, https://hbr.
       org/2019/12/what-happens-when-your-career-becomes-your-whole-identity.

5   T. J. Morgan and K. N. Laland, "The Biological Bases of Conformity,"
       Frontiers in Neuroscience 6, no. 87 (2012), doi:10.3389/fnins.2012.00087.

6   Anna Kaufman, "How Many 'Bachelor' Show Couples Are Still Together?
       The Final Rose's Success, Analyzed," *USA Today*, March 12, 2024, https://
       www.usatoday.com/story/entertainment/tv/2022/09/19/bachelor-
       bachelorette-couples-still-together/10381061002.

7   Wikipedia, s.v. "Confirmation bias," last modified March 20, 2024, 18:42,
       https://en.wikipedia.org/wiki/Confirmation_bias.

8   Nathalie Claus, Keisuke Takano, and Charlotte E. Wittekind, "The Interplay
       between Cognitive Biases, Attention Control, and Social Anxiety
       Symptoms: A Network and Cluster Approach," *PLOS ONE* 18, no. 4 (2023):
       e0282259, https://doi.org/10.1371/journal.pone.0282259.

9   Awakening Joy YouTube, "James Baraz on 'What is Mindfulness?'," YouTube
       video, https://www.youtube.com/watch?v=-3-VaV4JpHY.

10   Abraham P. Buunk and Frederick X. Gibbons, "Social comparison: The end
       of a theory and the emergence of a field," *Organizational Behavior and
       Human Decision Processes* 102, no. 1 (2007).

11   TED Blog Video, "Two Monkeys Were Paid Unequally: Excerpt from Frans
       de Waal's TED Talk," YouTube video, https://www.youtube.com/
       watch?v=meiU6TxysCg.

12   University of California, Santa Barbara, "The universality of shame,"
       ScienceDaily, September 10, 2018, https://www.sciencedaily.com/
       releases/2018/09/180910173734.htm#:~:text=Summary%3A,feel%20
       about%20a%20potential%20action.&text=Shame%20on%20you.

13   Larry Diamond, "Defending Liberal Democracy from the Slide Toward
       Authoritarianism" (keynote address, European Democracy Conference 2017,
       Bratislava, Slovakia, November 21, 2017), https://diamond-democracy.
       stanford.edu/speaking/speeches/defending-liberal-democracy-slide-toward-
       authoritarianism.

Chapter 3: Getting Connected

1   Mihaly Csikszentmihalyi, *Flow: The Psychology of Optimal Experience* (New York: Harper & Row, 1990).

2   Mihaly Csikszentmihalyi, *Flow: The Psychology of Optimal Experience* (New York: Harper & Row, 1990).

3   Cass R. Sunstein and Richard Thaler, "The Two Friends Who Changed How We Think About How We Think," *The New Yorker*, December 7, 2016.

4   DBT stands for dialectical behavioral therapy, a therapeutic approach that helps people regulate emotions and find a balance between acceptance of who a person is and their challenges as well as the benefits of change.

PART II: CONNECTION TO OURSELVES

Chapter 4: Connecting to Who You Are

1   Martin E. P. Seligman, *The Hope Circuit* (New York: PublicAffairs, 2018).

2   C. G. Jung, *Collected Works of C.G. Jung,* eds. Gerhard Adler and R. F. C. Hull, volume 13 (Princeton: Princeton University Press, 1967), http://www.jstor.org/stable/j.ctt5hhqv1.

Chapter 5: Connecting to What You Need

1   Itai Berger et al., "Maturational Delay in ADHD: Evidence from CPT," *Frontiers in Human Neuroscience* 7 (2013): 691, https://doi.org/10.3389/fnhum.2013.00691.

2   "Heart attack first aid," Mount Sinai, accessed March 26, 2024, https://www.mountsinai.org/health-library/injury/heart-attack-first-aid.

3   Terri A. Ammirati, "When Is It a Good Time to Seek Counseling?" The Gottman Institute, https://www.gottman.com/blog/when-is-it-a-good-time-to-seek-counseling/.

4   Ben Singh et al., "Effectiveness of Physical Activity Interventions for Improving Depression, Anxiety and Distress: An Overview of Systematic Reviews," *British Journal of Sports Medicine* 57 (2023): 1203–1209.

5   B. E. Wampold et al., "A Meta-Analysis of Outcome Studies Comparing Bona Fide Psychotherapies: Empirically, 'All Must Have Prizes,'" *Psychological Bulletin* 122, no. 3 (1997): 203–215, https://doi.org/10.1037/0033-2909.122.3.203.

6   K. Kamenov et al., "The Efficacy of Psychotherapy, Pharmacotherapy and Their Combination on Functioning and Quality of Life in Depression: A Meta-Analysis," *Psychological Medicine* 47, no. 3 (2017): 414–425, https://doi.org/10.1017/S0033291716002774.

7   Elaine N. Aron, *The Highly Sensitive Person: How to Thrive When the World Overwhelms You* (New York: Broadway Books, 1997).

8   Kristin Neff, "Self-Compassion, Self-Esteem, and Well-Being," *Social and Personality Psychology Compass* 5 (2011): 1–12, https://doi.org/10.1111/j.1751-9004.2010.00330.x.

9   Kyle Benson, "The Magic Relationship Ratio, According to Science," The Gottman Institute, https://www.gottman.com/blog/the-magic-relationship-ratio-according-science/.

10 Loghman Ebrahimi et al., "Attachment Styles, Parenting Styles, and Depression," *International Journal of Mental Health and Addiction* 15 (2017): 1064–1068, https://doi.org/10.1007/s11469-017-9770-y.

Chapter 6: Connecting to What You Want

1   In *Motivational Interviewing: Helping People Change and Grow* (2013), by William R. Miller and Stephen Rollnick, Motivational Interviewing is defined as "a collaborative, goal-oriented style of communication with particular attention to the language of change. It is designed to strengthen personal motivation for and commitment to a specific goal by eliciting and exploring the person's own reasons for change within an atmosphere of acceptance and compassion."

PART III: CONNECTION TO OTHERS

Chapter 7: Connecting to a Significant Other

1   H. Jackson Brown, *Life's Little Instruction Book: Simple Wisdom and a Little Humor for Living a Happy and Rewarding Life* (Nashville, TN: Thomas Nelson, 2012).

2   Molly Howes, *A Good Apology: Four Steps to Make Things Right* (New York: Grand Central Publishing, 2020).

3   Zoe Chance, *Influence Is Your Super Power* (New York: Random House, 2023).

4   "Study: 10 Percent of People Admit to Checking Phone During Sex," CBS News Philadelphia, June 7, 2018, https://www.cbsnews.com/philadelphia/news/study-10-percent-people-checking-phone-during-sex/.

5   "Courtney C. Stevens Quotes," Goodreads, accessed March 26, 2024, https://www.goodreads.com/quotes/7304033-if-nothing-changes-nothing-changes-if-you-keep-doing-what.

6   Save the Children's Resource Centre, "Tronick's Still Face Experiment," July 27, 2022, YouTube video, https://www.youtube.com/watch?v=f1Jwo-LExyc.

7   Tracy P. Alloway, "What 20 Seconds of Hugging Can Do for You," *Psychology Today* blog, January 19, 2022, https://www.psychologytoday.com/us/blog/keep-it-in-mind/202201/what-20-seconds-hugging-can-do-you.

8   Logan Ury, "Want to Improve Your Relationship? Pay More Attention to Bids," The Gottman Institute, accessed March 26, 2024, https://www.gottman.com/blog/want-to-improve-your-relationship-start-paying-more-attention-to-bids/.

9   Emily A. Impett, Haeyoung Gideon Park, and Amy Muise, "Popular Psychology Through a Scientific Lens: Evaluating Love Languages From a Relationship Science Perspective," *Current Directions in Psychological Science* (open access), January 12, 2024, https://doi.org/10.1177/09637214231217663.

10   According to Imago Relationship Therapy cocreators Dr. Harville Hendrix and Dr. Helen LaKelly Hunt, the practice is "a form of relationship and couples therapy that focuses on relational counseling to transform any conflict between couples into opportunities for healing and growth." ("What is Imago?" accessed November 13, 2023, https://harvilleandhelen.com/initiatives/what-is-imago/).

11   Ester Perel, *Mating in Captivity* (New York: Harper, 2006).

12   Catherine Pearson, "She Wrote a Best Seller on Women's Sex Lives. Then Her Own Fell Apart," *New York Times*, January 18, 2024, https://www.nytimes.com/2024/01/18/well/family/emily-nagoski-book-come-together.html.

13   *Oxford English Dictionary*, 2nd ed. (Oxford: Oxford University Press, 2004),
s.v. "Chronotypes," https://languages.oup.com/google-dictionary-en/.

Chapter 8: Connecting to Family

1   Irvin D. Yalom, review of *Momma and the Meaning of Life*, by Nancy Glimm,
Psychiatric Services 51, no. 11 (2000): 1460, https://ps.psychiatryonline.org/
doi/10.1176/appi.ps.51.11.1460.

2   S. M. Toepfer, K. Cichy, and P. Peters, "Letters of Gratitude: Further
Evidence for Author Benefits," *Journal of Happiness Studies* 13 (2012):
187–201, https://doi.org/10.1007/s10902-011-9257-7.

Chapter 9: Connecting to Children

1   Arseny A. Sokolov et al., "Gender Affects Body Language Reading,"
Frontiers in Psychology 2, no. 16 (2011), https://doi.org/10.3389/
fpsyg.2011.00016.

2   https://www.atlasobscura.com.

3   J. W. Moore, "What Is the Sense of Agency and Why Does it Matter?,"
Frontiers in Psychology 7 (2016): 1272, https://doi.org/10.3389/
fpsyg.2016.01272.

4   Andrew Solomon, *Far from the Tree: Parents, Children, and the Search for
Identity* (New York: Scribner, 2012).

5   Becky Kennedy, *Good Inside: A Guide to Becoming the Parent You Want to Be*
(New York: Harper, 2022).

6   L. Ebrahimi et al., "Attachment *Styles, Parenting Styles, and Depression*,"
International Journal of Mental Health and Addiction 15 (2017): 1064–1068,
https://doi.org/10.1007/s11469-017-9770-y.

Chapter 10: Connecting to Friends

1   Marco Iacoboni, "The Human Mirror Neuron System and Its Role in
Imitation and Empathy," in *The Primate Mind: Built to Connect with Other
Minds*, eds. Frans B. M. de Waal and Pier Francesco Ferrari (Cambridge,
MA, and London, England: Harvard University Press, 2012), 32–47, https://
doi.org/10.4159/harvard.9780674062917.c3.

2   Zara Abrams, "The Science of Why Friendships Keep Us Healthy," *Monitor
on Psychology* 54, no. 4 (2023).

3   Census Bureau, "Calculating Migration Expectancy Using ACS Data,"
     https://www.census.gov/topics/population/migration/guidance/
     calculating-migration-expectancy.html.

4   Daniel A. Cox, "The State of American Friendship: Change, Challenges,
     and Loss," Survey Center on American Life, June 8, 2021, https://www.
     americansurveycenter.org/research/the-state-of-american-friendship-
     change-challenges-and-loss/.

Chapter 11: Connecting to Animals

1   Jon Johnson, "What to know about Animal Therapy," Medical News Today,
     July 10, 2020, https://www.medicalnewstoday.com/articles/animal-therapy.

2   Gregory Berns, *How Dogs Love Us: A Neuroscientist and His Adopted Dog
     Decode the Canine Brain* (New York: New Harvest, 2013).

3   Beth Anstandig, *The Human Herd: Awakening Our Natural Leadership* (New
     York: Morgan James Publishing, 2022).

PART IV: CONNECTION TO THE WORLD

Chapter 12: Connecting to Work

1   Leigh Campbell, "We've Broken Down Your Entire Life Into Years Spent
     Doing Tasks," *Huffington Post*, October 18, 2017, https://www.huffpost.com/
     entry/weve-broken-down-your-entire-life-into-years-spent-doing-tasks_n_6
     1087617e4b0999d2084fec5?ncid=engmodushpmg00000004.

2   John Hagel III et al., "If You Love Them, Set Them Free," Deloitte, June 6,
     2017, https://www2.deloitte.com/us/en/insights/topics/talent/future-
     workforce-engagement-in-the-workplace.html.

3   Viktor Frankl, *Man's Search for Meaning: An Introduction to Logotherapy*
     (Boston: Beacon Press, 1962).

4   Viktor Frankl, *Man's Search for Meaning: An Introduction to Logotherapy*
     (Boston: Beacon Press, 1962).

5   Joshua Gold and Joseph Ciorciari, "A Review on the Role of the
     Neuroscience of Flow States in the Modern World," *Behavioral Sciences* 10,
     no. 9 (2020): 137, https://doi.org/10.3390/bs10090137.

6   Adam Grant, "Instead of asking kids what they want to be when they grow up, ask them what they want to do," LinkedIn post, https://www.linkedin.com/posts/adammgrant_instead-of-asking-kids-what-they-want-to-activity-6522841963639689216-4bhK/?originalSubdomain=rw.

7   Jeffrey Davis, "The Science of Weekend Recovery," *Psychology Today*, March/April 2023: 24–25.

8   *Positive Psychology and Psychotherapy: A Conversation between Martin Seligman, PhD, and Randall C. Wyatt, PhD*, produced by V. Yalom and R. C. Wyatt, online video, 2008, psychotherapy.net.

9   Jim Baker, "The Story of Three Bricklayers—A Parable about the Power of Purpose," accessed November 13, 2023, https://sacredstructures.org/mission/the-story-of-three-bricklayers-a-parable-about-the-power-of-purpose.

10 David Zax, "Want to Be Happier at Work? Learn How From These 'Job Crafters,'" *Fast Company*, June 3, 2013, https://www.fastcompany.com/3011081/want-to-be-happier-at-work-learn-how-from-these-job-crafters.

11 Hadley Hall Meares, "The Love Goddess: Rita Hayworth's Tragic Quest," *Vanity Fair*, September 23, 2020, https://www.vanityfair.com/hollywood/2020/09/rita-hayworth-biography-trauma.

Chapter 13: Connecting to Community

1   Johann Hari, *Lost Connections: Why You're Depressed and How to Find Hope* (London: Bloomsbury Publishing, 2019).

2   Angela Thoreson, "Helping People, Changing Lives: 3 Health Benefits of Volunteering," Mayo Clinic, August 1, 2023, https://www.mayoclinichealthsystem.org/hometown-health/speaking-of-health/3-health-benefits-of-volunteering.

3   *Arnold* (documentary series), Netflix, 2023.

4   Johann Hari, *Lost Connections: Why You're Depressed and How to Find Hope* (London: Bloomsbury Publishing, 2019).

5   Elizabeth Hopper, "How Volunteering Can Help Your Mental Health," *Greater Good Magazine*, July 3, 2020.

6   Sonja Lyubomirsky, *The How of Happiness* (New York: Penguin Books, 2008).

Chapter 14: Connecting to Art and Inspiration

1   Maxime Aubert and Adam Brumm, "What the World's Oldest Cave Paintings Tell Us about Our Human Ancestors," Griffith University, accessed March 26, 2023, https://www.griffith.edu.au/research/impact/worlds-oldest-cave-paintings.

2   Beverlee Warren, "The Top Five Regrets of the Dying: A Life Transformed by the Dearly Departing by Bronnie Ware," *Proceedings* 25, no. 3 (2012): 299–300.

3   Jordan Bates, "Make Your Soul Grow: 84-Year-Old Kurt Vonnegut's Wonderful Letter to a Group of High School Students," High Existence, August 24, 2023, https://www.highexistence.com/make-your-soul-grow-84-year-old-kurt-vonneguts-wonderful-letter-to-a-group-of-high-school-students/.

4   Morra Aarons-Mele. "It Isn't Failure, It's Data: Dorie Clark On Failing Without Blame Or Fear," *Forbes*, February 28, 2017, https://www.forbes.com/sites/morraaaronsmele/2017/02/28/it-isnt-failure-its-data-dorie-clark-on-failing-without-blame-or-fear/?sh=3633f9224395.

5   Associated Press, "Steve Jobs' First Girlfriend Writes about His Young-Adult Years in *Rolling Stone*," *Denver Post*, October 13, 2011, https://www.denverpost.com/2011/10/13/steve-jobs-first-girlfriend-writes-about-his-young-adult-years-in-rolling-stone/.

Chapter 15: Connecting to Nature

1   Pierre A. Geoffroy et al., "Efficacy of Light Therapy versus Antidepressant Drugs, and of the Combination versus Monotherapy, in Major Depressive Episodes: A Systematic Review and Meta-Analysis," *Sleep Medicine Reviews* 48 (2019): 101213, https://doi.org/10.1016/j.smrv.2019.101213.

2   Dorothy Day Huntsman and Grzegorz Bulaj, "Healthy Dwelling: Design of Biophilic Interior Environments Fostering Self-Care Practices for People Living with Migraines, Chronic Pain, and Depression," *International Journal of Environmental Research and Public Health* 19, no. 4 (2022): 2248, https://doi.org/10.3390/ijerph19042248.

3   Julian Treasure, *How to Be Heard: Secrets for Powerful Speaking and Listening* (Ontario: TMA Press, 2017).

4   Michael Gass et al., "The Value of Outdoor Behavioral Healthcare for Adolescent Substance Users with Comorbid Conditions," *Substance Abuse: Research and Treatment* 13 (2019): 1178221819870768, https://doi.org/10.1177/1178221819870768.

Chapter 16: Connecting to Ancestry and Tradition

1   JAMESP0WER, "Paul McCartney on Bertrand Russell," YouTube video, August 23, 2010, https://www.youtube.com/watch?v=N3m2r0Ln0rU.

2   Life in the 1800s, "My Grandfather Met Napoleon: Bertrand Russell Interview 1952," YouTube video, April 23, 2022, https://www.youtube.com/watch?v=4OXtO92x5KA.

3   William Faulkner, *Requiem for a Nun* (New York: Vintage, 2012).

4   Randy Cordova, "Maya Angelou's 2011 *Arizona Republic* Interview," *Arizona Republic*, Ma 28. 2014, https://www.azcentral.com/story/entertainment/books/2014/05/28/maya-angelou-arizona-republic-interview/9682587/.

PART V: CONNECTION TO SOMETHING GREATER

Chapter 17: Connecting to Spirituality

1   Maya Spencer, "What Is Spirituality? A Personal Exploration," 2012, https://www.rcpsych.ac.uk/docs/default-source/members/sigs/spirituality-spsig/what-is-spirituality-maya-spencer-x.pdf?sfvrsn=f28df052_2.

2   Laura Upenieks, "Unpacking the Relationship Between Prayer and Anxiety: A Consideration of Prayer Types and Expectations in the United States," *Journal of Religion and Health* 62, no. 3 (2023): 1810–1831, https://doi.org/10.1007/s10943-022-01708-0.

3   Lisa J. Miller, *The Awakened Brain: The New Science of Spirituality and Our Quest for an Inspired Life* (New York: Random House, 2021).

4   Elie Wiesel, *Somewhere a Master: Hasidic Portraits and Legends* (New York: Schocken, 2005).

5   Thich Nhat Hanh, *The Miracle of Mindfulness: An Introduction to the Practice of Meditation* (Boston: Beacon Press, 1999), 9.

6   Seyma Bayram, "Billions of People Lack Access to Clean Drinking Water, U.N. Report Finds," NPR, March 22, 2023, https://www.npr.org/2023/03/22/1165464857/billions-of-people-lack-access-to-clean-drinking-water-u-n-report-finds.

7   Wikipedia, s.v. "Savoring," last modified January 15, 2024, 19:17, https://en.wikipedia.org/wiki/Savoring.

8   Benjamin Hoff, *The Tao of Pooh* (New York: Penguin Books, 1983).

9   Matthew 6:34.

10 Adam Dorsay and Jonah Paquette, "The Science of Awe," June 22, 2020, in *SuperPsyched*, podcast, https://podcasters.spotify.com/pod/show/superpsyched/episodes/15-The-Science-of-Awe--Dr--Jonah-Paquette-efnlvt.

11 Martin Buber, "Lost in It," Becoming Thou, accessed March 26, 2024, https://www.becomingthou.com/lost.

ABOUT THE AUTHOR

Dr. Adam Dorsay is a licensed psychologist and a certified executive coach working in private practice. He specializes in assisting high-achieving professionals—including tech executives, entrepreneurs, and professional athletes—with relationship issues, stress reduction, easing anxiety, and attaining more happiness in their lives.

He delivers lively and well-received keynotes and trainings at institutions like Microsoft, LinkedIn, and the California Psychological Association. He is also the host of the award-winning psychology podcast *SuperPsyched*, which in nearly two hundred episodes has featured interviews with everyone from NBA coaches to rock stars to world-famous comedians to bestselling authors and many more.

He lives and works in San Jose, California, and is happily married with two children and an Australian Labradoodle named Raffi.